When the Stars Align

When the Stars Align

Reflections on Astrology, Life, Death, and Other Mysteries

Ray Grasse

Inner Eye Publications/Chicago, Illinois 2022

Also by Ray Grasse:

The Waking Dream: Unlocking the Symbolic Language of Our Lives

Signs of the Times: Unlocking the Symbolic Language of World Events

Under a Sacred Sky: Essays on the Philosophy and Practice of Astrology

An Infinity of Gods: Conversations with an Unconventional Mystic

Urban Mystic: Recollections of Goswami Kriyananda

StarGates: Essays on Astrology, Symbolism and the Synchronistic Universe

The Sky Stretched Out Before Me: Encounters with Mystics, Anomalies, and Waking Dreams

"We have lost the cosmos. The Sun strengthens us no more, neither does the Moon. . . Now we have to get back to the cosmos, and it can't be done by a trick. The great range of responses that have fallen dead in us have to come to life again. It has taken two thousand years to kill them. Who knows how long it will take to bring them to life?"

~ D.H. Lawrence, *Apocalypse*

TABLE OF CONTENTS

ACKNOWLEDGMENTS

I want to express my heartfelt thanks to those who offered feedback or support over this last year. They include Judith Wiker, Laurence Hillman, Eric and Devi Klein, Bill Hogan, Sharon Harms, Barbara Keller, Swami Pranananda, Bess Demopolous, Ken and Kamala Lee, Dawn Silver, Dave Gunning, Jane Wodening, Perry Fotopoulos, Gale Ahrens, Mia Feroleto, Normandi Ellis, Elizabeth Avedon, Kevin Korody, Claudette Baker, Gary Lachman, Greg Silka, Sharon George, Debby Sher, Victoria Martin, Victor Oliver, Thomas Tiernan, Jon Parks, Zoli Althea Browne, Eileen Ruffer, Robert Baracani, Sue Neill, Ed Maslovicz, Mark Springle, Olga Chapa, Michele Gaspar, Diana Mauriello, Jill Neilson, Claudia Bader, and Eileen Grimes.

Also, Paul Broucek, Nancy Bragin, Greg Taylor, Livia Alessandrini, Tom and Sue Wilkens, Georgia Stathis, Donna Haddad, Doyle Armbrust, Richard Tarnas, Kate Sholly, Christine and John Cianciosi, Beth Melnick, Naomi Greene, Pamela Kokott, Hilary Spector, Kay Gardner, Al Paoletti, Whitley Strieber, Omari Martin, Valerie Baker Easley, Mimi Betinis, George Gawor, Allison Gawor, Greg and Alice Grasse, Edith Hathaway, Thomas Tiernan, Gary Wager, Elaina Raspolich, Kirsty Jackson, Katrina Boomer, Chris Bolger, Edward Moskowitz, Margaret Cahill, Ed Weber, Tony Howard, Bill Kavanagh, Karin Hoffman, Pat Eddishaw, Julie Van Gieson, Dav Ero, Nancy Cotton, Maria Hildalgo, Colleen Mauro, Ken Bowser, Sam Reynolds, Rebecca Langley, Lynn Hayes, Amanda Alford, Megan Smeaton, Anne Lindgren, Karen Tlusty, Susanne Hoepfl-Wellenhofer, Bill Kavanagh, Kirk Baldwin, Kairos Cuilann des Rosiers, John Culp, Annette Mckinney, John David Ebert, Frederick Woodruff, Lynn Staudacher, David Metcalfe, Toni Surdo, and Rebecca Fyffe.

As always, I owe a massive debt of gratitude to Shelly Trimmer and Goswami Kriyananda, whose teachings formed the basis for much of my own thinking on all matters mystical and esoteric, as well as to the memory of John Daido Loori. A special thanks goes to Richard Smoley, for both his editorial advice and friendship. Finally, I want to express my profound gratitude to Jonathan Powell and the Urania Trust, who helped with their eleventh hour support.

To anyone I may have overlooked, my sincere apologies!

INTRODUCTION

L ike many others, I've experienced an assortment of challenges in my life these last couple of years. It's been a time of profound change for the whole world, but in my case that primarily took the form of some pesky health issues, which as of this writing seem to be under control, I'm happy to report.

But experiences like that can have a silver lining, not only in forcing one to take stock and re-examine one's priorities, as you might expect, but also in stimulating one's thought processes and creative impulses in unexpected ways. Lying in bed for a number of months might not be very good for getting out and experiencing the world, that's true, but it can be helpful for thinking through ideas and questions that have been percolating in one's mind for months or even years. As a result, this was a hugely productive time for me in terms of writing, and this volume is one result of that.

Of all the works I've written, this is by far the most eclectic, and features an assortment of essays across a wide range of topics that include astrology, sacred geometry, cinema, Egypt, psychedelics, science, kundalini, God, the Beatles, sex, and even aliens. (But no sex with aliens, sorry to say.) A few of the essays in this collection are older pieces that have been published in journal or blog form before, and along the way I also revisit some themes introduced in earlier works, but the majority of the essays are new, the fruit of this last year's hibernation.

I've always enjoyed that sort of kaleidoscopic diversity. That isn't just because it helps to "keep things from getting boring" (as one friend characterized the Gemini syndrome—not altogether inaccurately), but because I find that unusual new alchemies can arise from the intermingling of wildly diverse ingredients in a single stew. The result is that what initially seemed "wildly diverse" on its surface sometimes gives rise, in the end, to a unique new fusion of elements greater than the sum of its parts.

In the case of this book, that amalgam wound up weaving itself around certain recurring themes, including fate, free will, the nature of time, suffering, synchronicity, patterns of history, consciousness, the soul, and last but not least, death. I can't predict whether you will like the result, of course, but I think I can safely say you've probably not read anything quite like it before. As with my book *StarGates*, I've reserved some of the more technical or esoteric discussions for later chapters, and for the appendices. As I've said with earlier books, I'd suggest that if you come across parts that are difficult to understand, simply skim through those and come back later on, after they've had a chance to steep in your unconscious a bit.

The roller coaster we've all been on these last two years doesn't seem to be drawing to an end anytime soon, and I conclude that as much from simply watching the news as from studying the stars. But I keep recalling something Thoreau said: "Read not the times, read the eternities." I'm a student of history, so I pay close attention to what's happening in the news, but at the same time I'm careful to look for the universal themes and archetypal patterns which underlie those developments, and which give a very different perspective on things. It's my hope that these chapters might help you do the same.

—Ray Grasse, March 2022

CHAPTER 1

THE FORTUNE TELLER

I was 18 the first time I encountered a living, breathing astrologer. She was a college classmate, an intelligent young woman who happened to mention between classes that she did horoscopes on the side. I had no experience with the subject besides reading a paperback by Joseph Goodavage about astrology during my teens, but I was intrigued enough to set up an appointment and find out what all the fuss was about. We scheduled to meet up at her apartment on the city's north side the following Saturday.

I was nervous standing outside her building, wondering what she might tell me. Did horoscopes give someone the ability to peer into your soul, X-ray style, and uncover your deepest foibles? Did they show if something terrible might happen? Might they even foretell when I was going to die? Questions like these swirled around in my head as I pressed the buzzer.

She welcomed me in, and I sat myself down on the floor opposite her, my horoscope laid out on the rug between us. My experience that next hour was surprising, but not in the gloom-and-doom way I feared, fortunately. She said things she couldn't possibly have known about me, such as the possibility of abdominal surgery early in life, or the crippling shyness I experienced as a kid. She even seemed to know about the huge emotional deflation I'd just experienced several weeks earlier. How was *that* possible, I wondered?

"It all has to do with the positions of the planets when you were born," she explained.

There was something astonishing about all of this. That's because if it was true—that someone could really know all this just from looking at the patterns of the planets when I was born—what did that say about my life? Or life itself, for that matter? About free will? It raised a host of new questions that buzzed through my head. I asked her to explain more.

She described the role of various symbols in my horoscope—or, as she referred to it, *"the chart."* Each of the planets represented a different part of one's personality, she explained, and the different "houses" in the chart showed where those energies were focused. "Your Gemini planets up there in the Ninth House suggest that you could become involved with teaching, or even publishing. I have the feeling you'll do a fair amount of traveling in this life, too."

"Your Moon is aligned with Neptune, which makes you a bit of a mystic. But there could be some addictive tendencies with that, too, so you need to watch out for that. You've got a good imagination, and you're extremely sensitive. Maybe a little *too* sensitive."

How can someone be *"too* sensitive," I wondered?

"Well, you could be a bit thin-skinned. You might take things a little *too* personally sometimes."

Fair enough.

My Sun was really fortunate, she said: "Three trines and a sextile"—whatever that meant. "You have a strong creative urge, and you could get recognition for what you do."

But when it came to my Uranus, though—"Well, that one's *out of control."*

What in the world did *that* mean?

"Don't get me wrong. I'm not saying that's *bad*. Nothing is innately 'good' or 'bad' in the horoscope. It depends on what you do with it. But looking at how your Uranus is configured with all those squares, I imagine you feel a really strong need for freedom, a 'don't fence me in' kind of attitude. There's a lot of restlessness with that aspect, and independence. Also, people might see you as a bit eccentric. Or, you might just be *attracted* to subjects other people regard as 'offbeat' or eccentric. Maybe even astrology!"

She paused a bit, then continued: "Along those same lines, I think you're going to have an unusual life, or what other people might consider unusual. It's even possible you could become a pioneer in whatever field you go into, but that could take place mainly behind the scenes rather than on center stage—a 'power behind the throne'-type situation, if you know what I mean."

That was all very intriguing, and I tried to take it in without judging it too quickly one way or the other. But I had to admit it was impressive. While most of what she said hit home, however, a few things didn't click for me. Like her comment about my strong Mercury showing a potential for writing, and I might even become a writer. That was something I had no real interest in at the time.

Then she elaborated: "I have the feeling you'll experience a real struggle between writing and the arts. To be honest, my sense is that writing will win out in the end, since the Gemini and Mercury in your chart is even more dominant than your Venus." That was *clearly* a misfire, I thought, since my allegiance was to the arts, not to writing. I was in an arts program, after all, not a literary one. But no one's perfect, so I gave her a pass on that one.

One more thing. While my horoscope indicated a good potential for creative success, there could be a lot of delays and detours along the way, and probably more than a few disappointments. "That could happen in the area of romance, too," she said. "That's because of how your planets are configured." I'll need to be patient, she affirmed.

That frankly wasn't what I wanted to hear. I nervously asked her to explain.

"Well, it's due to how your Saturn is placed. It touches virtually everything in your horoscope. To top things off, it's placed right in your *First House*, which is the area of your chart associated with the personality. Talk about heavy...! You need to lighten up, Ray. I imagine your childhood was pretty rough in some ways, at least in terms of how you felt inside, emotionally.

"The flip side of all that Saturn energy is that you're a late bloomer. You have a lot of hidden talents and resources, but it could take a long time for them to surface, or to get recognized. That slow-developing quality will probably characterize all kinds of situations in your life, actually."

Right then a loud crashing noise echoed from outside of her apartment door, as though a large pot had fallen in the hallway. It was followed by the sound of children squealing, then a chorus of laughter.

"On the bright side, it also means that any setbacks or detours you'll experience early on will probably turn out to be stepping stones to bigger and better things down the road. Don't take things at face value, in other words. When you're older you'll probably look back on the twists and turns of your life with a different perspective than you did at the time. In that respect, it's actually a good horoscope. A *really* good horoscope."

But what did she mean when she said "down the road"? Or by *"when you're older"*? Was she really saying things might not work out for me until I'm 30? Or worse yet, not until I'm 40? That was too discouraging to even think about, so I did my best to just put it out of my mind.

CHAPTER 2

STUMBLING ACROSS THE SCRIPT

While searching through my 2002 book Signs of the Times *for a lost bit of info, I came across a "thought experiment" I introduced in that book which relates directly to some of the themes I'm exploring in this one, so I've chosen to revisit and reformulate some of that material here.* —R.G.

I 'd invite you to imagine a small village where everyone goes about their daily business, enjoying what they believe is a perfectly ordinary existence, thinking they are all perfectly ordinary people, when there is actually something quite un-ordinary going on.

What none of them realize is that each and every one of them in the village has been hypnotized at some point by a master hypnotist who has given them all elaborate inductions for acting out pre-assigned parts in a play he's written, while also programming them to forget they'd ever been hypnotized or playing pre-written roles. They've even been hypnotized to forget *he* exists, so that they wouldn't even recognize him if they passed by him on the street.

It's all part of a grand experiment for the master hypnotist in mass mind control. Of course, not every single thought or movement of the villagers has been pre-determined by the script, just most of the major ones. Consequently, all of them in this village are simply acting out their parts as little more than puppets on a string, mechanically reciting scripted lines to one another. They all genuinely believe that they're acting out of free will, yet the fact is, none of them are.

But then something unexpected happens one day.

Due to a flaw in the master's plan, one of the young villager-actors happens to be wandering around in one of the buildings in the village, and stumbles onto a copy of the script the master hypnotist has written for the villagers. The hypnotist carelessly left it in a certain room of that building, and none of the villagers were ever supposed to see it. Leafing through the pages, the villager-actor finds his own role delineated right there before him, with most of his life's decisions clearly laid out—the kind of work he does, who he marries, his triumphs and tragedies. Also shocking is the experience of thumbing forward a bit in the script and seeing the major actions and lines of dialogs he is personally set to deliver in the days ahead, in exactly the ways he himself had roughly planned.

Now, try to imagine how *you* would feel in such a situation? It might well trigger an existential crisis of sorts, since you'd be forced to question virtually everything you believed about your life and personality. You'd realize you really weren't in control of your existence much at all, and that you weren't much different from a robot, acting out someone else's programs.

From that point on, you'd probably be second-guessing everything you thought or did, and what was or wasn't scripted by this hidden figure you've just learned about.

However, there's a flip side to this realization, and a more positive one at that. Because now that you *know* about the script, you'd have a certain element of *choice* in what you do, some degree of free will. Why? Because, you could decide now whether or not to act on that script—an option not available to the other actors in the troupe, since they'd have no way of knowing which actions and conversations were truly theirs and which weren't. Through the gift of knowledge, you'd now have a degree of freedom you never experienced before.

Astrology and the "Script" of Our Lives

One of the reasons I introduce this story is because I think it says something useful about astrology. You may recall the encounter I described in the previous chapter, involving my first meeting with an actual astrologer. There was that sense of astonishment I felt about what I was hearing, which made me wonder how in the world someone could tell me about my life just from looking at patterns based on celestial bodies millions of miles away. It also made me question whether or not I was really the master of my own fate.

Astrology, I'd like to suggest, is a way of getting a peek at the script of one's life, from a more objective and detached viewpoint, like what the young villager-actor in my story experienced. And with that peek also comes—ideally, anyway—a certain sense of freedom and free will. Because having seen the *astrological* script, you could now choose whether or not to act out its storylines. Before seeing the horoscope, you never really had that option. (As a teacher I knew once put it, you can't be free from your karma until you first know what it is!) For instance, you might see that Mars is coming up to form a difficult relationship with your Moon, and decide ahead of time not to respond by getting angry; or you might notice that Jupiter is about to cross over your Venus, and decide to take advantage by signing up for a dating site, going to Vegas, or perhaps even by *not* acting on your gambling instincts, whether romantic or financial. Generally speaking, you'd now have more choice in your range of responses than you had before.

In pop culture, I think this is partly why astrology has always been accorded a certain mystique by outsiders, as though it represented a special key into something mysterious and powerful. Because in fact that's partly true; astrology *is* a Promethean "fire" all its own, since it gives you a certain *edge on the gods*, as it were. Those armed with astrology can peek backstage, mess with the stage instructions or dialogue, and just generally do things in a different way or time than laid out in the script. That doesn't make such people any better than anyone else, of course, but it does give them a certain edge on those who *don't* have that knowledge.

(I'm reminded here of a talk show interview with the late comedian Norm MacDonald, in which he described a twitter exchange he had with famed biologist—and avowed materialist—Richard Dawkins, which seemed to have left Dawkins somewhat stumped. Norm tweeted: "Professor, if a man is hard-wired to survive, but is aware of that hard-wiring, isn't he therefore no longer hard-wired?" Dawkins responded, "That's a very interesting and more difficult philosophical question. I need to think more about it." That exchange has obvious implications for astrology, too, since to some extent astrology also suggests we are "programmed"; consequently, if someone becomes aware of their horoscope, are they no longer "hard-wired"?)

The Uranus Connection
In turn, this all connects in a deep way with the symbolism of the planet Uranus, the body most often associated in modern times with astrology.

It's important to remember that Uranus represents *a step outside of the orbit of Saturn*. Why is that so important?

Because Saturn represents the limits of our visible solar system, the "established order" of our conventional laws and boundaries, the status quo, and what is or isn't normal and "acceptable." Uranus exists outside of all that, symbolizing all that doesn't quite fit inside those boundaries, and therefore represents all that is *un*conventional, all that is *apart from* the norm. But more importantly, it can look in on everything contained inside those boundaries with a certain detached understanding. It can think outside of the Saturnian box, rather than from inside it, and act accordingly.

It's thus only natural that Uranus would be associated by so many astrologers with the principle of free will. The advantage given by this planet is similar to that enjoyed by our villager-actor who's able to perceive his life from a more detached and rational viewpoint, due to that peek at the script, rather than from the vantage point of being completely immersed in the story. Or, saying it a little differently, Uranus is a bit like the lab rat that figures a way out of the maze not by exhausting every possible pathway, but rather by standing up and peeking over the top in order to see the layout from above. The perspective given by Uranus is similar to that, and one can easily see why astrologers like Richard

Tarnas and Stephen Arroyo associate it with the mythical figure of Prometheus, the titan who stole fire from the gods and passed it on to humanity.

The "Air" Element and the Aquarian Age

The principle I'm describing here applies just as well to the role and function of the *Air* element in charts, the astrological principle of rationality and mind (and which is strongly connected in meaning to planets like Uranus and Mercury).

The four archetypal elements—Earth Water, Fire and Air—represent uniquely different modes of experience, but Air represents a critical step above and beyond the others, and represents a particularly decisive move beyond animal instincts in its ability to reason in a prolonged way. By contrast, a lion doesn't deliberate over whether it is right or wrong to eat the gazelle, or stop to put its desires on pause to reflect on the significance of what it *means* "to kill"; it simply does what it does. Same goes for your ordinary house plant, the rock in your garden, or a river winding through the mountains.

But the element of Air-rationality goes beyond that, and opens the door to a much broader range of responses. It gives you a certain distance, an ability to extract yourself from experience and observe it more objectively so that you can make decisions based on thinking and analysis rather than pure emotion or even blind fate.

Roughly since the discovery of Uranus, science has essentially been acting out the Air mythos, the archetypal drama of rationality. By extracting itself from the influence of dogma, beliefs, and emotion, rationality attempts to examine nature—whether that be cosmic and human—through the crystalline eye of pure reason, and in doing gain knowledge about how best exploit the properties of the world, for good or ill.

In turn, I naturally see all this as an expression of the larger Great Age we're entering, the era of Aquarius. But one doesn't even need to believe in astrology or "the Great Ages" to recognize there's something to what I'm describing here, in essence. The expanding influence of rationality in our world these last few centuries is obvious enough for anyone to see, *whatever* label you choose to slap on it.

But for those of an astrological bent, the Aquarian Age is clearly shaping up to be an extremely mental one, in which humanity views the world less in mythic, religious or emotional ways than in rational, detached terms, relying more on observation, evidence and induction rather than belief.

As a result, you could well say that humanity has itself stumbled across the "script" which describes the hidden laws underlying both the universe and human psychology.

You can even find signs of this evolutionary shift within the imagery and symbolism of various films and TV shows. In the coming chapters we'll be looking at some of the clues hidden in works like *Citizen Kane* and TV series like *Midnight Mass,* among others. But this shift is even more explicit—and literal—in films like 1998's *The Truman Show,* where the lead character (played by Jim Carrey) gradually realizes he's in a vast production in which he's the unwitting star, living out a story scripted by someone else.[1] And last but not least, there's *The Matrix,* with its story of Neo waking out of the illusory world he's been imprisoned in without even knowing it.

But notice that in these last two films, this process of awakening is actually depicted as *a movement from water and into air.* In *The Truman Show,* the film's final scene shows Jim Carrey leaving a watery world behind to literally walk into the sky (those who have seen the film will know what I'm talking about). In *The Matrix,* Neo's awakening is depicted as a transition from life in a watery amniotic sac to an air-breathing existence. Did the creators of these films understand the archetypal symbolism they were tapping into? Most likely not, but that doesn't mean they weren't intuitively drawing on something deeply archetypal about our times.

To be clear, the collective "awakening" I'm talking about here isn't the same as *spiritual enlightenment*. The great Aquarian shift is far more rational and mental in nature than that; which isn't to minimize its importance, since that represents a pivotal enough stage in our evolution. The awakening of rationality is a turning point, since we can now take that knowledge revealed by the hidden script in several different directions. For instance, rationality allows us to see (and use) the complex laws which underlie our world, as well as those which govern our psychologies (via studies in personal or group psychology, brain chemistry, childhood conditioning, and so on). And while astrology may not ever be *fully* accepted by mainstream science, I have no doubt that it, too, will be a subject of growing interest throughout the coming Great Age, providing us with a look at the even subtler laws governing our world and psyches. With all of this comes a certain amount of power and freedom, since one now one has more control over one's world, more choice in influencing our destinies.

But there is a less constructive side to this emerging Air-rationality—such as the fact we can become so encased in ideas and mental laws that we lose a vital connection to our world, and find ourselves living a relatively "cold" existence. Think of the person who experiences their world largely mediated through smart phones, TV sets, radios, or video games, and so on. We could—and to some extent already have—become a population isolated within our own techno-bubbles, shelled off from reality by machines, ideas, laws, plastic and steel. It might make for a perfectly stimulating life of the mind, but a potentially imbalanced and somewhat "dead" one as well.

More problematically, that awakening of rationality, coupled with our newly heightened individualism, confers huge powers that can be lethal when not harnessed constructively. The

Promethean fires of Uranian rationality have awakened a sleeping giant. With our newfound knowledge of nature's hidden workings, we can create either an Internet or an atom bomb, while awakening the hidden powers of human nature can give us an Albert Einstein or an Adolf Hitler. Humanity has begun tapping into something very powerful, on both the outer and inner fronts; but like the sorcerer's apprentice, it hasn't quite figured out how best to control it.

And if we're not careful, we might very well wind up wishing we'd never stumbled across that script in the first place.

CHAPTER 3

HOMAGE TO ASTROLOGY

I had what seemed an unusually productive session with a client not long ago. Which is to say I offered some information she seemed to find helpful, while managing to hit a few "home runs" along the way, as far as coming up with specific insights into her life and personality.

One of those home runs involved my describing some challenging situations she probably experienced in childhood that were likely coming back into focus for her at the time—the very same week I was talking to her, in fact. (The reason I said this was because of transiting Pluto exactly squaring her natal Moon in the Fourth House.) She looked fairly stunned upon hearing that, and it led her to open up about some of the feelings she had been bottling up inside for a long time.

Now, I normally don't spend much time thinking back about readings once I've finished them, mainly because I'm usually so drained from talking by that point that I just want to decompress. But this time felt different to me for some reason, and I found myself reflecting on the points I made to her—but, more importantly, *why* I made them.

I thought about how I'd synthesized what I'd learned about astrology over the years, connecting this planet over here to that one over there, looking at the signs and houses they were placed in, and the various degrees involved, then drawing certain conclusions about how all these indicators might manifest for her in the real world.

And it all reminded me of just how weird and even miraculous this system really is in some respects. In a way, it evoked some of that same sense of wonderment I experienced on first coming into contact with this system so many years ago, when I was both baffled and mesmerized by what I was told by the teachers I studied with, as well as that first astrologer I met.

NASA photo

For those of us who have worked in this field a long time, of course, it's easy to take it all for granted, and forget that original sense of wonder. But I think it's good to step back on occasion and take a fresh look at what we *actually do*, as a way to reawaken that sense of wonder and awe, as a way to keep some perspective on it.

How to do that, though? Here's one more thought experiment that might help.

Imagine you could be transported back in time a hundred thousand years to life in a wandering tribe existing out in nature somewhere, with nature's elements all around you—the wind, plants, animals, and of course the stars, those sparkling pinpoints of light up there in the nightly dome.

But then try to imagine that your memory had somehow been wiped clean of anything having to do with modern-day astrology. You'd be allowed to retain a memory that there *was* something called "astrology," and how it's based on the idea that the patterns in the sky relate in some way to our affairs down here on earth; but beyond that small inkling of information, you'd be starting completely from scratch.

So there you are, standing beneath the sky, looking up at all those points of light, and you're assigned the challenge of creating an astrology from the ground up all by yourself, of crafting your own system of "astrology."

Where would you even start?

It's safe to say you'd probably pay special attention to the most obvious things seen over the course of a 24-hour day, like the broad movements of the Sun, especially sunrise and sunset, as well as the movements and phases of the Moon. Would you think to even focus on those wandering stars we now call "planets," or no? And which star constellations would you pay more attention to, out of all of those that are visible across the entire sky? For that matter, would you even *recognize* groupings of stars as "constellations"? I suspect you would also pay special attention to any unusual phenomena in the sky, like shooting stars, comets, perhaps the aurora borealis, and of course, eclipses.

But having done that much, just what *meaning* would you start ascribing to any or all of these things? And just how far do you suppose you would have gotten with this project during a single lifetime? Probably not very, to be honest, judging from the glacial pace of astrology's development from its earliest beginnings, from what scholars have been able to piece together.

Fast forward now 100,000 years back to our own present day, to our current level of astrological understanding. You've just come from that bare bones state of knowledge out there in the wild, and find yourself confronted with the extraordinary intricacies that have been built up through the centuries around this discipline, to where we now not only have the luminaries and the planets (including ones not previously visible to the naked eye), but their "aspects," the twelve signs and houses, the various nodes, our knowledge of predictive techniques like transits and progressions, the meanings of specific stars, as well as the mountain of measurements and techniques that have been developed in astrological systems both East and West. With all these tools at your disposal, you'd now be able to build up a picture of someone's inner and outer life that can be astonishingly accurate, sometimes down to weird little details about their experience—some of them so far out in left field that it hardly seems possible one could extract those just from abstract measurements drawn from the sky.

Like that item about my client's childhood issues coming back into her life the same week I spoke to her. Think about that for a second: how can you deduce things about a person's emotional and family life from measurements of a planet so distant it's not even visible to the naked eye, from its placement and precise angular relationship to other bodies in the sky? What could these two realms—terrestrial and celestial—possibly have in common with each other?

Occasionally I find myself thinking, *this is insane, it's bonkers*. It really *shouldn't* work—deducing all manner of things about someone's life just from looking at these little notations on a computer screen, drawn from the sky—and yet it *does*. Time and again, it works.

Here's another example to illustrate just how crazy this could all seem to the untutored eye.

Take the case of famed basketball player Michael Jordan, born on February 7, 1963. One of the many distinguishing features of his horoscope is the fact that Jupiter is the highest planet in his chart, positioned in the sign of Pisces. As I've written about elsewhere, Jupiter elevated in the horoscope can sometimes be an indicator of success or popularity (providing the rest of the horoscope is supportive), and that was certainly true in Jordan's case.

But as I was watching the documentary series about Jordan and the Chicago Bulls basketball team titled "The Last Dance" not long ago, another interesting fact caught my attention. The documentary mentioned how he made 90 million dollars playing for the Bulls, but he actually made far greater amounts of money in endorsements outside the basketball court—a staggering *1.6 billion dollars'* worth, in fact. Not bad money at all for a kid who rose up from humble circumstances.

And what was the product he endorsed which brought in the lion's share of that fortune?

Shoes. ("Air Jordans," to be specific—pretty fitting name, actually, considering Aquarian Michael Jordan is himself an "air" sign.)

Now, remember what zodiacal sign I said his natal Jupiter was located in when he was born? It was *Pisces*—the zodiacal sign traditionally associated with *the feet.* So he was not only born with a possible indicator of success and wealth in his horoscope, but that indicator was specifically located in the zodiacal sign associated with the feet—and Jordan not only wound up becoming successful on the basketball court due to a good deal of fancy footwork, he made even more money outside the basketball court hawking a product *associated with the feet.*

This would all seem perfectly sensible to anyone well-versed in astrology, but from a non-astrological or purely mechanistic standpoint, it would indeed seem bonkers. By making some precise calculations about the positions of planets, signs, houses, I can somehow relate all these back down to someone's life, even down to specific body parts. How is *that* possible?

As I said, it really shouldn't work, not to the skeptical eye, yet work it does. And it's all because of the secret language of symbolism encoded within those myriad points in the sky and their complex movements, all involving a hidden level of correspondences and meanings not readily visible to the naked eye.

And it's all come down to us thanks to the efforts of countless astrologers and skywatchers throughout the millennia who toiled to decipher that extraordinary hidden language, with all its subtle meanings and mysterious linkages, until many generations later we now possess what we have today—namely, a rich body of esoteric knowledge about the universe, more impressive in many ways than anything created by Michelangelo, Bach, or Homer, crafted by countless hands over time and readily available to anyone now as easily as ordering a book or chart online.

Over the years I've come to view astrology as nothing short of a divine gift, one that I've become increasingly grateful for, since it reveals secrets to us about existence not readily found through other avenues. In that same spirit, I would invite my fellow astrologers to consider these factors as well, and remember that each time you practice this art, you're holding in your hands an ancient and infinitely rich treasure, one with the power to not only understand but transform personal lives, perhaps even the entire world.

CHAPTER 4

THE BEATLES ~ HARBINGERS OF THE AQUARIAN AGE?

While I was in college during the 1970s, I had a debate one afternoon with a fellow student about popular culture—in particular, the Beatles. My friend was an unabashed elitist, a true believer in the superiority of classical music and art to anything currently offered up by modern pop culture. When the subject turned to rock music, specifically the Beatles, he literally turned up his nose and suggested they offered nothing of lasting value to culture.

"100 years from now," he said, "they'll be completely forgotten."

I politely disagreed. My sense then was that they'll still be listened to long into the future, not much different from how people still listen to the compositions of George Gershwin, Cole Porter, or for that matter standards like "Greensleeves" or "Ave Maria."

Several decades have passed since that discussion, and I feel just as strongly now in that opinion than before, and that's for several reasons.

For one, the Beatles were actually involved in the cultural revolutions of the last century on *several* fronts, which gave their work an importance beyond the purely musical one. Their influence extended to the realms of politics, media, cinema, fashion, religion, and even mind-altering drugs. Viewed together, it would be hard to overestimate how far-reaching their impact on global culture has been—an influence that continues to ripple on up through our own time.

But what I'd like to suggest here takes it a bit further, in that the Beatles may well hold an archetypal significance relating to the unfolding zeitgeist of the next two millennia. Far-fetched? Maybe. But first consider this simple question:

What accounts for the extraordinary popularity of the Beatles?

Sure, there were obvious musical talents at work there, along with considerable charm, humor and personality. But whenever a major cultural phenomenon comes along and grabs the entire world by the throat, like the Beatles did, there is usually something deeper taking place, as if greater archetypal chords were sounding in the collective unconscious. With that in mind, I've come to believe the Beatles had the impact they did because of how closely they resonated to the impulses of the emerging Aquarian Age. In a variety of ways, they were the spearheads of trends specifically related to that global transformation. We'll look here at a few examples of what I mean.

The Uranus/Pluto Conjunction of the 1960s

But first, it's important to realize that the period during which the Beatles became popular, the 1960s, was characterized by a number of powerful astrological influences—central among those being the epic Uranus/Pluto conjunction which colored that entire decade (and which hadn't happened since the mid-1800s). Technically, that aspect became exact in 1965 and 1966, so it's hardly a coincidence that those two years were the epicenter of the Beatle's most extraordinary work: *Help!, Rubber Soul* (1965), *Revolver* (1966) and, following close behind, *Sgt. Pepper* (1967). Shakespeare wrote, "There is a tide in the affairs of men which, taken at the flood, leads on to fortune." Clearly, the Beatles were riding that tide of the Sixties to their own fortunes, along with quite a few others (like Bob Dylan, who came out with his most critically acclaimed albums in 1965 and 1966 —*Bringing it All Back Home, Highway 61,* and *Blonde on Blonde*).

As I've remarked elsewhere,[1] I've come to regard major planetary configurations like this on the cusp between Great Ages as "cosmic triggers" in the way they serve to activate and illustrate the transition from older epochs to newer, different ones. They are the "micro-triggers" within the larger "macro-phases" of the Great Ages (a point we'll come back to in chapter 34). In this case, the significance of this configuration is due partly to the role of Uranus—the planet believed by most modern astrologers to rule (or co-rule) Aquarius. Even without Uranus, though, I've come to believe that *any* major planetary configuration on the cusp between Great Ages can serve as just such a trigger, helping to usher in the energies of a new paradigm. The upshot is, the cultural manifestations of the mid-60s can be seen as foreshadowing what lies ahead for us, in both constructive and destructive ways. With that said, let's look now at some of those trends the Beatles reflected, and how they can be related to the archetypal currents of the Aquarian mythos.

The Power of the Collective
At the most basic level, we need to look first at the fact that their primary impact was, first and foremost, as a *group*—a band of friends. That by itself is obviously Aquarian. But at its most constructive, Aquarius isn't about just any "group"; note how all four of the Beatles were distinct *individuals*. By comparison, can you name any one of the musicians who backed up Elvis? Or Sinatra? Or Duke Ellington? Sure, a few aficionados can, but most cannot. But virtually everyone knows the names John, Paul, George and Ringo. While Aquarian group consciousness does have its darker side, in representing a sort of faceless "mob" consciousness, at its most creative it represents the power of community, of group activism, of individuals working together in harmony. In the process it shows us what each of us can do "with a little help from our friends."

Let me explain a bit further. I've written frequently about the importance of *jazz* as a symbol for the higher potentialities of

Aquarian group consciousness, and we'll come back to that later.[2] Whereas the Gregorian choir of the fading Piscean Age required that singers surrender their individualities for the sake of a higher ideal, a typical jazz band *encourages* personal creativity and individuality within the group. That's a uniquely different, and very Aquarian, form of collective.

Nor is it just in jazz or music where we find that archetypal dynamic in play. Besides being the essential dynamic of democracy, the same essential symbolism underlies the story of *The Wizard of Oz*, where four distinctly different beings join together on a great quest. Unlike the classic mythic quests of ancient times, like the search for the Holy Grail or the Golden Fleece, each member of L. Frank Baum's group is searching for something distinctly different, yet despite that they are able to work together harmoniously.

I'd suggest that this same dynamic applies to the Beatles. Their music may not have been strictly "jazz" in style (although they toyed with the genre in songs like "I'm Only Sleeping"), but their individual contributions to the group definitely involved a jazz-like merging of personal and group energies, in a way dramatically different from the strictly anonymous Gregorian choirs of old.

From the Bottom Up: Working Class Heroes

It's also important to note that the Beatles represented a distinctly populist, grass-roots effort. These weren't upper crust, "trust-fund" kids, let alone descendants of royal bloodlines; all four hailed from working class roots. That's Aquarian as well, with this zodiacal sign's "We the People" democratic emphasis holding forth from the other end of the zodiac from more kingly and queenly Leo.

As such, the Beatles came to represent what might be called *the triumph of the average person*. Aquarius represents the influence of ordinary men and women, whether for good or ill, whether for mob rule or group activism and creativity. We're entering an age where, thanks to the internet and media, virtually anyone can become influential or famous. The Beatles gave hope to young people around the world that even those from modest backgrounds and means could rise into positions of wealth, influence, and authority. That's a relatively new phenomenon in global society, and hints at one of the manifestations of what Aquarius has begun introducing into the world.

Apostles of Freedom
But there was something even deeper involved with the Beatles' lingering impact, and that had to do with the notion of *freedom*. With their long hair, irreverent attitudes and unconventional lifestyles, as depicted in films like *A Hard Days Night* and *Help!,* there was something about them which spoke to young people about a different attitude towards life, an attitude of rebellion, self-expression and creative possibility. It's worth noting that when they first became famous, all four were wearing corporate-style black suits—"uniformity" in the most literal sense of the word—and only later abandoned those uniforms in favor of more personalized outfits. As such, they were a microcosm of what was happening throughout the culture, as society itself began moving away from corporate uniformity and towards more individualized forms of self-expression.

Indeed, that spirit of freedom and rebellion had some surprising social consequences, not just in the U.S. and Europe but across the world. I hinted earlier at the political influence of the Beatles. Aside from their public and musical statements on such matters ("Give Peace a Chance," "Revolution"), there were some real-world decisions on their part which left a formidable imprint on history. For instance, in 1964 they showed their support for the civil rights movement in the U.S. by refusing to play a show for a segregated audience in Jacksonville, Florida. "I'd sooner lose our appearance money," Lennon remarked at the time. With the threat of their backing out of the concert potentially causing a major controversy, the officials overseeing the event finally caved and allowed the segregated audiences to merge.

In addition, there are a growing number of historians and social commentators who attribute the break-up of the Soviet Union and its brand of communism (a distinctly Piscean Age phe-nomenon—the economic version of a Gregorian choir) in large part to Western pop culture, but particularly the Beatles. They embodied a new spirit of freedom for young people that reflected itself not just in musical and artistic areas but in attitudes towards politics. "Beatlemania washed away the foundations of Soviet society," explained Mikhail Safonov at the Institute of Russian History. The Russian rock musician Sasha Lipnitsky added, "The Beatles brought us the idea of democracy. For many of us, it was the first hole in the Iron Curtain." [3] While it's no doubt true that the wave of change in the U.S.S.R. triggered by the Beatles would have happened even without them, it likely wouldn't have hap-pened nearly as soon, nor quite as colorfully.

From Religion to Secularism
On another front, the shift from Pisces to Aquarius signifies the transition from a religious era to a more secular one. It's not that Aquarius is *anti*-religion, simply that it doesn't demand unques-tioning fealty to a specific faith, religious leader, or ideology; it's more decentralized and kaleidoscopic than that. By contrast, Pisces is inextricably religious and ideological. (If Aquarius is dogmatic or ideological about anything, it would more likely be science or technology.)

This stand-off between worldviews came to a head in 1965, exactly during the peak of the Uranus/Pluto alignment, when John Lennon made his controversial statement, "We're more popular than Jesus" during a press conference. It set off a firestorm of reaction from conservative Christians everywhere, causing religious devotees to gather in protest and destroy their Beatles records. In truth, Lennon didn't mean to suggest they were *better* than Jesus, he was simply commenting on a social reality. The fact is, and was, fans of The Beatles *did* shower a degree of near-religious devotion on the band in ways previously reserved for spiritual figures and movements—which was exactly Lennon's point. The times they *were* a-changin', and doing so in ways that reflected a shift from the religious values of the Piscean era to the more secular ones of the Aquarian one. (Something was definitely in the air throughout that time; several months after Lennon's statement, for instance, the editors of *Time* magazine famously stirred up controversy when they printed the words "Is God Dead?" on their front cover.)

Ushering in the New Global Culture

Finally, it's important to mention the role the Beatles played in drawing together social and artistic influences from around the world towards the emergence of a true global culture. They weren't the first to incorporate foreign musical elements from other traditions into their own, nor were they the first to travel to the Far East in search of mystic wisdom. Yet their enormous fame led them to have a far greater impact in those ways than anyone else had before.

Suddenly, musicians from distant lands began appearing on musical stages across Europe and the U.S., while Western musicians were returning the favor by touring in far-off countries and incorporating previously exotic elements into their own recordings. For the Beatles, that cultural cross-pollination was underscored by John Lennon's marriage to Japanese-born (and Aquarian) Yoko Ono. In fact, the Beatles synthesized elements from *many* musical tributaries, including folk, blues, rock, classical, jazz, pop,

Motown, experimental, even heavy metal—which is Aquarian in spirit, since this sign is less concerned with monolithic styles or genres than with a more inclusive or "kaleidoscopic" integration of myriad perspectives.

In the process, the Beatles became a worldwide media phenomenon—itself a modern development—uniting audiences from countries and their citizens beyond just Great Britain and the U.S. As a child I remember watching their first appearance on the Ed Sullivan show in 1964, a broadcast garnering 23 million viewers. That was followed by their appearance in 1967 performing "All You Need Is Love" for a live satellite telecast that reached an astonishing 350 million viewers around the world. In some ways, that telecast was similar to the first Moon landing in 1969 in uniting masses of people in the same moment of time for a singular event. Here, too, there was a dissolving of local boundaries in service of a world culture, along with a linking of minds toward a larger "group consciousness."

"And in the end..."
These, then, are a few of the ways the Beatles embodied themes intrinsic to the emerging Aquarius mythos. While I see this as being a largely positive development, there are always two sides to everything, and besides their impact on creativity and global culture we have to consider the potential darker side of their influence and symbolism as well, however inadvertent and unintended that may have been. Here are a couple examples of that.

While the Beatles ostensibly represented non-conformity, they influenced millions of people to be, act, and look just like them, in ways that were, ironically, extremely conformist. In its own way, this led to a kind of "hive-mind" situation—which is one of the dangers of Aquarian society at its most negative and extreme.

As world-famous celebrities, they also represented the pitfalls of the Aquarius/Leo epoch in terms of the extraordinary lack of privacy they experienced, as the eyes of the world scrutinized their every move and statement. That's been increasingly happening to *all* of us, actually, as we find ourselves plugged into a worldwide electronic network, exposed to the prying eyes of countless unseen individuals and companies.

But despite problems like these, I think it's clear the Beatles represented the more harmonious potentials of Aquarian group consciousness. In the end, the Beatles weren't simply a product of the 60s, but of the ages—the *Great Ages*, to be precise. Even for those who may not like their music, it's still possible to speculate that, centuries from now, the 1960s will be studied by scholars and historians just as we now do with the Roaring 20s, *fin de siècle* 1890s, or even the Renaissance. And when that happens, the Beatles phenomenon will be at the forefront of those studies, emblematic of a tectonic social change that will reverberate long after they left the world stage.

CHAPTER 5

BRAIN KOAN

I magine if you could look at someone and actually see their brain. Crazy idea, I know—except that's exactly what happens every time you look into someone's eyes. That's because they are the one part of the brain that actually reaches the surface of the body—the retina, anyway. That means that when you see their eyes, you're really seeing their brain.

So now you know.

There are boatloads of interesting facts like that about the brain, of course. Here's another one, or set of them, actually.

I once asked a brain surgeon if he could give me a basic description of how the brain works. He said it essentially boiled down to a combination of brain chemistry and electrical impulses; maybe a few other things, but those were the basics. Now, compare that to something the mystic and yogi Shelly Trimmer said to me in passing during a conversation about possible future technologies, and how they might involve the psychic sciences. We wandered onto the topic of possible technologies for tapping into the "akashic records" (the so-called cosmic records of all that's happened since the dawn of time). I asked him how would one even go about *creating* something like that—that is, a machine or computer that "not only matches the human mind but even taps into paranormal information." In response, he quickly rattled off the following points about the workings of the human mind, and by implication, the brain:

> You first have to decode the human mind, so that you know how a person thinks. The human mind uses FM, AM,

analog, and digital, and it uses single-sideband in order to process information. It uses chemicals, it uses electricity—it uses everything you can conceive of to process information, including things they haven't even discovered yet. So you need to use all of these factors...In fact, if you're going to create a *really* smart computer that's comparable to man, also incorporate laser devices for the computer, since those are dealing with much higher frequencies, and you can include more bits of information per unit of time with a laser than with any other system. So you'd be using fibers and lasers associated with it. And of course, electronics too. Once you've built an intelligent computer, you then have to go into the field of 'psi-tronics' in order to get into the psychic memory banks. So far you don't know how to decode that stuff, but if you keep going, you might find out how, and then you can telephone into the memory banks of the cosmic dream of God—or for that matter, anyone else's memory banks. [1]

Considering he wasn't a doctor or a psychologist, I found his comment quite a bit more interesting than what the neurosurgeon said to me. I can't say whether it was more important or more valid, but it was certainly more interesting, and was just one of the reasons I became intrigued by Shelly's knowledge on any number of subjects.

But this all still leaves open the question: *what actually is the "brain"?* There's a reason I ask this—and it may be a bit different from what you might expect.

Not long ago I came across a scientific paper which attempted to explain, in strictly materialistic terms, how everything we perceive in the outside world is really just a construct in one's brain. In a very matter-of-fact way, it explained how the colors we see, the sounds we hear, and the meanings we ascribe to phenomena and people—that's all put together and re-presented in this lump of meat up here in my skull. It's all taking place in my brain. All that got me thinking about a question I've been pondering ever since I was back in college:

Doesn't the idea described by that paper mean that our concept of the brain is *also* a construct of the brain? And if that's so, where is all of this—including your perception of these words right now—taking place, if indeed the brain is nothing but a construct in and of itself?

And what exactly is doing the thinking?

What exactly is doing the observing?

CHAPTER 6

AVATARS, GENIUSES, AND CHANNELING THE DIVINE

The term has become a buzzword in pop culture these days largely because of its association with the blockbuster film of director James Cameron. But look up the word "avatar" in the spiritual literature and you'll sometimes find it defined as the "direct incarnation of the Divine into our world." In Hinduism, for instance, we're told of the ten appearances of Vishnu in a variety of forms that include a fish, tortoise, boar, a half-man/half-lion, as well as more developed figures like Rama, Krishna, Buddha, and last but not least, Kalki. In the *Bhagavad Gita*, Krishna tells Prince Arjuna:

> Whenever there is a decline of righteousness (dharma) and rise of unrighteousness then I send forth Myself. For the protection of the good, for the destruction of the wicked, and for the establishment of righteousness, I come into being from age to age.

It's an inspiring concept, to be sure. Yet I've long felt there was something vaguely paradoxical about the avatar concept, and that centers around the fact that in some of these accounts the avatar in question talks about having had *numerous past lives.* For instance, Krishna also says this to Arjuna,

> Many, many births both you and I have passed. I can remember all of them, but you cannot.

Why is that paradoxical? Because if the avatar is indeed a *direct* incarnation of the divine, as distinct from other mortal beings, why would these accounts also speak of a *multitude* of past lives, just like any other mortal? Note that Krishna didn't simply speak about eight, nine, or ten past lives, but of "*many, many* births"—almost as if he were an ordinary human enduring the interminable round of rebirths himself. (And by the way, aren't we *all* incarnations of the Divine?) So, just how direct of a "direct incarnation" is the avatar, anyway?

Here is my take on all of this.

Becoming a Suitable Vessel

For the sake of discussion, let's assume that it's indeed possible for the Divine to enter into our world, whether we think of that in terms of God him/herself, or simply as a highly evolved being who chooses to come down and help us out, a divine emissary of sorts. Either way, it's safe to say that this divine intelligence would necessarily be far more evolved than ordinary mortals.

If so, though, how could that spiritual being simply incarnate directly into ordinary human society? To use an analogy, try to imagine a human—say, Martin Luther King or St. Francis of Assisi—trying to incarnate down to the level of the ant kingdom to help out the ants. How could he adjust to the massive constriction he'd encounter in the conversion? And how would he be able to relate to the profoundly different mindset and biology of the ant kingdom?

In a somewhat similar way, we need to ask: How would a massively evolved divine entity—like God herself—simply slip into ordinary human form and relate to us on *our* level?

There's a relatively simple solution to this problem. The divine intelligence could simply employ *a human conduit through which to operate.* In other words, if there was a human on Earth who had evolved enough over many lifetimes to resonate with that lofty divine impulse, he or she could then serve as a *channel* for that divine being and their intentions. They'd be a suitable "host," in a manner of speaking.

Indeed, that concept resonates closely with one of the central features of the life of Jesus, as depicted in the Bible. Notice that up to around the age of 30, Jesus acted like a comparatively normal person, and hadn't yet risen to the full status of his appointed destiny. If we are to believe the written accounts, even *he* didn't seem to consider his transformation complete until he was formally baptized. (Think about it: why would a purported "Son of God" feel a need to be baptized by a mere mortal?) And so it was, climaxing in his baptism in the river Jordan, that the Holy Spirit descended into him—actually appearing in the form of a dove, we're told—at which point a voice issued from heaven saying, "This is my beloved son, in whom I am well pleased." At that point, you could say he transformed from simply being *Jesus the carpenter* to *Jesus the Christ,* having now become a conscious conduit for God the Father, a humble channel for the Divine Will.

(Interestingly, even up to the end of his life Jesus seemed to exhibit ambivalence about that dual existence, both mortal and divine. That's especially obvious in the Garden of Gethsemane as he struggled with God's plan. The Gospel of Matthew described it this way: "…he became anguished and distressed. He told them, 'My soul is crushed with grief to the point of death…' He…bowed with his face to the ground, praying, 'My Father! If it is possible, let this cup of suffering be taken away from me. Yet I want your will to be done not mine.'" [Matthew 26:37-39, NLT]. This clearly implies there was still a very human personality right alongside the Divine one, and they hadn't completely fused into a single entity yet.

The Avatar/Genius connection

To my mind, there is something analogous here to what we see in the lives of great geniuses, whether they be artistic, literary or scientific in nature. Every now and then we come across a true genius who produces a work that seems nearly transcendent in its brilliance, as if he or she had tapped into something far beyond ordinary human capacity and which brought down the "fire of the gods" into tangible form.

For example, we'll see a great writer like Shakespeare, Tolstoy or Herman Melville pen a work that somehow seems to operate on multiple levels simultaneously and opens itself up to countless interpretations for years or even centuries to come, sometimes in ways even the author him or herself didn't fully comprehend. It's not uncommon to hear artists, songwriters, or poets themselves claim they don't feel entirely responsible for their work, as if their creativity was more akin to "channeling" something from beyond themselves.

So where does it come from?

In ancient Greece, of course, this was sometimes explained in connection with the notion of the "muse." There were nine of them in all, and they were regarded as the source and inspiration for all great achievements in art, dance, poetry, comedy, astronomy, music, and history. A related notion is implied in the Latin root for the word "genius," which concerns the guardian deity or spirit which watches over each person from birth, as well as in the concept of the "genie," familiar to most now in those Middle Eastern tales about spirits in bottles that possess unusual powers.

But whereas the notion of the avatar would seem to require an extraordinary degree of moral and spiritual purification over multiple lifetimes for any mortal to qualify as a host, I think it's slightly different in the case of artistic or intellectual geniuses. Here, it seems to be more a matter of developing one's *creative and mental* qualities over time, more than any explicitly spiritual or moral ones. (Just consider how so many of our greatest artists have been seriously flawed human beings). Or, if one isn't comfortable with the reincarnational model involving multiple lives, you might instead think in terms of Malcolm Gladwell's proverbial "10,000 hours," which suggests that one achieves a certain degree of excellence only after so many hours and years of practice within a discipline. The Beatles were one example of that, having spent years refining their talents as performers and songwriters before they recorded their music in the studio.

Either way, this more explicitly creative or artistic form of genius requires that a person hone their talents to such a degree that the necessary motor skills become instinctual, after which the "higher" influence can enter in and guide their faculties, whether one chooses to think of that as involving an external intelligence or simply one's own higher intuitive powers. As someone who has been involved with various creative projects over the years, I've come to think that most of those involved in the creative arts for any length of time have probably experienced such moments of inspiration, however fleeting, to where it may indeed feel like something's been handed to you, and you wind up being surprised by the outcome.

But I think we can bring this all closer to home and talk about it in even more mundane contexts, since the process I'm describing here can occur in *any* area where one has developed mastery. One example of that can be seen with sports players. I remember watching an interview with a pro football player in which he spoke about those special moments during games where he felt completely "in the zone," where time seemed to slow down and he made precisely the right moves throwing the ball to a downfield receiver. It's safe to say that he tapped into his own personal "genius" in those moments, or what I've sometimes called *samadhi-in-motion* The psychologist Mihály Csíkszentmihályi described something similar with his concept of "flow." One sometimes hears of similar experiences from martial artists, skiers, and baseball players, as well as dancers, master chefs, or even those participating in religious or magical rituals.

I once took part in a Buddhist ceremony during my time at a Zen monastery in upstate New York when, at one point, my movements and those of my fellow participants synchronized and "flowed together" in a way that almost seemed to suggest a telepathic connection amongst us. In a way very difficult to describe, it felt like something bigger than our surface personalities had been choreographing the show. Similarly, it's not uncommon to hear musicians describe improvising with fellow musicians and experiencing heightened moments of communion with each other, as if something larger had taken over and was synchronizing their actions.

What exactly is happening during such moments? Should we chalk it up to an external deity, muse, or *daemon* guiding our consciousness? Or does it involve one's own "higher self"? Or might it simply be a matter of higher brain functions, with no need whatsoever for theories of God, angelic beings, or spiritual factors of any sort? I'm not entirely sure it matters, since either way the result seems to be the same.

Mastering One Thing

I'd like to close off by suggesting a very specific way we can cultivate and develop this ability in our own lives, and it stems from something I heard a spiritual teacher once say to his students. As a prerequisite for studying with him, he insisted that they take the time to "master one thing"—whether that be a subject, talent, manual skill, or spiritual practice—and to "become the best or most knowledgeable in the entire world at that thing."

The more I've thought about that over the years, the more I think this closely relates to what we've been looking at here. By taking a given skill or subject and developing a degree of mastery with it, several things begin to take place. For one, it serves as a "grounding" or centering force that organizes one's mental and physical energies, and brings one's life into sharper focus. In a sense, it actually offers a path towards mastering *yourself.*

But it also paves the way for that higher intuitive genius to enter in and operate from a level beyond the conventional mind. By analogy, it strikes me as being a bit like knocking a hole in one's ceiling to create a skylight so that sunlight can pour in. By mastering a given skill or subject, you might say that it helps create a skylight in *oneself,* through which one can develop a back-and-forth communication between the "lower" and "higher" levels of one's nature.

And in so doing, one eventually becomes an "avatar" to oneself—and quite possibly, others as well.

This essay first appeared in Quest magazine, Spring 2020.

CHAPTER 7

CLASSROOM EARTH

A client recently confided to me how depressing it had been for her looking at the news lately, what with all the cruelty, greed, and dishonesty that seemed rampant around the world these days, and which only seems to be getting worse. She'd become "disappointed in the human race," as she put it.

She then asked me, "Do you ever think there will be a time when humanity finally grows up and becomes enlightened?"

Well, yes, I do, I said, but "maybe not in the way you might expect, or possibly even like."

Think of it this way, I told her. Imagine someone walking into an ordinary grade school on a particularly "off" day and seeing a few of the third graders in the classroom acting up—fighting with one another, throwing spitballs, acting unruly, and so on— prompting that visitor to ask, "Why is there so much poor behavior with these kids?"

Well, my answer to that question would probably be that some of that behavior is due to the fact that kids in third grade act pretty much like—wait for it—*third graders*. As a result, they probably shouldn't be expected to act like seventh or eighth graders, let alone college graduates, not every one of them, anyway. (There are always a few who are mature beyond their years, I know, but just a few.) In fact, I'd say that in any halfway decent school, third grade is reasonably well-suited to deal with kids at that level of intellectual and emotional development.

In turn, I'd like to suggest that our Earth is, in a sense, analogous to third grade—a *cosmic* third grade, you could say. Looked at symbolically, the Earth is the third planet from the Sun, and represents a sort of "way station" between Mars and Venus, between the third and fourth planets of our system.

In terms of their equivalents within the chakra system, that puts the majority of us humans somewhere between the third and fourth chakras in our *spiritual* growth.

The Solar System as Symbolic Mirror
According to some schools of thought, the various bodies of our solar system mirror our inner chakras—"As without, so within," as the saying goes. According to this model, the Sun corresponds to the "third eye," or *ajna* chakra, representing the higher spiritual potentials of consciousness, with the planets fanning out from there relating to the other chakras on down the line. Mercury thus relates to the throat chakra, Venus to the heart chakra, Mars to the naval chakra, Jupiter to the second chakra, with Saturn at the bottom relating to the root center, or *muladhara* chakra. (The outer planets have their place in this system as well, but that's a subject beyond the scope of this discussion.)

Let me explain. For those unfamiliar with this system, the "chakras" are the psycho-spiritual centers of consciousness located along the length of the spine, as described in the esoteric teachings of yoga. While there are supposedly thousands of different chakras located throughout the body, most teachers identify six or seven *primary* ones, each relating to a different level or state of consciousness. To astrologically-minded mystics, these primary chakras correspond in surprisingly close ways in their meanings to the visible celestial bodies of our solar system (as illustrated above). As a result, the Sun and Moon reflect the qualities of the dual chakric centers in the head; Mercury corresponds to the mental qualities and concerns of the throat chakra; Venus to the aesthetic or loving concerns of the heart chakra, and so on. (I've written in more detail about these correspondences in other books, most notably chapter ten of *The Waking Dream*, and chapter five of *An Infinity of Gods*, although my most detailed discussion of the subject was in an essay I contributed to the 1997 Weiser anthology *Eastern Systems for Western Astrologers*.)

So what does all this mean for those of us here on Earth, positioned as we are between the planets Mars and Venus?

To me, it suggests that the primary lessons of this planet have to do with managing the tug-of-war between the relatively animalistic instincts of Mars and the more loving and artistic impulses of Venus. Perched between those two, the Earth is a transitional world, an archetypal battleground of sorts where humans struggle between their impulses toward anger and love, fear and desire, horror and beauty.

Fortunately, the higher exemplars of those next-level, Venusian energies do walk among us, whether that take the form of spiritual teachers, avatars, or just plain ordinary folks doing good and decent things. But that doesn't apply to everyone on this planet, so expecting all of Earth's inhabitants to act like highly-evolved beings is not much different from expecting third graders to act like eighth graders or college graduates.

So just as third grade is pretty suitable for most children of a certain age, I'd say this planetary classroom is probably the right place for humans to work through the sorts of issues we see being acted out here—however imperfectly that may seem to us most of the time.

But there's another key point to add to this discussion, which speaks to the uniqueness of this particular rung on the evolutionary ladder. Precisely *because* we straddle this "midpoint" between worlds, between the animalistic and the angelic, there's an element of free will here that may not exist on other rungs of the evolutionary ladder, at least not to the same degree. The angels above can't really be other than angels, nor can the demons below really be other than what they are. But in this transitional no-man's land we find ourselves in, betwixt heaven and hell, we can choose to go in *either* direction. We are not quite as bound by our destinies. Which of course is a precarious position to be in, since the stakes are that much higher as a result. That freedom to choose is a gift in its own way, but it's a razor's edge as well.

With that in mind, our best hope as students in this classroom may be to simply do our best to resonate to those higher potentials, while helping others to lift their sights upward as well. If we can achieve that, that's quite a lot. The American-born yogi Goswami Kriyananda[1] put it well when he said, *"What the spiritual life is about is becoming nobler than the civilization you are in."*

CHAPTER 8

THE CITY OF BIG SHOULDERS

I was walking toward the north end of the Michigan Avenue bridge late one afternoon in the early 1970s when a large black car pulled up quickly next to the curb. This was an area normally off-limits to parking, so I suspected someone prominent must be inside.

The passenger door in the back opened, and out of it emerged, like shot out of a cannon, a short man in an expensive black suit. I recognized immediately it was Mayor Daley, the elder—or as some of the locals referred to him, *Hizzoner*. He was defiantly proud-looking, with shoulders back and chest puffed out like some human/bulldog hybrid. Paradoxically, there was also something almost childlike about his face that hinted at something very different behind that bravado. Though we nearly collided, he looked past me like I wasn't even there, disappearing fast into the plaza of sunlit bodies.

He was the archetypal big city mayor in some ways, but he was in some ways also the archetypal Chicagoan. This city has seen its share of colorful characters over the years, and Daley was certainly one of those.

I grew up on the Chicago's borders, and during my childhood the city felt forbidding to me in some ill-defined way. Venturing into it with my parents by car or train was simultaneously a source of both wonderment and fear. As a child, that latter impression was influenced partly by my experiences just across the city line into Chicago's "Austin" district, where my cousins Billy and Alfred lived, on the 900 block of Waller, and with whom we spent many weekends. My brother and I would get together with them to watch horror films on Saturday afternoons at the Rockne

Theater, or stay up till midnight on Saturday nights to watch horror movies on a weekly TV show called "Shock Theater."

Like now, gangs were a problem in that area; that neighborhood had the highest crime rate in the city at the time. But unlike
now, where the gangs are largely black, in those days the gangs
were largely Italian. I recall all too well the sight of gang members
milling about street corners and alleyways. I was frightened when
I heard stories of one or another of our friends from that neighborhood being beaten up by those menacing fellows in their t-shirts.

The older I grew, though, the more I came to see it as great good fortune to live near such a large city. This was partly for the all the obvious reasons—museums, libraries, musical and theatrical events. I attended many great lectures and classes there, as well as meeting some extraordinary astrologers and spiritual teachers.

But even the simple act of mingling with the hordes of pedestrians on its city streets fed my soul in undefinable ways, which made for quite a contrast to the agoraphobia that afflicted me early on. I always enjoyed seeing the variety of characters that graced the big city streets. There were stories in all their faces and body language. Sometimes that included a few surprises along the way, like seeing Frank Zappa standing outside the Palmer House eating potato chips from a bag and looking ahead with a 1000-yard stare (likely to dissuade conversations with possible fans like myself); Bob Hope in Marshall Fields department store holding forth for throngs of admirers; or jazz trumpeter Dizzy Gillespie flashing his million-megawatt smile in front of Rose Records; composer Aaron Copland shuffling past me at the Chicago Public Library on his way to a music recital; writer Stephen King looking like a deer in the headlights on his first national book tour, signing copies of *The Shining;* or talking to media scholar Marshall McLuhan without even knowing it was him I was conversing with.

But there are subtler factors at work in any city's personality, including that quality philosophers sometimes refer to as the *spirit of place.* This is the distinctive character unique to each locale and which shapes its inhabitants in ways both obvious and subtle. We're usually too close to it to recognize it with any clarity, and for me, anyway, it's taken the better part of a lifetime, and many travels away from home, to truly understand or appreciate what comprises that spirit of Chicago.

And what most surprised me over the years was how the very thing I most disliked about this city early on turned out to be one of the things I grew to appreciate about it.

Diesel and Dust

The elder Daley, like him or not, had it in spades: a quality of earthiness and no-nonsense toughness. Chicago has its more beautiful and refined face—its exquisite architecture, the lakefront, and the "Magnificent Mile" which plays host to the Art Institute and various parks at one end and upscale stores on the other. But I always saw those as masking this city's less appealing side, like glamorous make-up on a backstreet thug. In my late teens and twenties, I worked a couple of jobs in a run-down part of town on the city's near-West Side, along a stretch of Halsted Street, which was referred to then as "skid row" (but which has since been yuppified beyond all recognition). Every day I would take the elevated train to the Halsted train stop and maneuver my way past the listless bodies of drunks lying along the sidewalk. That was definitely a side of Chicago I could do without.

Then there is this city's longstanding association with organized crime, and iconic figures like Al Capone and Bugs Moran. To this day go into almost any foreign city and mention you're from Chicago, and the listener might well say, "Rat-a-tat-tat-tat!" while gleefully mimicking machine gun fire with their fingers. That association wasn't altogether unjustified, of course, and it was one of the reasons I never really considered Chicago to be a particularly spiritual town, toddling or otherwise. Quite the contrary, I tended to think of it as being very Saturnian, or "root chakra"—that is, too focused on earthy, materialistic values.

But there is more than meets the eye to such things, and over time I came to view even *that* side of Chicago differently. To my surprise, I even saw that element of earthiness as one of its virtues. There are more glamorous cities in the world, and others with more exotic scenery, that's true, but the sheer grit of this city, along with its nuts-and-bolts practicality and overall geographical flatness, confer on residents a certain authenticity I haven't found in many other places. Just about when I start to feel stymied by this city's occasional narrow-mindedness and materialism, features which can make it harder to push the envelope here than in some other places (except when it comes to architecture and comedy, curiously), I'll discover an almost Zen-like "realness" to that part of the city's character.

For one, it's given rise to a quality of directness and honesty in its citizens, an ability to cut through bullshit and simply call a spade a spade. *Groundedness* is a word that comes to mind. For instance, I've encountered spiritual teachers from other parts of the country, especially the West Coast, and have been surprised by how some of them seem to be just a bit *too* ethereal, a little *too* "holy." That's why I found it refreshing coming across a Chicago-based teacher like Goswami Kriyananda, who shot from the hip and was someone you'd feel perfectly comfortable having a drink with, if only he drank. He never presented himself as better than anyone else, and never wore his spirituality on his sleeve. That always felt to me like it was due to his Chicago roots.

The Spirit of Chicago Blues

When I meet fellow Chicagoans in other parts of the world, I immediately notice that sense of directness and authenticity, which is often paired with a certain humor and humility (those latter qualities possibly resulting from Chicago's "second city" status). Living here, you don't really appreciate how special that is until you experience it from afar, from the perspective of distant cultures.

Consider the seeming paradox of how so many music-lovers in a country like France appreciate Chicago-style blues, which are so completely different in style from the refinements of their own cultural heritage. Chicago blues may be taken for granted by many of the locals but it's fascinating how it seems to possess an almost "exotic" quality to some listeners from afar. I once heard actor (and former Chicagoan) Bill Murray say during an interview how the French may love blues, but they can't play it worth a damn. Try listening to Debussy's "Claire de Lune" and Muddy Waters' "Hootchie Kootchie Man" back to back, and you'll see why: the sensibilities informing those two styles spring from completely opposite ends of the spine, one top, the other bottom.

But in a way, that's precisely why they complement each other so well. American blues was born in the South but grew up in Chicago, and couldn't have developed in the beautiful environs of Big Sur or the French Riviera. Detroit or Philly? Sure, maybe. Blues is a fundamentally secular, earthy music that celebrates, even *sanctifies* life's carnality, as well as its suffering. When performed by figures like Albert King or Koko Taylor, it becomes a kind of musical Haiku, with so much said using so few notes.

It was that raw energy and "complex simplicity" that attracted 60's British musicians like the Rolling Stones and John Mayall to this city, for whom Chess Studios on Michigan Avenue became a kind of Mecca. Resurrected by foreigners and echoed back from afar, those transformed creations held up a sonic mirror to teenagers like myself to hear our city's music anew—which in its own way, wound up transforming world culture, and served as one more catalyst in the shift from the old world of Pisces into the new, more secular one of Aquarius.

Life in the Border Town

But as I mentioned, I grew up mainly on the city's fringes, in the near-West suburbs. This is a no-man's land between urban and pastoral, and it's a world I also had ambivalent feelings about. I appreciated the relative tranquility of the suburbs, along with the beauty of features like the Frank Lloyd Wright buildings I encountered almost daily, not to mention the nearby forest preserves which I explored as much as possible.

At the same time, I abhorred the suburbs' hyper-stability and overly sanitized qualities. These are features which can anesthetize the sensitive soul and prompt restless types toward extreme measures. I suspect it was a big part of the reason why Hemingway was so eager to get away from Oak Park and see the larger world in all its untamed wildness and spontaneity.

That same borderland reality sometimes gives rise to a certain split personality syndrome, a Jeckyll/Hyde duality between cosmetic surfaces above and turbulent forces below, not unlike that portrayed in David Lynch's *Blue Velvet*. For me, that split was especially obvious in the suburbs' intimate relationship with organized crime. Whereas the city was where the mob earned its money, its ruling chiefs lived away from the city and settled in the comfort of those pastoral fringes.

The neighborhood I grew up in, Oak Park, was one of the domiciles of choice for many of them. A few blocks to the west of us in River Forest was Tony "Big Tuna" Accardo and Paul "the Waiter" Ricca; while a few blocks to the East of me, in Oak Park itself, was mob boss Sam Giancana. But the mob presence came even closer to home for me, when a notorious hit man and his family moved into a house across the street from my family on Belleforte Avenue. His name was Richard Siegel, related to his considerably more famous cousin, Bugsy. He had a suitably brutish look, with a large hook nose that earned him the nickname "the Beak" amongst colleagues. They all had nicknames like that, it seems. His name or picture appeared periodically in the Chicago newspapers, for one or another crime, and he would sometimes disappear from sight for several months at a time, once for a couple of years.

It was clear to me his family suffered terribly for his actions—his wife, their daughter, and especially his eldest son. Early on, he struck me as a highly sensitive kid, but after his dad's arrest hit the front page just one too many times, he was taunted mercilessly at school and developed a hard shell, and took to wearing leather jackets and a scowling countenance. I went out of my way to extend myself to the mother and kids whenever possible, since they were so isolated from the other neighbors. On one occasion, I carved a wooden toy in high school woodshop class for their young daughter, and when I went to their front door to hand it to the mother, she was clearly holding back tears from the gesture. I didn't hear anything about the "Beak" again until 2007, when his face was plastered all over the Chicago newspapers for turning informant on his mob pals, to avoid a lengthy prison sentence for various murders and armed robberies.

He wasn't our only unusual neighbor, however. To our direct left was an FBI agent, who may or may not have had his eye on the mob family, while to our immediate right lived a proverbial mad scientist, Dr. Richard Seed. A true character in every sense of the word, he was an in-vitro specialist with degrees from Harvard and elsewhere. Years after I moved away, he wound up making world headlines for boasting that he'd become the first man in the world to clone a human being. For weeks afterwards, late night talk show hosts like Jay Leno and David Letterman had a field day with him, making light of this eccentric doctor out of Illinois named *"Dick Seed."* As a direct result of Seed's boasting, nearly 20 nations around the world enacted a ban on human cloning. That was his 15 minutes of fame, rest assured.

We had long debates standing out in the driveway between our houses, about topics like science and religion. I spoke to him a couple of times about astrology, and he patiently listened, not expressing a strong opinion one way or another. On one occasion I went back to the neighborhood and loaned him a copy of Rupert Sheldrake's book on morphogenetic fields, *A New Science of Life*, just to get his reaction. After reading it, he gently dismissed Sheldrake's work, saying "Nah, he's just too speculative. I just don't think we should theorize beyond the available evidence."

I replied, "Well, okay. So you think that Einstein should have kept his mouth shut and not published any of his theories until all the confirming evidence had first came in?"

That seemed to catch him off guard. He paused a bit and said, "Hmm…let me get back to you about that."

(He never did.)

CHAPTER 9

A QUESTION FOR CARL, WHO IS STILL DEAD

Doctor Seed's comment about not theorizing beyond the available evidence brought something to mind I've often wondered about involving the issue of "broad-mindedness"— that is, being open to new ideas, speculating about unusual possibilities, as well as determining exactly where skepticism and "critical thinking" fit into all of that.

As you might suspect, I'm quite fond of broad-mindedness and Big Ideas. After all, it's what gave us the Civil Rights movement, space exploration, and virtually every scientific advancement of the last few centuries, including that little Theory of Relativity I asked Dr. Seed about. These and many more developments were made possible by people thinking outside the box, by figures who stretched beyond the bounds of what was normal and acceptable for their time.

But I also know the dangers of being *too* broad-minded, because—well, *here be dragons*, as the old maps used to say. One needs to temper far-flung speculations and theories with healthy skepticism and critical thinking lest one become vulnerable to hucksters and cult leaders, not to mention propaganda, harebrained theories of all stripes, and the influence of the herd mentality. Without critical thinking, it doesn't take much before one can find oneself cocooned in a web of illusions and toxic lies.

That was a point scientist Carl Sagan became emphatic about towards the end of his life (which is somewhat ironic, considering he was thought to be a bit too broad-minded himself by colleagues early on in his career). I remember listening to an interview National Public Radio did with him not long before he died, in which he spoke about his recently published book *Demon-Haunted World*. Similar to what I mentioned above, he stressed the need for skepticism and critical thinking so that people don't fall prey to "irrational" beliefs in subjects like UFOs, bigfoot, astrology, ghosts, and other such balderdash. He suggested a few tools for helping to cultivate a more rational approach to our world, such as carefully examining all available evidence, not blindly relying on authority, and taking into account opposing viewpoints.

Though I disagree with some big chunks of what he said—like his derision of astrology or his simplistic take on religion—I also know the value of the general point he was making. As someone who traffics in fairly far-out ideas and speculative possibilities, I know that if you leave the door *too* wide open, you not only invite in all sorts of crazy ideas, but sometimes all sorts of crazies. I've had my share.

But I also know how tricky it can be knowing just where to draw that line, not only in terms of determining what does or doesn't constitute "evidence" but for that matter "critical thinking." After all, what one person considers compelling evidence may be another person's worthless noise. As a case in point, I'd like to have posed the following question to Carl, were he still alive today, and I'd frame it in the context of the following episode from recent history.

In 1912, the German geophysicist Alfred Wegener first proposed the theory of continental drift, which suggested that the continents were slowly moving around the Earth. He based this partly on the curious way the shorelines of the different continents seem to fit together like a jigsaw puzzle, so that the continental shelf of the Americas fits closely to Africa and Europe, for example. He also analyzed both sides of the Atlantic Ocean for rock types, fossils and geological structures, and noticed there was significant similarity between matching sides of the continents that way as well.

It may not seem like it now, but Wegener's theory was a huge conceptual leap for its time—so huge, in fact, that it was roundly criticized, in some cases even ridiculed, by many of his colleagues. Their criticism was based largely on the fact there was no known geological mechanism to account for how continents could move that way. To their minds, then, Wegener's theory wasn't supported at all by the evidence—the evidence as it was accepted back in 1912, that is. As things turned out, it wasn't until the 1950s that the scientific community finally came around to saying that, well, whaddya know, old Alfred was right after all—and we were wrong.

Which brings me to my question for Carl, if he were still alive to hear it:

When you look at those opposing viewpoints back in the early 20ᵗʰ century—on the one hand, Wegener with his speculative ideas about how the Earth changed shape over eons of time (which proved to be right), and on the other hand, his critics who claimed his theory wasn't supported by the evidence (and who turned out to be wrong)—which of those two do you feel demonstrated better "critical thinking" in examining all the available evidence?

CHAPTER 10

VINCENT

As a child, I became so obsessed with horror movies that my mother became seriously concerned about my mental health. I read all the monster magazines I could find, purchased plastic models of all the major film monsters from our local toy store, and watched TV shows like The Munsters and The Addams Family every week.

But it was when I asked my carpenter father to build me a coffin out of plywood that my mother definitely knew I wasn't quite right in the head. (He kindly obliged, by the way, kind-hearted man that he was.) Some of that early obsession was probably the result of a certain melancholy or even depressive temperament I had as a kid.

But on another level, I now look back at that attraction to horror as the first inklings of what later became my interest in mysticism, the occult and the paranormal, not to mention a lingering fascination with death. Horror films were my gateway drug to all of that, you could say. I wasn't drawn to gore-for-gore's sake, mind you, or the blood-and-guts horror of war films or crime dramas. What genuine horror films possessed that none of those others had was an element of the ethereal, of the otherworldly. They hinted at something *beyond the veil*.

Whatever it was exactly, I was particularly drawn to the Universal films of the 1930s and 1940s, and when it came to actors, I was most drawn to the holy trinity of Boris Karloff, Bela Lugosi, and Vincent Price. I'd enjoyed all of Price's "Poe" films for Roger Corman, especially *Pit and the Pendulum* and *Fall of the House of*

Usher. I fantasized about meeting these actors in person, although that didn't seem at all realistic, especially considering one of them (Lugosi) was already dead.

My parents drove my brother and I out to California in 1965 to spend time with her relatives in Los Angeles, and while we were there we went on the tour through Universal Studios, which was thrilling to me. It was huge fun seeing the house from Hitchcock's *Psycho,* as well as the house from The Munsters TV show, which was still in production at the time. As our tour bus drove past, in fact, I saw actress Yvonne di Carlo walking by in full Mrs. Munster make-up, which was especially cool, I thought.

But when I heard that Vincent Price was going to be presiding over the opening of an art show in Chicago, for the Merrill Chase Gallery, I pleaded with my father to drive me down there in hope of seeing him. It was slated to be held in the Prudential Building, a structure my dad had actually worked on as a construction worker years earlier, so he knew exactly where to go. Looking back on that period from the vantage point of my twenties, I discovered that Jupiter was crossing over my Gemini Sun at the time, so the stars were certainly well-aligned for me to meet someone important to my world then.

When we arrived, I walked into the large room where the gallery was situated, and immediately saw Price standing amongst all the partitions adorned with paintings, looking seemingly eight-feet tall and surrounded by fawning admirers. I walked up and nervously said, "Mr. Price? Mr. Price?" His back was turned towards me, and he pivoted around to see who was calling his name.

After blinding him with my flashbulb at close range, I reached into my pocket and pulled out a small photo I received from his fan club months earlier, and asked if he would autograph it for me. The contrast between his youthful appearance in the well-lit publicity photo decades earlier and how he looked to me now in the flesh was frankly extreme, at least to my young eyes. I struggled to make some conversation, and having no idea how rude it was, I asked him, "Umm...when was this photo taken?"

Rather than be offended, his response was gracious. Leaning over, he smiled and said, with that trademark swooping voice of his, "Oh, well, you *know,* when photos are small like that, they make you look *so much younger.*"

I had no idea what he meant by that, so his comment went completely over my naïve little head. It was years before I grasped just how witty that response of his really was.

CHAPTER 11

A FEW QUESTIONS (AND POSSIBLE ANSWERS) ABOUT REINCARNATION AND THE AFTERLIFE

W hat happens when we die?

If we're to take the teachings of the mystics seriously, we have a few good clues to go on. I'm as curious as anybody about what to expect, and have spent a great deal of time studying what those mystics taught on the matter.

Below are some of the queries I've fielded from students or clients over the years, along with a few of my answers based on those teachings, drawn largely from the yogic tradition, along with what I've learned from experiencers of near-death episodes themselves. Of course, none of us will know the full truth of the matter until we've crossed that bridge ourselves; but until then, it's worth venturing some educated guesses as to what lies ahead. After all, it's where we're all going to wind up.

"I'm afraid of dying. What can you tell me to ease my concerns?"

I once heard it said that fearing death is akin to fearing orgasm. That's because of the expanded sense of bliss and hyper-awareness that occurs for many upon leaving their bodies, or so the mystics claim. As the old Tibetan saying goes, "When we're born, we cry and the world rejoices; when we die, the world cries and we rejoice."

I once spent time visiting a battlefield where much carnage had taken place centuries earlier, and was surprised at how peaceful the feeling was. When I asked Goswami Kriyananda later on what he thought accounted for that, he paused a bit and said, "That might

be due to all the souls leaving their bodies on the day of the battle."
The implication there was that leaving one's body upon death was
an intrinsically pleasant, maybe even ecstatic experience, and that
the mass exodus on that battlefield probably left its mark that way.
Survivors of near-death experiences often describe just such a state,
with the release from their bodies likened to escaping from a tight-
fitting suit or cage—and conversely, returning to it felt relatively
unpleasant, like being "stuffed into a sardine can," as one NDE-
experiencer described it to me.

It appears from all accounts that most souls eventually drift
into a kind of semi-dreamlike state, where a person's consciousness
dims as they go on to relive various experiences or mental patterns
developed and cultivated during their waking life. In my book *An
Infinity of Gods*, I related a conversation I had with Shelly Trimmer
about something said to him by Paramahansa Yogananda (author
of *Autobiography of a Yogi*), which hinted at this point:

> Yogananda told me that when one of his disciples was
> dying, she made him promise he would come and see that
> she was all right over there. Now, he had a little difficulty
> finding her, since it's not very easy finding someone over
> there, and when he found her, he called out to her—several
> times, in fact. In her semi-dreamlike state, she was tending
> a garden, but she looked up at him and thanked him for
> coming. Of course, when he came, she woke up just a *little*
> bit more, but then she went back to her semi-sleep stage
> and continued gardening.

Shelly went on to say:

> You see, we gravitate to those things over there which suit
> us, in other words. Another example would be a man who
> worked hard all his life. He might just sit and rock back

and forth in his rocker, because his idea of heaven would be not having to go to work. See?

"Is that eventual dimming of awareness you describe true for all people who die?"

I'd answer it like this. While most people do experience that dimming of awareness, some later than others, one of the goals of mysticism is retaining heightened awareness into the death state so that one not only has more control of one's experience there, but one can reincarnate with one's memory and hard-earned knowledge relatively intact. How to cultivate that thread of continuity, though? One way is by maintaining a regular meditation practice, and in so doing, cultivate a state of heightened awareness during one's waking hours that carries over into both the sleep and afterlife states. A simpler method is learning to fall asleep more slowly and consciously every night, which serves as a way to prepare for that larger "sleep" of dying.

"Do we stay at the same age over there as when we died?"

In contrast to the world of "the living," so to speak, aging seems to work in reverse on the other side, the result being that we grow younger with time rather than older. One perspective holds that one gravitates to the age at which one felt to be at one's "best." Over a longer span of time, our superficial memories are gradually wiped fairly clean—something hinted at in ancient tales about drinking from Lethe, the river of forgetfulness—to the point where we can then reincarnate as a young child again with relatively fresh consciousness, harboring only vague memories of past incarnations.

It does seem, though, that very young children often *retain* many of those memories, which gradually fade as they grow older, similar to how we can remember our dreams on awakening but then lose that awareness afterwards. I'll never forget how my nephew, Sean, when he was just three years old, said to his mother: "Do you remember when I was your mommy, and you were *my* child?" His recollection of that memory remained consistent throughout that period—but within a year or two, he had no more memory of it at all.

"Do you think when we enter into this life that we know in advance everything that's going to happen to us—including when we're going to die?"

Based on various teachings and NDE accounts I've come across, I believe we certainly know the *broad outlines* of what's in store for us, possibly even the finer details as well. As for the manner of death, I'm sure we have a good idea of that too. On a deep intuitive level, we may even know when *that's* going to happen right before it actually does. I say that because of all the accounts I've heard over the years of people saying or doing things shortly before their passing which indicates they sensed—if only subtly—what was about to happen.

Take the story I read years ago about a boy who rode the train to school every morning, but one day before leaving said to his mother, "Do trains ever crash head-on into one another, mom?" He'd never asked that question of her before—and about one hour later he was dead from a head-on train collision. Or look at all the songwriters whose death seems to have been foretold in songs they released shortly beforehand. Like John Lennon having his first hit song in years when he died, titled "Starting Over"; or Hank Williams' most popular recording when he died having the title, "I'll Never Get Out of This World Alive"; or Buddy Holly dying in a plane crash in 1959 just as his song "It Doesn't Matter Anymore" was experiencing widespread popularity. The singer Kirsty McCall had a song titled "Can't Stop Killing You" which had the line, "When you're swimming in the water, I'm the hand that drags you under"—and she died not long after while swimming off the coast of Mexico, hit by a speedboat.

Sometimes those hunches can take the form of dreams, as it did for Abraham Lincoln. On the morning of his assassination he told cabinet members how he'd dreamt of sailing across an unknown body of water at great speed; also, several days before, he dreamt of seeing a covered corpse guarded by soldiers and surrounded by mourners. When he asked one of the soldiers in that dream who had died, the soldier reportedly replied, 'The president. He was killed by an assassin." Finally, there is the story of Lincoln leaving for the theater the night of his death. Turning to his bodyguard, William H. Cook, he said, "Goodbye," instead of his usual "Good night"—something he'd never said to Cook before. What caused him to change his wording that particular night?

"How long does one remain on the astral between lives?"

Theories about that vary widely, with some traditions claiming a precise number of days, weeks or years for that interval. I tend to go with what Goswami Kriyananda said when asked about that: "It can be anywhere from a thousand years to almost immediately." There is no one-size-fits-all time frame for everyone, in other words, and the difference can depend on many factors. For instance, one's own destiny may be linked to a given person or group, in which case that timetable may hinge heavily on those factors. If one is closely linked to a spiritual teacher, say, one will likely choose to incarnate sometime during that teacher's lifespan, so as to reconnect with them in the physical world.

I also believe individuals sometimes incarnate during a specific period in order to take advantage of the unique planetary energies in play then. If one is an aspiring artist, one might choose to incarnate when the energies are especially ripe on Earth for accessing great ideas or feeling states, as we saw during the 1960s or 1990s, or the 1890s. In 1769 and 1770, there was a rare grand trine involving the outer three planets—Uranus, Neptune and Pluto—which is precisely when Beethoven and Napoleon were born. Or take the 6th Century BCE, when *all three* outer planets joined forces in an even rarer conjunction for the first time in thousands of years. If I let my imagination wander, I can easily picture some pretty fierce competition amongst hovering souls over who gets to come in when the stars aligned in potent ways like that.

And while there's something to be said about being born exactly when these celestial energies trigger, there are certain advantages to being born twenty or thirty years *earlier,* so that one can best take advantage of those mounting forces when one's own talents and sensibilities have fully matured. Consider some of the brilliant singer/songwriters of the early 1940s—Paul McCartney, John Lennon, Brian Wilson, Bob Dylan, Leonard Cohen, Joni Mitchell, and others—who then blossomed two decades later during the powerhouse Uranus/Pluto conjunction of the mid-1960s. Writer Herman Melville had it good at both ends, actually, having been born in 1819 just as the powerful Uranus/Neptune conjunction of that period was culminating, but then reaching his creative peak with *Moby Dick* three decades later under the Uranus/Pluto conjunction of the early 1850s.

"What is this so-called 'life review' I've read about that supposedly happens when one crosses over?"

Many mystics and near-death survivors describe a stage in the death and dying process where individuals witness a review of their entire life, experienced as a 3-D "movie" of sorts. This review shows everything they've experienced or done during their incarnation on Earth. One of the unique features of that life review is the fact that one experiences one's actions towards others from *the vantage point of those others*. If you've chiefly done kind or generous things towards others, you'll experience that kindness from their perspective; on the other hand, if you've done hurtful things towards others, you'll feel those hurtful actions or comments as they experienced them.

Importantly, this is generally described as an impartial, completely non-judgmental process, with no blaming or assigning of guilt involved. Several years ago, I came across an anonymous comment posted online by someone describing their own encounter with dying, and while there's no way to verify the truth of their account, it articulates something I've come across any number of times in NDE accounts. This person wrote: "I was dying on the ER bed. I lay my head back, closed my eyes and thought, 'Should I confess my sins?' I was answered by a living Spirit. I was startled. It answered, 'That's irrelevant.' I thought, 'Irrelevant'? The Spirit answered, *'It was all experience.'*"

"If reincarnation is real, then why don't I have any memories of past lives?"

For much the same reason that you probably don't have much if any memory of what you dreamt last night—or for that matter, any memory of your first two or three years of life in *this* incarnation, or memories of being born. Memories fade tremendously over time. But as Shelly Trimmer said, we actually *do* remember our past lives, but in the form of our *emotional tendencies*—our fears, desires, talents, skills, and so on.

I also believe that the more quickly a soul reincarnates, the more likely they'll have clear memories of their previous life, and in turn the more quickly the skills or knowledge acquired in that life will resurrect in the new one. This would likely explain the phenomenon of child prodigies who from an early age pick up a musical instrument and know how to play it well, or who quickly gravitate towards certain professions and master them in no time. Those skills or knowledge sets are probably still fresh in their memory banks.

Along those lines, I don't believe we ever really lose any effort we put towards a given skill or ambition. We build on whatever momentums we've established through past lives. If someone works hard in this lifetime towards being a violinist, they'll pick that skill up more quickly in the next life than someone who has never worked at it at all. By the same token, however, someone who works hard at being a career criminal will probably *also* be much better at it than someone with no background in that lifestyle! Needless to say, they'll also have more problematic karma to contend with as well.

"What is the evidence for near-death experiences actually being true, and for the reality of what those people say they've experienced?"

The most compelling evidence I've come across has to do with accounts by individuals who describe perceiving, while in their disembodied state, situations out of their sensory range which later turn out to be accurate. That sometimes involves details of conversations had by nurses or doctors in other rooms from where the flatlined patient was. These are broadly termed "veridical" accounts, and my colleague Greg Taylor writes eloquently about that phenomenon in his book *Stop Worrying! There Probably is an Afterlife.*

Another compelling point for me was hearing NDE expert Elizabeth Kubler-Ross say that of all the children she dealt with who experienced NDE's, not a single one described encountering a still-living family member on the other side; it was invariably a deceased family member or friend. Considering both the vivid imagination and emotional needs of your average child, one would logically think they would conjure up images of a mother, father, or other living family member; yet that never once proved to be the case, she claimed.[1]

"If reincarnation is really true, how come there are so many more people on Earth now than there were millennia ago? Where did they all come from?"

To my mind, that's a bit like looking at Grand Central Station in New York during rush hour and asking, "How come there are so many more people around now than there were a few hours ago? Where did they all come from?" In other words, the opening question assumes that Earth is the only celestial body in the cosmos where souls incarnate, or that there is a limited number of souls in existence—neither of which is likely true.

But another factor to consider is, how many souls have lived on the Earth over the last several million years or so? Do we really know for *sure*? Isn't it possible that many of those who have been waiting for bodies to become available are now rushing in while the opportunity presents itself, leading to a kind of spiritual "rush hour" on the planet?

"How can I best prepare for a good afterlife?"

The answer from most mystics tends to be much the same regarding that question—namely, *live as happy and balanced a life in this incarnation as possible.* Here's what Yogananda said about it:

> You are exactly the same after death as you were before. Nothing changes; you only give up the body. If you are a thief or a liar or a cheater before death, you don't become an angel merely by dying. If such were possible, then let us all go and jump in the ocean now and become angels at once! Whatever you have made of yourself thus far, so will you be hereafter. And when you reincarnate, you will bring that same nature with you. To change, you have to make the effort. This world is the place to do it. [2]

"When I look at Hollywood movie depictions of the afterlife, it's usually shown in terms of cloudy or misty environments, or some such thing. What is it really like over there?"

According to most mystics, environments and worlds on the other side are as varied as they are on this side, if not more so. And rather than being foggy or vague, our subtle senses are said to be more heightened on the other side, rather than dulled, at least initially. Again, Yogananda:

> The astral planes are of different atmospheres, or vibrations, and each soul that passes on from this earth is attracted to whichever atmosphere is in harmony with its own particular vibration. Just as fish live in the water, worms in the earth, man on the earth, and birds in the air, so souls in the astral world live in whichever sphere is best suited to their own vibration. The more noble and spiritual

a person is on earth, the higher the sphere to which he will be attracted, and the greater will be his freedom and joy and experience of beauty.[3]

"Is it true that what you're thinking about or experiencing at the moment you die, determines the direction and quality of your next life?"

I know that's sometimes claimed, but I have to go with what my dear departed friend Georg Feuerstein suggested on the matter. Those last few moments may have some significance, but they're not likely to outweigh an entire lifetime's worth of thoughts and actions. For instance, a person who spends their lifetime helping the homeless and doing charitable acts but then dies tragically in a house fire doesn't simply have all of their earlier good deeds canceled out by those final moments of pain and fear. Or conversely, a mob boss who orders multiple hits on enemies throughout his life but dies peacefully in the garden (like Don Corleone in *The Godfather*) doesn't simply have all of *his* prior history of criminality wiped clean by a few nice moments playing amongst the flowers. Rather, the legacy of an entire lifetime's thoughts and actions is what determines the direction of future incarnations more than any passing thoughts or emotions at the very end.

"Is *déjà vu* an example of remembering something from a past incarnation?"

In some instances, I think that's possible. For example, I've heard of many cases where a person visits a foreign country for the first time and somehow knows the area like the back of their hand, as if it were extremely familiar to them. Or a person might be engaged in a particular activity and suddenly remembers doing something exactly like it long ago, but with subtle differences and in a different setting. I once read about an actor sitting in his dressing room preparing to go on stage for a play, shaving his chin and neck as the sound of the audience in the theater echoed in the background. As he sat there before the mirror, moving the long razor across his throat, he suddenly flashed back to seeming memories of being executed by guillotine during the French Revolution, to the sound of cheering crowds. He had little doubt this was a past-life experience being triggered. The small details of the two situations were different, but they were clearly similar in their symbolism.

But there are other possible causes of *déjà vu*. I remember having a dream when I was 16 where I stepped off a bus in a remote land and looked around to see beautiful mountains all around me. On awakening, the dream was still vivid in my mind and I wrote it down, not giving it any further thought. Then, several years later, I traveled to a remote region in Norway, first by train and then by bus. When I stepped off the bus, I had a powerful sense of déjà vu because the entire situation was *precisely* as I had dreamt it years earlier, down to the smallest detail. In that instance, the sense of déjà vu seems to have stemmed from having a prophetic dream years earlier, then living it out in waking life years later.

But in the most prosaic and non-metaphysical cases, I think many déjà vu experiences are simply instances where one is engaged in an action that's similar to something one has done before in *this* life, and which had been partially forgotten. That similarity between experiences hits one with such force that it *feels* like something almost paranormal or past-life must be involved.

"I've had a very hard and disappointing life. Does that mean I'm probably destined to just have more of the same in the afterlife?"

It's not that simple. As far as the afterlife is concerned, my understanding is that, if anything, it's a relief from the trials and tribulations of this one, much in the same way that falling asleep after a rough day is a relief compared to what one dealt with during the waking hours. True, there is a continuity from this world to the next, as I mentioned, but for the most part it's said to be considerably easier on the other side.

As far as the quality of one's next *incarnation* is concerned, my understanding is that karma can vary tremendously from lifetime to lifetime, in terms of its expression or even quantity. For instance, Goswami Kriyananda once suggested that a soul might choose to take on an exceptionally heavy load of karma in one life in order to burn it off quickly, in so doing speeding up their evolution—but that might be followed up with a relatively R&R, "rest and relaxation" lifetime where things are more comfortable. After all, one can only work the cosmic treadmill of existence so long before one needs (and is entitled) to take a break!

"Can we really communicate with people who have crossed over? And can they really reach out and get in touch with us?"

My understanding is, yes, it's indeed possible, to some extent. From our side of the divide, that communication could be achieved through prayer, rituals, "channeling," or simply directing one's thoughts and intentions to the departed; while from the other side, it can come to us in the form of psychic impressions, the smell of perfume or food, or dreams. That happened to my friend George. After his wife of several decades died, he had an unusually vivid dream in which she appeared to him walking in a beautiful field, wearing her wedding dress and looking happy, with their deceased dog Maggie prancing alongside. It was not like any normal dream, he said.[4] (Curiously, the same night his wife died, the clock in their house stopped at the time she passed.)

Or that interdimensional communication might take the form of synchronistic "messages" in our environment. I've heard countless stories over the years of possible communications from the departed involving butterflies or birds, which appear at particularly important moments. I know of one poignant story where a woman got into her car and hurriedly backed out of the family garage—tragically running over her two young children, causing their deaths. She was so traumatized by the experience that she couldn't even attend the children's funeral. It was a full year before she mustered up the strength to visit the gravesite of the children—and when she did, there were two butterflies perched on the headstone of the children's joint grave. They remained there for some time before flying off. She had a powerful intuitive sense it was a message letting her know that the children were okay and she could finally "move on." Was it a sign from the children themselves? Or from the universe? Or just a coincidence? She felt sure it was the children, and no one could possibly convince her otherwise.

But I also believe the longer a soul has been on the other side, the harder that interdimensional communication becomes, not only because the departed are living in a different time continuum but because of that awareness-dimming effect I mentioned, which makes it especially difficult for them to hear us, or even be motivated to contact us. (The exception to this may be elevated "masters" who can transcend those problems and freely communicate freely to those of us on this side of the veil.) For much the same reason, I'm dubious about claims from mediums and channelers who say they've contacted famous individuals who have been dead for many decades or even centuries—not to mention the fact those souls might have reincarnated into new bodies since their earthly passing, which would make direct communication difficult if not impossible.

This might be a good point to mention an experience I had while still a teenager, which I semi-seriously refer to now as my "experiment in necromancy." A close friend of mine in high school, a charismatic young man named Harmon Cooper, died unexpectedly of spinal meningitis. It came as a huge shock to those of us who knew him. It was several weeks after his closed-casket wake that I traveled with my family to visit some relatives overseas, who lived in an old structure from the 1800s.

One night in the upstairs bedroom I was staying in, I got it in my head to see if I could communicate with Harmon. So after everyone else had gone to sleep, I laid there with the lights on in the room and decided to send out an intention to Harmon in his new realm, wherever that might be. Mentally, I said, "Harmon, if you can hear me, send me a sign of your presence. Perhaps move the light fixture hanging from the ceiling here to show me that you've heard me." I kept that up for a good hour, but by the end of that hour nothing had transpired, so I finally gave up, turned out the lights and went to sleep.

Several hours later, probably around 3 AM in the morning, I awoke to see a glowing human form at the foot of my bed, motionless. I rubbed my eyes, thinking this must surely be a problem with my vision. But after clearing my eyes, the phantasm only became sharper—at which point I realized I might well be looking at a ghost. I thought my heart would explode from sheer fright, and I instinctively rolled over to bury my face in the pillow, hoping the disembodied form would simply go away. I laid that way for several more hours, coward that I was, refusing to turn around until dawn arrived and light began to fill the room.

It wasn't until the next morning that I put two and two together and realized it might have been Harmon that I saw, responding to my call. Looking back on the experience now, of course, I do wish I'd had my wits about me enough to try and communicate with that ghostly form, so as to find out for sure. But if it was Harmon, I have no doubt it was possible because only a short amount of time had elapsed since his passing, since I doubt such a striking connection could have been made three or four years later.

I should also mention that there are certain *times* when the proverbial "veil" seems to be thinner, making communication between dimensions that much easier. Samhain and the Day of the Dead are two of those. Another is the German and Austrian tradition of *Rauhnacht*, the period between Christmas Day and epiphany on January 6, when the doorway to the underworld opens and interaction between realms becomes more fluid. (Interestingly, Charles Dickens' story *A Christmas Carol* describes Scrooge being visited by the Ghost of Christmas Past during that very period.) The same "veil-thinning" quality likely holds true for powerful configurations involving Neptune, or certain zodiacal times of the year, such as the months of Pisces or Scorpio. It hardly seems accidental that Samhain, Day of the Dead, and Halloween all happen when the Sun is moving through Scorpio—the sign most associated with hidden mysteries and the occult! In the yogic tradition, it's believed that the 49 days following a person's passing are a time when that veil is especially thin.

"Some texts talk about the various 'stages' of the death process, in terms of what happens once the body dies and a person is 'reborn' on the other side. What is that all about, really?"

That's difficult to answer partly because it can be approached from several different angles. But one of those angles was summed up nicely by Goswami Kriyananda—this, from my book, *Urban Mystic*:

> At some point in the death and dying process, the soul passes from the physical realm into the astral realm by moving through a tunnel of light, which has three sections, each section being larger than the previous one. The first section is colored yellow, the next is blue and the last one is white. The yellow zone indicates the astral world, where most people go and then are forced to return to the earth plane because of their karma. The blue zone is the causal world, where a few souls stay in-between incarnations and then choose to return to the earth plane to help humans mature and evolve. The white zone is the divine zone, in which souls who exist here generally do not choose to return to the earth plane, or they may choose to descend into the lower two zones—the astral and causal—and help beings who reside there.
>
> As the soul moves through this tunnel, it senses other souls—some moving in the same direction, others moving in the opposite direction. (Notice the similarity here with the Old Testament story of "Jacob's ladder," by the way—R.G.) On the left side there is a cool, snowy path. On the right side there is a warm, dry path. Most people take the dry, warm path. However, the yogis say to take the cool, snowy path if you wish to speed up your evolution. On both sides you will meet some of your closer

relatives and friends who are there to greet and help you. On the eighteenth day after death, you can choose to stay within the force-field of the earth or pass through it, and enter the blue zone. Almost all souls remain in the yellow zone level and later reincarnate back on one of the earth planes.

"Some traditions claim that the personality or 'self' is essentially dissolved during the death and dying process, and that there's relatively little of your ego-personality which survives the process, or that carries over into the next lifetime. What do you say about that?"

First of all, the notion of your personality and your ego "dissolving" is actually something you experience every night as you fall asleep. That's a smaller version of what happens when souls are crossing over at death, or part of what happens, at least. For the vast majority of souls, this isn't some dramatic or traumatic process; it's much more natural than that. But what actually survives into the next lifetime? A good deal of superficial knowledge might be lost, or more accurately, buried, but your basic personality patterns and karmas are pretty entrenched, so it doesn't take long for them to reformulate and reassemble. In *An Infinity of Gods*, Shelly Trimmer made this interesting comment:

> Your emotional pattern is almost identical to what it was in your past incarnation, and so your response to stimuli is almost the same. You may not remember the *intellectual* things which you carry on from one incarnation to another, but *emotionally* you do…In order to see a great deal of change in your emotional pattern over lifetimes, it takes about three to four incarnations. If I take a picture of you now, and a picture of you at the same age in your past incarnation, and I put them

together here, you would say it's the same person. Everyone would recognize you. But after about three incarnations, no, they wouldn't recognize you anymore. And after seven incarnations, there would be a tremendous difference.

"Why would someone even want to come back here to earthly existence, when it can be so painful here?"

Part of that surely has to do with karma. If we have unfinished business from past lives, we need to come back and tie up loose ends until those karmas are cleared up. In some cases, in other words, it may not be so much a matter of *wanting* to come back as *needing* to. And on our return, we take on those circumstances which we feel will balance out those karmic legacies.

Another reason for returning has to do with the tangible allures of the physical world; because despite all its pain and disappointments, we're simultaneously drawn to its enticements as well. That may include physical pleasures like sex or food, of course, but it may even involve negative experiences like violence, revenge, or addictions. Some souls are trapped in negative "tape loops" and drawn over and over again to those "dark" experiences as much if not more than to more pleasurable ones. Because in their own way, those experiences *are* pleasurable to them, or at least comfortable, like any deeply ingrained habit tends to be.

Sometimes, a soul will take on difficult challenges in connection with some long-range goal, like an athlete who submits him or herself to a grueling regimen over years in order to compete in the Olympics. Or imagine a soul who has the dream of becoming the world's greatest blues singer; would you expect them to incarnate into a wealthy childhood where they're raised with a silver spoon in their mouth—or would they be drawn to a more painful life beset with an assortment of challenges? It seems obvious to me the latter scenario is more likely. In that case, the problems encountered by that person would be part and parcel of their broader life-goal, rather than representing any sort of karmic debt or "punishment."

Then there are examples of true *bodhisattvas,* spiritual beings who consciously choose to descend into this world with all of its pain and disappointment, not necessarily out of karma or desire but simply to assist and heal others. I can put this in simple terms which I think almost anyone would understand.

Imagine you were offered a chance to go by yourself on a luxurious cruise to one of the most beautiful regions in the world, with all your needs and desires attended to; but right when you're scheduled to leave, a beloved child of yours (or a pet, if that's more applicable to you) undergoes an injury or illness, and suffers terribly as a result. Could you really still go on your trip and enjoy your time away, knowing of the suffering that your loved one back home was experiencing? The bodhisattva is like that—the sensitive soul who cannot really enjoy "heaven" knowing that souls down here are suffering and need help.

Yet apart from all that, it's important to mention that there are also extraordinary *riches* to be found in this highly limited realm, because of the ways it allows one to develop aspects of psyche and soul probably not available to those outside those limitations. The French poet and novelist Anatole France said, "Until one has loved an animal, a part of one's soul remains unawakened." But we could just as well add to that by saying that until one has also loved a child, a mother, a father, a sibling, or a friend, *many parts* of one's soul remain unawakened. Strange as it may sound, one could even make a case for *grief* being one of those riches, because of how it scours out spaces in the soul that make room for compassion and wisdom. But whether pleasant or unpleasant, all such things are available only within the worldly limitations of time and space.

I'll add one more point to that list of mortality's "fringe benefits." It's something of a truism to say you can't truly appreciate freedom until you've been deprived of it, but I suspect that holds true for the Transcendent Ones as well. That is, can any being who's never experienced physical embodiment truly appreciate either infinity or eternity, or realize just how "good they've had it" as a Transcendent One? There's a marvelous bit of dialogue uttered by Achilles (played by Brad Pitt) in the film *Troy*, which seems apropos here:

> I'll tell you a secret, something they don't teach you in your temple. The gods envy us. They envy us because we're mortal, because any moment might be our last. Everything is more beautiful because we're doomed. You will never be more beautiful than you are now.

In short, this realm offers an abundance of opportunities for soul-enrichment unique to mortal beings and their woefully transitory lives, despite all its hardships—and in some cases, specifically because of them.

"You mentioned grief—so where does that fit in here? Is there really any value to *suffering*, ultimately?"

As it so happens, that's a question we'll be taking up in our next chapter.

CHAPTER 12

SUFFERING AND SOUL MAKING ON THE MEAN STREETS OF PLANET EARTH

"Call the world, if you please, 'the Vale of Soul Making,' Then you will find out the use of the world..."

—John Keats in a letter to his brother, 1819

I had a client who enjoyed a short-lived career on Broadway many years earlier, strictly doing bit parts as an extra in various theatrical productions—an office worker in one play, a soldier in another, a street thug in yet another, and so on. He never landed a major role in any of those shows but still valued that period of his life because (in his words) "even the smallest part in those spectacles was a great experience. Everyone wanted to be in on the action," he said.

Hearing that, I couldn't help but wonder if that wasn't comparable to the situation we humans find ourselves in here on Earth, in terms of souls clamoring to be on this planet and "get in on the action"—no matter how small or mundane the part.

In fact, there may even be something of particular value in those seemingly "small" parts that's quite different from the more extravagant lead roles. Let me explain what I mean.

On a number of occasions, I've watched a celebrity being interviewed on TV where they talk about coming from humble beginnings, whether that was growing up in poverty, working for years or even decades as a dishwasher or waitress, or having survived on the mean streets of Chicago or Philly. But what I find intriguing about those accounts is how those celebrities generally seem quite proud of having come from those hard backgrounds, as if they'd "paid their dues" in a way someone raised with a silver spoon in their mouth wouldn't have experienced.

In some cases, though, it actually turns out later on that the person exaggerated or perhaps even *lied* about those early "hardships," and that they really hailed from a perfectly middle-class background. They just *wanted* everyone to think they rose up from hard circumstances.

Think about that for a moment.

Why would anyone do that—that is, lie or even brag about how bad they had it as a kid, how much they suffered, and the hardships they endured?

My guess is it's because there's a certain sense that dealing with hard circumstances and surviving early struggles builds character, or gives one a certain toughness or even depth which those who grew up in comparatively easier circumstances might not share.

It reminds me of the time when I was a kid and watched two older gentlemen discussing their battlefield experiences in World War II. It was almost like they were trying to outdo each other with the hardships they endured, and were practically boasting about the suffering they'd experienced. ("Yeah, but you should have seen what I went through at the *Battle of the Bulge...!*")

I find that fascinating. We clearly dislike suffering, and try to avoid it at all costs. Yet once we've gone through it, we sometimes look back on it with a certain pride over having survived it, wearing it almost like a badge of honor. And like those veterans I overheard as a kid, we might even *brag* about it when comparing notes with others, with an attitude of one-upsmanship, thinking, "So you think *that* was bad? You should see what *I* had to deal with!"

Why am I bringing all this up? Simply because I think this has something to tell us about the role and value of earthly existence itself, in terms the role it plays in our spiritual evolution.

I've sometimes conjured up the image of two angels sitting on a cloud high up on some astral plane, their harps alongside them, and they're swapping stories about their past sojourns down here on Earth, comparing notes about what they went through down in these lowly nether regions.

So the one angel says to the other, "Boy, in my last lifetime I was sick all the time, poverty-stricken and completely deaf to boot, and in the life before *that* one, my parents and I were refugees in a war-torn country. You can't imagine the hardships we endured." But the other angel says, "Oh, don't get me started! I was sold into slavery in my last lifetime and beaten daily by my master; and a few lifetimes before that I was trapped in a house fire and suffered third-degree burns all over my body, which plagued me my entire life. So shut your mouth!" And they argue back and both like that, each trying to outdo the other over what they did or didn't contend with during their physical incarnations.

But then another angel comes along, one who has *never* descended down into an earthly body, and thus never experienced either the joys or sorrows of living down here in this physical realm. This neophyte angel is a very pure soul, a proverbial babe in the woods (or clouds, as the case may be), but also lacking in a certain awareness, as well as a certain depth. This angel never had to "leave the garden," as it were.

So the two veteran angels look at each other and roll their eyes over this innocent, who they know is relatively inexperienced and has no idea of what existence is *really* about, not in its fullness. They also know there's something substantially different about their own souls as a result of having spent those thousands or perhaps millions of years down here on Earth, a quality not just of depth or complexity but of *compassion*, which can only come from having suffered and dealt with great struggle and resistance. That's because a soul both develops empathy and grows spiritual muscles from pushing up against obstacles, and contending with "friction."

That's one of the subtle messages of the ancient "Hymn of the Pearl," a passage from the apocryphal Acts of Thomas. It tells the tale of a boy, the "son of the king of kings," who is sent down into Egypt to retrieve a pearl from a mysterious serpent. But while on his mission, he is seduced by Egypt and its ways, and consequently forgets his home country and family. A letter is then sent to him from the king to remind him of his background and royal heritage, at which point he remembers his mission, retrieves the pearl, and returns home.

In terms of symbolism, "Egypt" in that tale represents worldly existence itself, in which we can likewise easily become lost—and will forever remain lost until we receive that message from our higher Self reminding us to complete our mission and return home again. One of the key points of the story is that our sojourn in this realm is not a waste of time, nor is it meaningless; there is a treasure to be gained from enduring this mortal existence, which is symbolized by the pearl.

That choice of symbols (as opposed to, say, a treasure chest or golden crown) is not insignificant, when you consider that a pearl's beauty arises from the interaction of a rough irritant (like a grain of sand) with the surrounding clam it's found its way into. In a sense, one's soul is similarly polished as a result of its sojourn through this "rough" world. That's not to say that one *seeks out* suffering, because even the mystics say the wisest option is to learn without it, if at all possible. But as the Buddha himself pointed out, that's *not* always possible; suffering is, to some extent, part and parcel of mortal existence, with its rounds of life and death, beginnings and endings.

Let me toss one more idea into the mix, to help round out this picture a little more.

One summer between freshman and sophomore year of college, I worked a summer job to earn some money for a trip through Europe, a kind of "pilgrimage" where I'd visit as many of the major art museums in Europe as I could within a four-week period. I didn't have much money, so I purchased a "Eurail pass" and slept on the trains at night and went from city to city, a new one each day, to study the great masters up close. The chief focal points of my study were artists like Leonardo, Velasquez, Ingres, Vermeer, Caravaggio, van Gogh, and Rembrandt, although there were many others I drew inspiration from.

When I got to the great Rijksmuseum in Amsterdam, I had an interesting thought while standing before Rembrandt's large canvas commonly called "The Night Watch," completed in 1642. This work is essentially a military group portrait painted in Rembrandt's inimitable style. In a way that almost prefigured the later Impressionists, the Dutch master was notable for his manner of depicting figures and forms with richly textured swabs of color along with atmospheric plays of light and dark.

When I stood up close to the painting to examine it in detail, I saw that some of those splotches of brown or black paint were nothing particularly beautiful when seen up close—in fact, taken strictly by themselves, they might be considered somewhat ugly. But when you stood further back, all of those splotches and dabs of paint, both light and dark, colorful and drab, coalesced to form a larger tapestry, and the result was majestic.

It was some time later that I thought to myself: if we indeed experience thousands or perhaps even millions of lifetimes over the course of eons, then each lifetime might be like one of those individual dabs of paint on Rembrandt's large canvas. As a result, a given lifetime might seem dreary or even painful when experienced up close and in isolation, yet might actually play an integral role within the larger "canvas" of spiritual evolution—and that would become clear if you stood back far enough. I could imagine that even a lifetime spent seemingly "wasting away" in a medieval dungeon could play as important a role in that evolutionary arc as any dab of black or brown paint did in Rembrandt's painting, complementing the rich gold and white highlights right alongside it.

So I do believe there is something profoundly important about surviving the "mean streets" of planet Earth, on any number of levels. It is indeed a life filled with disappointments and seemingly endless struggles, right alongside great beauties and awe-inspiring wonders. But whatever you may think about it, it certainly doesn't seem *meaning-less.*

At least not if you stand back far enough.

CHAPTER 13

ON THE MYSTERIES OF SOUL

We've been taking a brief look at the process and the value of soul making.

But what exactly *is* the "soul"? And how does it differ from spirit? One simple explanation would be to say that spirit is what you *are,* whereas the soul is something you *have.*

Or, as Shelly Trimmer explained it, the spirit is the I AM AWARE THAT I AM, the transcendent witness at the foundation of one's being. By contrast, the soul consists largely of one's *memory track*—the vast body of emotions, thoughts, and personality traits accumulated by the spirit over lifetimes, and which serve as its clothing or "sheath" (with the physical body being the crystallized embodiment of those soul patterns).

A rough analogy from astronomy and astrology would be the layout of our solar system, with the Sun at the center representing spirit and all the outlying planets and moons symbolizing the various components of soul. Just as the various planets mark off orbital harmonics extending outward from the Sun, so the soul can be said to possess various "layers" as well, relative to that core source of being. Those layers are analogous to the various chakric levels along the spine, in descending order from the source of consciousness in the head down to the root chakra at the bottom.

In turn, any new memory that's generated is "logged" into the soul-layer (or chakric level) corresponding to its vibration, such that imprints of anger or courage are logged into the third, "Martian" chakra; ideas and intellectual imprints are absorbed into the throat or "Mercury" chakra; while memories of love or beauty are embedded in the heart or "Venus" chakra, and so on.

In fact, most soul-impressions are a *combination* of one or more chakric centers or soul-layers, such that a scientist engaged in the study of physical matter might be expressing a combination of throat and root-chakra concerns (Mercury and Saturn), rather than just one or the other; or an artist who paints pictures of battlefield scenes would be expressing a combination of both heart and navel-chakra energies (a combination of Venus and Mars). In this way, the human soul is a patchwork quilt of karmas and memories gathered by the spirit over the course of its journeys through the phenomenal realms. Or, recalling the analogy from the last chapter, the soul is not unlike that great Rembrandt canvas I spoke of, comprised of thousands of brush strokes of varying colors which together form a cohesive picture.

The astrological chart is a diagram of one's soul-patterns, symbolically illustrating one's accumulated memories and experiences from many (though by no means all) past lives, with the different houses and signs signifying the various soul-compartments into which those energies and memories have been stored.

But while it may tell us much about the soul, the horoscope doesn't really say anything about one's *spirit*, not directly. For while the Sun may come the closest of all the bodies in our system to illustrating the self-illuminating principle of spirit, the spirit is ultimately beyond the horoscope, and beyond any tangible symbolism altogether—except perhaps for the symbolism of pure light. The spirit expresses itself through the horoscope much in the same way that sunlight moves through the stain glass windows of a cathedral, with pure white light going in, multi-colored light coming out.

Ideally, the process of soul making referred to in the last chapter isn't simply a matter of acquiring more or better memories, valuable as that may be, but of harmonizing those elements toward creating a more purified and balanced soul-garment through which the spirit expresses itself.[1] The spirit "wears" the soul much like a person wears a suit or dress, and the style and condition of that outfit is a reflection of their consciousness. In 1990, on the occasion of his 89th birthday, I attended a talk by the esoteric scholar Manly Palmer Hall at his center in Los Angeles, shortly before he passed. He spoke during that talk about something he referred to as the "golden wedding garment," and explained how all of one's virtuous thoughts and deeds over time generate flashes in the soul, or aura, that eventually coalesce to create a luminous vestment that reflects the purity and elevation of one's consciousness.

The spirit and soul are uniquely different in their roles, and each one needs the counterbalance of the other. For example, as important as spiritual awareness is for opening someone to profound insights and experiences, it can be overly "dry" if left entirely to itself, and even show a certain lack of empathy or "juiciness" at times—like the yogi who comes down from the cave to the nearby village after meditating alone for years, all enlightened now but without a clue how to relate to ordinary people, let alone have a grounded relationship.

On the other hand, *soul* is vitally important in its own way; for me, that's best expressed by the image of your classic Italian or Jewish mother feeding a room full of family members during the holidays, all of them enjoying the warmth and humor of their companionship. She might not be able to expound on the intricacies of theology or philosophize about consciousness and the various dimensions of existence, but she could rightly be considered *rich in soul*, in terms of her ability to actually *live* the teachings, and "feed" the world not just through food but the healing energies of love and nurturance. This is the so-called feminine dimension of being, and it's a critical one in personal growth. Yet *too much* soul poses its own set of problems—like the person so immersed in their own melodramas that they never emerge from those murky depths to see the fresh light of day. Such a person isn't merely "rich" in soul; they're drowning in it.

It's when these two aspects of spirit and soul are held in balance that the brilliance of spirit fuses with the emotional and compassionate energies of soul to produce the most vibrant and awakened personality.

The Spirit and Soul of God

If the teachings of mystics like Shelly Trimmer are to be believed, this distinction between spirit and soul applies even to God, in terms of the contrast between the "transcendent" and "immanent" aspects of the Divine—which is to say, *God the Father* versus *God the Mother.*

In other words, God's "spirit" is the timeless I AM, or transcendent cosmic witness; whereas God's "soul" is the divine memory track, the entirety of creation on all its levels of manifestation, from subtle to gross, and which emanates out of that divinity as it continues evolving towards ever greater states of balance.[2] And just as the individual soul has levels and layers, so the *cosmic* soul does as well, sometimes referred to by mystics as "planes," of which we're said to be occupants of the lowest level.

This soul-dimension of God can be thought of as the *cosmic feminine*, which in Kabbalistic thought is known as *Shekinah*, in Gnosticism as *Sophia*, and in Hindu thought as the principle of *shakti*, the dynamic feminine energy of the cosmos. We also find it in the notion of the *anima mundi*, or "world soul" found in some traditions. But whatever name or label we give it, this is the *emotional* dimension of God's being. Whereas God's transcendent spirit cannot by itself know our suffering, it can experience it through that more feminine and immanent dimension of its nature—which is to say, *God's soul*. It is this feminine, soul-dimension of the Divine that feels the suffering of all those creatures within its embrace, and which expresses compassion towards those beings, whether recognized and accepted or not.

This naturally raises the question: are we ourselves just products of that Divine soul, the progeny of that creative effulgence—or are we independent, self-existent beings who have simply *entered into* God's soul where we benefit from the myriad offerings and challenges of that memory tract, but are ourselves more like *brothers and sisters* of the Divine rather than its children? [3]

It's not a trifling question, and how we choose to answer it makes a world of difference not only in how we see the world but ourselves.

CHAPTER 14

APOCALYPSE NOT

E arly one afternoon in the summer of 1979, I received a long-distance call from a childhood friend who I'll call Mark.

"I've landed a job working on a new film by Francis Coppola," he said. "It's called *Apocalypse Now*, and it's in post-production. They're looking for someone to fill a position in the department I'm working in. I can't guarantee anything, but if you make it out here within a week, I think you'll stand a good chance of landing the job."

I was definitely interested, but I needed to know a bit more. "What kind of work?"

"You'd be alongside me and a couple other guys on the post-production soundtrack. They're desperately trying to finish the film in time for the premiere, and could use an extra hand in the mixing room. We're helping out Walter Murch, who's the main man in charge at this point."

After high school, Mark had moved from Illinois out to Oregon and eventually made his way down the coast after college to San Francisco, setting his sights on making it in either the music or film industry, maybe both. He helped me find work once before, but that was just a summer job in nearby Cicero when he was a punch press operator and I landed a position as a mail courier between company branches. This was the movie industry, though, and it was a different situation altogether.

His phone call came through in the wake of several big disappointments I'd experienced in recent years with various creative projects. A year earlier I watched as the experimental film I'd labored on for seven years was partially ruined in a processing mishap at the film lab I was using downtown. And though I continued painting for a while after graduating from the Art Institute of Chicago, I found myself feeling blocked with my art; it was as if my inspiration for the craft simply evaporated into thin air. Combined with still other setbacks, it all left me feeling discouraged about my future direction.

So when Mark pitched the possibility of working with Coppola, I was anxious to give it a try, even if that meant entering into the commercial end of the movie industry—something that would have been anathema to me a few years earlier. I was in the midst of some challenging Saturn energies taking shape in my chart, as the ringed planet inched closer to my Ascendant, so I knew I could run into obstacles. But I've never wanted to let my knowledge about the horoscope dictate my actions *too* rigidly, since I've had valuable life-experiences result from problematic times as well as more pleasant ones, so I thought I'd give it a go out there as well, come what may.

So after wrapping up some personal business back home, I boarded a train with a few essential belongings and headed out from downtown Chicago to San Francisco.

Zoetrope Studios

Mark and his girlfriend met me at the station, and they drove me back to their apartment in the heart of the city. They kindly offered to put me up for a short time while I tried my hand finding work with Coppola's crew. The very next day, I made some calls and took the city bus over to Coppola's Zoetrope studio.

Normally when one hears the word "studio," the image that comes to mind is a sprawling complex with movie backlots and soundstages, but that wasn't the case here. Coppola's studio was a relatively modest pre- and post-production office complex on one of the city's streets. If you walked past the front of the building, you might not suspect anything important was taking place inside. But something certainly was, at least cinematically.

I came in and spoke with the woman in charge of personnel, Kristina, who was friendly but very professional. There were people bustling about the office tending to paperwork and phone calls. I was extremely nervous but hopeful about my chances at finding work there. At the end of our short talk, she said she'd give me a call to let me know of their decision.

The next day she phoned me and asked if I'd come back down to the studio. I assumed she wouldn't ask me to go through the effort of heading all the way down there if I didn't actually have the position, so my hopes were high. But less than a minute into our conversation she politely informed me that she was sorry, the position was already filled. I put on a good face, but walked out of the studio feeling like my heart had been crushed in a vice. Rather than take the bus home, I decided to walk around for a few hours to sort out my feelings about what had just happened. I'd traveled all the way out to the West Coast for this, but in the blink of an eye realized I'd have to come up with another strategy for surviving out there.

A few days later, I moved out of Mark's apartment into one of the city's downtown hotels. The first night was a strange one. I looked out from my seventh floor window to see a string of fires necklacing the city streets. I had no idea what that was all about, but wondered if it might be some special tradition unique to San Franciscans, perhaps. It was beautiful in its own way, but it was certainly odd thinking that cars being set on fire might be part of the festivities. The next day I learned that riots had broken out across the city over a controversial court decision involving the murder of city mayor George Moscone and gay supervisor Harvey Milk.

Those next few weeks and months I continued looking for work, surfing through several low-grade hotels in or around the downtown area, but that was proving to be costly. I had some savings to fall back on, but knew I could go through those in no time if something didn't turn up soon. I applied for work in stores, business offices, even at George Lucas's studio in Marin County, where they were working on the second *Star Wars* feature, *The Empire Strikes Back*. But none of it bore any fruit. All I could muster up were a number of horoscope readings for a variety of colorful local residents, including drag queens and prostitutes, which I conducted out of my tiny hotel room not far from Union Square. I was grateful for every one of them.

© 1979 United Artists

Behind the Scenes

Things took an unexpected turn with Coppola's studio, thanks to Mark. He and his coworkers were focused on finishing work on the film, with Mark working the graveyard shift along with two other young apprentices, while lead sound editor Walter Murch sat off in his adjoining room. The arrangement was such that Murch made his decisions off in a sound-mixing room while speaking to the others via intercom through a pane of glass, with the young men cueing up the various reels of audiotape in line with his directions.

It was into that environment that Mark began sneaking me into the studio late at nights without any of the higher-ups knowing about it, just his two young co-workers. Even Walter Murch didn't seem to notice me, since he had his back to the glass partition most of the time, and probably wouldn't have cared one way or another anyway, since he was so tied up with his work.

And so it was for an average of three to four times a week over the next two months I'd walk up to the side door and Mark would let me in to observe post-production activities on the film, along the way treating me to a host of intriguing glimpses into Coppola's moviemaking process.

That first night, he took me on a tour around the facility, and we eventually ended up in one of Coppola's two personal offices, where I saw shelves of videocassettes lined up and labeled. Pointing to the chair by Coppola's desk, Mark said, "If you want, you can sit here and look at these cassette tapes, just try not to disturb anything in this office."

I felt like the proverbial kid in a candy store, and that night would be the first of many where I'd rummage through scores of videocassettes containing scenes from the movie in their raw form, unassembled and unedited. What I viewed over those nights gave me a window not only into Francis Coppola's imagination, but the mechanics of mainstream moviemaking itself, which was new to me.

Most of the footage I watched consisted of unassembled shots from different sequences, or some of the film's classic sequences in various stages of editing. The famous "Ride of the Valkyries" sequence which had helicopters descending on a village to the blaring strains of Wagner, appeared on these videocassette tapes in four or five different versions, and it became obvious that it took shape very slowly over numerous edits. The earliest version had the scenes cut almost precisely to the rhythms of the music, which seemed a little too neat and tidy, whereas the later versions juxtaposed the music and the imagery in a way that was more complex and syncopated.

But a large amount of what I saw consisted of outtakes, scenes or sequences that never made it into the finished film. Mark explained that Francis filmed a virtual mountain of footage for the movie—200 hours or more—and most of that wound up on the cutting room floor. One especially large batch of outtakes involved what Mark called the "French plantation" sequence. In it, Martin Sheen's character docks his cruiser and is met by a group of commandos emerging from out of the mist. He eventually has dinner with a group of French colonial hold-outs still living their lives as if nothing had changed since the old days. That sequence eventually became a much-talked about topic not only among cinema fans but other directors; several years later I read an interview with Japanese director Akira Kurosawa where he said the one thing he'd like to see before he died was that "French plantation" footage from *Apocalypse Now*. When I saw it, though, it was largely a series of disjointed shots. Years later I watched those same shots edited and assembled in a "director's cut" version of the film Coppola eventually released, at which point I finally understood what Francis was aiming for with that sequence.

But most interesting to me were all the outtakes involving Marlon Brando, some of which never made their way into any of the released versions of the film. One of those involved a daylight sequence where Brando spoke to Sheen as he languished in a bamboo cage. Though Brando was charismatic, I thought it was a smart move for Coppola to delete it from the finished film, since the darker, nighttime shots of Brando conveyed more mystery.

As much as I enjoyed those evenings at the studio, it only consumed an hour or two a few nights each week, which left the rest of my days and evenings open. When I wasn't out looking for work, I spent much of my energy exploring San Francisco and its environs, drinking in as much of the city as possible. These forays became an emotional necessity for me, since a couple of the hotels I stayed in were located in a run-down neighborhood, with tenants who settled disputes via screaming matches or fistfights in the hallways. I spent hours each week in the nearby library doing research, often followed by bus rides down to the ocean when it was shrouded in light fog, where I'd sit and observe the waves cascading out to the horizon, or hike the paths snaking their way in and around the area's cliffs. I started attending weekly astrology meetings conducted by San Franciscan astrologer Jayj Jacobs. Some evenings after leaving Coppola's studio, I'd head over to Mabuhay Gardens, a lively music club where figures like Jim Carroll debuted their work.

Taking a selfie in San Francisco's Exploratorium, 1979

First Light

During the weeks I watched those snippets of Coppola's film, I wasn't sure what to make of it, since I was seeing it in such a disjointed way. The individual shots were stupendous, but how did it all fit together? I couldn't get a feel for the overall flow or its dramatic power from seeing the images in isolation.

As the August date of the premiere drew near, the tension amongst the nighttime crew was palpable. Every time I'd walk into the anteroom where the young men worked, I'd see Walter Murch hunched over in his own mixing room, slaving away, never looking up from his mixing board. With the deadline approaching, it was obvious that he was getting little sleep.

But to everyone's relief, the film was completed on time. I wouldn't be going to the world premiere held in Los Angeles, but Mark said there was an advance screening for employees and their families planned for the Northpoint Theater in town. He had an extra ticket for that, if I wanted it. Well, of course.

Arriving at the theater that next week, I was anxious to see what Francis had accomplished. Sitting there with all the others, the experience was simultaneously mesmerizing and disorienting. I was genuinely stunned by Vittorio Stararo's cinematography and its spectacular colors, which were richer and more exotic than anything I'd seen on the big screen before. That was especially true of the nighttime jungle sequences with their lush deep greens and blues that practically glowed off the screen.

At the same time, there had been so much ballyhoo leading up to the film that it was almost destined to be anti-climactic in some way. Something about the film didn't quite connect for me, emotionally. I'd experienced something like that once before, when I was a teenager in the late 60's and won tickets from a local radio station to see the Chicago premiere of Kubrick's *2001: A Space Odyssey*. The hype leading up to the film had been so great that nothing less than a song-and-dance by Jesus would have lived up to it. After the film finished and the house lights went up, the audience sat there largely silent, apparently unsure over what they'd just seen. Kubrick's film was beautiful, yes, but just so *different*.

It was similar with this screening of *Apocalypse Now*. Instead of a chorus of applause after it finished, there was mainly silence as audience members filed out. I read several months later about a similar situation in Moscow where the audience reacted in the same way: with silence. The news service which reported the Russian event interpreted it as a sign of how stunned viewers must have been by the film's message, but I suspect it was something closer to what I observed at the Northpoint Theater that afternoon: respect and a certain awe, but mixed with a dose of puzzlement.

Reflections

I wanted to stay in San Francisco, but knew that without a steady job I couldn't survive there, so as the year drew to a close I hopped on a train and made my way back to the Midwest, feeling fairly dejected. During those following months I continued to think about Coppola's movie, and discussed it with others. Over lunch the next year with my former film professor Stan Brakhage, I related my experience with the movie and asked for his thoughts about the film, artistically. After a brief silence he remarked, almost grudgingly, "Well...it's probably the only interesting film to come out of Hollywood these last few years."

Since 1979 I've had the chance to watch it several more times, and my reaction to it has deepened with each viewing. While there are elements I don't like, overall I've come to think it's a great film. Besides the film's well-crafted script, the film offers a smorgasbord of iconic images that linger in the mind long afterwards, from the scenes of Brando's face emerging out of the shadows to that montage of helicopters plunging headlong to the strains of Wagner. The film's editing is especially artful, I thought, like the beautiful dissolves and juxtapositions that weave their way around Sheen's rehabilitation in Brando's compound. Coppola's *The Godfather* was a great movie, beautifully photographed, stunningly so, but it wasn't particularly innovative with its editing or sound. This film was, I thought.

But if there was one aspect of the film that most haunted me most, it was the story's mythic resonance—a sense that deep below its surface archetypal chords were sounding. At the film's core was a story about a figure journeying deep into the proverbial "heart of darkness," with each stop along the way signifying a stage further back in time. Sheen's character was moving through progressively older levels of civilization, from modern day surfers to French colonialists, past archaic tribesmen wielding bows and arrows, until he finally arrives at his destination at Kurtz's compound, adorned with signs of carnage. This was something I'd been fascinated with since childhood: the idea of traveling back into the past, whether through archaeology or movies about time machines. This movie evoked much that feeling for me.

Final Thoughts

For years afterward I felt disappointed over not having landed that job at Coppola's studio, since I knew it probably would have opened doors for me. It certainly did for the other young men at the studio. One of Mark's two co-workers on that night shift, Doug, went on to work on films like *Blade Runner,* and won a couple of Academy Awards for his sound production on later films; while Mark himself went to work on films like *Dark City* and the *Lord of the Rings* trilogy, and eventually became a force over at Warner Brothers. It seemed like everyone associated with Coppola's film, from the actors to the production crew, saw their careers take off in the years that followed. The stars weren't quite so aligned for me like that, apparently.

Over time, though, I came to see that disappointment differently. I once heard someone suggest that our life's-paths are guided and shaped by our limitations and set-backs, and that's certainly been true for me. Had things worked out for me as I hoped back in San Francisco, my life likely *would* have gone in a different direction—but one probably less aligned to my true calling. One can never be sure about such things, of course, but it's a possibility I began taking more seriously after a vivid dream I had upon returning to Illinois.

In that dream, I lived in a rural area and learned that a well on my property had begun to dry up. That was distressing to me. But while contemplating my predicament, I happened to catch sight of another well located higher up on a nearby hill, which I somehow knew was more abundant with water. As I started walking towards it, I noticed this other well was inlaid with exotic gems and jewels, and around it was a pile of scrolls inscribed with beautiful hieroglyphics, all of them looking vaguely Egyptian in style, some of them even glowing faintly.

On awakening, I spent a good deal of time reflecting on that dream and what it might have meant. I had just begun to consider writing as a path to pursue, rather than painting or film. Could that be the other "well" represented in my dream? It was too early to really know, especially since I had no real experience with writing up to then. What I *did* know was that I needed to find a new pole star by which to orient my life, since the old one was growing dimmer by the year.

CHAPTER 15

THE MEETING OF JUPITER AND NEPTUNE IN PISCES

By the time many readers come across the ideas in this essay (originally written as a blog post for the Mountain Astrologer website in November, 2021), the event it describes taking place in April of 2022 will have already come and gone. On the plus side, that gives those readers the advantage of having some perspective about how it actually manifested. Understanding a bit more of the history behind this configuration, as we'll see here, can provide valuable perspective on what this configuration means for our own time, both for ourselves and the world. —R.G.

This coming April, 2022, a remarkable planetary configuration will take place that you'll probably want to note on your calendars: Jupiter will be aligning with Neptune in the sign of Pisces, during the second week of that month.

What's so "remarkable" about that?

For one, this particular aspect in this particular sign hasn't happened since *1856*, when they came together on March 17th of that year. Jupiter may cross through Pisces every 12 years, but Neptune's journey through this sign is far less frequent, making its meeting with Jupiter there a much rarer affair.

But also consider that both of those planets are directly linked in their symbolism to Pisces, Jupiter being the traditional ruler, and Neptune being the body most modern astrologers associate with the sign. Either way, it's obvious enough that both bodies enjoy a resonance with Pisces, the result being that this impending alignment certainly signals a major amplification of the Piscean principle, and all that implies.

So what exactly *does* that imply?

With Pisces being the symbol *par excellence* of the great "ocean of being," as it were, I see this configuration as signaling a potentially extraordinary opening up of the collective unconscious, a time when the proverbial "veil" thins and we suddenly can enjoy easier access to subtler ideas, concepts and creative impulses—perhaps even contact with intelligences beyond the veil. At the very least, it should be a time when the human imagination will be especially rich in its offerings, when ideas can be plucked from the collective mindstream like low-hanging fruit.

Like any important configuration, of course, it's not going to be all rainbows and unicorns—on top of which, it will be experienced differently by everyone depending on their charts and attitudes. No doubt, there will be those who use this energy to escape even further from reality than they already do, via drugs, alcohol, or even extremist ideologies and religions. It's even tempting to wonder if there won't also be some problems involving water, the ocean, floods, or oil.

But for those who *are* more creatively or spiritually-inclined, I think this aspect offers an especially rare opportunity to draw on the creative, imaginal, psychological and spiritual energies of the cosmos, whether through art, poetry, music, writing, photography, meditating, dance or travel.

(Speaking of which: I mentioned this upcoming configuration to several of my clients, one of whom informed me he had planned a trip right at that time to South America to partake in an ayahuasca ceremony, while another client said she had booked surfing lessons in Hawaii around then. To each his/her own!)

Looking to the Previous Jupiter/Neptune Conjunction

Looking deeper into this, I decided to go back and research what was happening around the last time these two combined, around March 17 of 1856, to see if any clues appeared as to what we might expect this time around. A few things stood out for me:

- Composer Richard Wagner completed his famed score for *Die Walküre* almost exactly on this conjunction, just six days later on March 23, 1856. (Those familiar with *Apocalypse Now* will know this work.)
- On May 1 of that year, Charles Dodgson formally chose the pseudonym Lewis Carrol (author of *Alice in Wonderland*), while also taking up photography that same day.
- The second of Eliphas Levi's 2-volume work, *Dogme et Rituel de la Haute Magie*, was published during this period, a work now regarded as inaugurating the modern age of occultism.[1]
- Mauviene, sometimes referred to as "the color that revolutionized the world," the first synthetic organic dye, was discovered that same month—and led to the birth of the chemical industry.

Even more interesting to me, though, were some of the individuals born during that period. They included:

- The great painter John Singer Sargent was born on January 12 of that year, just nine weeks before the actual conjunction. Sargent was known for his fluid style, sense of color, and spiritual kinship with Impressionism, but I'd particularly call attention to his remarkable murals in the Boston Public Library, featuring hugely imaginative scenes that would have made Salvador Dali proud.
- On April 5, Booker T. Washington was born. He was an American educator and prominent leader in the African-American community, widely regarded as a powerful inspiration both to his own community and beyond.

- Psychologist Sigmund Freud was born on May 6 (just two days before Jupiter departed Pisces and entered Aries). He would eventually be seen not just as the "father of modern psychology" but the individual arguably more responsible than any other for popularizing the idea of the "unconscious mind"—the notion that there is a vast ocean of being lying below the surface of our conscious life, akin to the submerged portion of an iceberg.
- Curiously enough, on that exact same day explorer Robert Peary was born, the figure generally credited with being the first to reach the North Pole. (Can we see a commonality between these two men in their shared exploration of previously uncharted landscapes of the imagination?)

And even though Jupiter left Pisces for early Aries on May 8 of that year, it's worth making note of a few of the other individuals born that year, since the influence of that Jupiter/Neptune energy continued for quite some time, whether the zodiacal sign Pisces was fully involved with both planets or not. Those include L. Frank Baum, author of *The Wizard of Oz*, born on May 15; H. Rider Haggard, fantasy novelist, born on June 22; Nikola Tesla, Serbian-American inventor, on July 10; Irish writer George Bernard Shaw, on July 26; the great architect Louis Sullivan, born on Sept. 3; and finally, the pioneering physicist J.J. Thompson, on Dec. 18. (It's worth noting that Thompson was born just a few months after Freud, considering they would both eventually open doors to vast new realms of experience, one of them internal and psychological, the other more material and sub-atomic.) Quite a remarkable assemblage of personalities and creative spirits!

Summing up, I'd say that examples like these make it clear this combination of celestial energies will indeed be a time when there will be a great opening up of our collective imagination, of the so-called "unconscious," and perhaps even *superconscious*. Though as the above examples illustrate, we may not know the *full* impact of these energies until the children born under its influence grow up to make their own mark on the world!

Timing Considerations

So when should we pay closest attention to this energy? While the conjunction in Pisces technically occurs on April 12 (at 23° Pisces), its influence will be especially strong for a week on either side, and somewhat less strong for one or two months on either side. It's even possible this energy will act as a subtle backdrop for the entire year, and several years to come, apart from whatever other chaos or insanity comes our way during 2022. (As Richard Tarnas reminded me, this energy will be strong again later in 2022, especially early November, when Jupiter backs up into Pisces and comes within spitting distance of Neptune.) And of course, whatever influence this pattern holds for *you* will depend heavily on how and where it falls in your horoscope.

In any event, have fun surfing the wave!

Postscript: I remember how in June of 2018, during a station point of Neptune in Pisces, there was a massive amount of media attention on the plight of refugees flooding across the southern U.S. border. That Piscean energy was evident not only in the massive suffering on display but in the sympathy and concern evoked by the plight of those people. As of this writing (mid-March of 2022), it looks like something similar may be happening with the burgeoning Jupiter/Neptune conjunction in Pisces, in terms of refugees flooding out of Ukraine, and the global wave of sympathy that's provoking. Jupiter expands whatever it touches, and the sheer enormity of what's happening now in Europe could well be another expression of this Piscean energy.

CHAPTER 16

A BRIEF MEDITATION ON THE HUBBLE "DEEP FIELD" PHOTO

It's been called one of the most important photographs ever taken. The so-called Hubble "Deep Field" photo is a composite image resulting from more than 23 days of exposure. In the space of a single picture, it shows thousands of individual galaxies, each one of which contains millions of stars, like our own galaxy.

To give a sense of proportion, the amount of sky actually covered by this picture equates to just a small fraction of the size of a normal Full Moon. The number of stars and galaxies that implies for the rest of the cosmos is beyond what the human mind can possibly comprehend. Dimensions like that have a paradoxical effect on the mind: on the one hand, making one's own life feel relatively insignificant, while simultaneously hinting at the incomprehensible vastness of our spiritual natures.

The very oldest galaxies in this image are up to 12 billion light years away. Because of the time it takes for light to travel, that means this image also gives us a window *back in time*: when we look at the furthest galaxies in this shot, we are looking 12 billion years into our past. (It's sometimes been pointed out how if the telescope were sufficiently powerful, an astronomer far enough away could look at the Earth and still see dinosaurs roaming around its surface.)

But it's interesting to flip that around. This also means that to any beings who may have lived in those furthest galaxies, *we are now living twelve billion years in their future.*

As mentioned, there are more stars implied by this photo than the human mind can conceive, and some of the stars in some of those galaxies are likely going *supernova*. That's when a star explodes in a flash of light and cosmic rays. We tend to think of these as being relatively rare events; for example, our own Sun probably isn't large enough to ever go supernova, but if it did, that wouldn't occur for several billion more years yet. But the universe is so vast that astronomers speculate that at least one supernova is going off *every second, somewhere*. In the time it's taking you to read this paragraph, a dozen or so solar systems somewhere are likely exploding; indeed, in the twenty-three odd days it took to take this photograph, thousands more supernovas undoubtedly occurred.

But this image raises another thought for me.

When we look at the Deep Field photo, we're actually seeing *very different points in time,* since each of these galaxies occupies a different distance away from us. Some are only a few hundred or thousand years old, others a few millions years old, and some are up to twelve billion years old.

That means this image is somewhat akin to having a photograph in which you see Napoleon, King Tut, a Neanderthal, Abraham Lincoln, Aristotle, "Lucy" the ancient proto-human, and Elvis Presley, all standing next to one another in a single portrait, as though they were all living at the same time. Implausible as that would be, that's exactly analogous to what we're seeing when we look at the Deep Field photograph.

So when someone says to you that we live in interesting "times," they probably have no idea just how right they are.

Anatomy of a Breakthrough

The Hubble Space Telescope which took this photo was, of course, named after the famed astronomer Edwin Hubble (who attended high school about 500 yards from where I'm writing this right now, funny you should ask). He rightly deserved that honor for the simple reason that he made monumental contributions to science and astronomy on not just one but two fronts: firstly, by showing that our galaxy wasn't the only one in existence, and that the universe was unimaginably larger than anyone previously suspected; and secondly, by discovering that the universe is expanding, he allowed scientists to then calculate backwards to a theorized "Big Bang" which birthed our universe.

As a result, it could well be argued Edwin Hubble was responsible for the greatest expansion of humanity's knowledge of the universe in recent centuries. For that reason, I thought it would be interesting to look at his horoscope, for which we seem to have a reasonably accurate birthtime: Nov. 20, 1889, 11:45 PM, Marshfield Wisconsin (data from his autobiography).

The first thing that jumped out at me was the fact he was born under the influence of the paradigm-shifting, once-every-five-hundred-year Pluto/Neptune conjunction, which was in effect most strongly from the late 1880s up through the 1890s. That was a window in time that gave birth to such historic figures as Mao Zedong, Dwight Eisenhower, Paramahansa Yogananda, Ernest Hemingway, Adolph Hitler, Charlie Chaplin, and J.R. Tolkien, among many others. This generational pattern took on personal significance for Hubble not just by being the most elevated pattern in his chart, but by having a strong connection to his personal planets as well, suggesting a more personal attunement to those broad cultural movements and Big Ideas. Specifically, that planetary duo is opposing his Sun, and is part of a T-square to his Saturn in Virgo on the Ascendant. Now, that may not be a very comfortable placement for someone's emotional life, it's true, but it's pretty much perfect for someone wanting to investigate matter and the secrets of the natural world.

But I was particularly curious to see what planetary energies he had firing around the time he made that first epic discovery, for which we have an exact date, since he inscribed it on a photographic plate: *Oct. 6, 1923.* After all, what could be more significant than revolutionizing our perception of the universe, in both its size and age? Not surprisingly, there were a number of interesting configurations happening around then, a few of which seem particularly important to me.

Aside from the fact that Pluto was stationing at the time, or standing relatively still—a planetary pattern often associated with the unearthing of hidden truths and deep truths—*expansive Jupiter was sitting right on his Mercury, firing exactly one day later, on*

Oct. 7. One could hardly find a more fitting aspect for someone in the midst of a mind-expanding intellectual breakthrough. In addition, Jupiter was about to cross over his Sun, a pattern that likewise showed an expansive new phase in his life and perception. (While it became exact on Nov. 20, its effects extended for months on either side).

But perhaps most important of all was the fact that he had several once-in-a-life progressions taking place during that period. In particular, progressed Mars was conjuncting his natal Uranus, the planet of revolution (that was exact on Oct. 15), while Uranus was, by "solar arc" progression, conjuncting his natal Sun, thereby igniting his whole personality with the spirit of revolution and innovation (that one fired precisely on Dec. 2 but was influential for a good year on either side).

So what does that all mean?

Simply, that this could have been a period of extraordinary expansion and revolutionary breakthroughs for him, and in turn for the world—and it certainly was!

Postscript: The Hubble Space Telescope was launched in 1990, under a Mercury retrograde, but due to technical problems it didn't become activated until 1993—the same year that the epic conjunction of Uranus and Neptune occurred. As befits a large, generationally-oriented configuration like that, our view of the cosmos has forever been changed by what we've learned since the Hubble became fully operational in 1993.

Towards the end of 2021, the James Webb Telescope—considered to be the next major step in space photography since the Hubble Telescope—was launched into space. Someone asked me for my astrological opinion about the horoscope for the launch itself, which took place on Christmas Day, December 25, 2021. I replied that my own hunch was to focus less on that launch time or date and more on the broader planetary energies in play around when the telescope becomes fully *operational*, which is scheduled to occur sometime in the Spring of Summer of 2022.

And as far as I'm concerned, the likely candidate to consider in that respect will be the Jupiter/Neptune alignment in April of 2022, as we discussed in the previous chapter, but which will have an impact well beyond that month or even year. As we saw, that's a potentially visionary and expansive combination that could well usher in a major opening of our minds to broader horizons, both internally and externally.

Will our sense of the cosmos be forever expanded or even altered by the Webb, said to be a hundred times more powerful than the Hubble? I, for one, will be watching closely.

CHAPTER 17

WHEN SOMEONE'S SATURN IS ON YOUR SUN

In the fall of 1969, when I was seventeen, I went to a Rolling Stones concert in Chicago with my close friend Rick Andresen. His father owned some upscale camera equipment, and Rick enlisted me to use his dad's 16-millimeter movie camera to film the group in concert. I'd been playing with 8-mm cameras since I was about twelve, so Rick figured that I would be the right person for the job. In exchange, he offered to pay for my ticket (which in those days cost less than buying a drink at a concert now, incredibly). I could hardly refuse.

As it turned out, the three-hour concert began with two opening acts: Terry Reid and Chuck Berry. It was held at the International Amphitheater down in the city, and we found ourselves situated in the back section of the venue that night. But over the course of those first two hours, I managed to gradually weasel my way up through the standing-only crowd until I got to the edge of the stage. There was little security in those days to prevent anyone from getting that close, so you could do that sort of thing then—assuming you had the gumption to try (and having the camera in my hands gave me just enough of that, despite my discomfort around crowds back then).

This was what some called the Stones' "Sympathy for the Devil" tour, when they were in their peak Jagger-dressed-in-black-flipping-a-red-sash days, dishing out songs like "Street Fighting Man, "Gimme Shelter," and of course "Satisfaction." Brian Jones had recently died, and Mick Taylor had just taken his place. The infamous tragedy of their performance at the Altamont Speedway in California was still three weeks away. They were all very young and seemed to be excited about performing in the city whose music meant so much to them.

Rolling Stone magazine eventually listed this tour among "The Fifty Greatest Concerts of the Last Fifty Years," and for a teenager, it was thrilling stuff. I've never thought the Stones were a particularly great live band, particularly in the larger venues, since it always seemed to me they were playing to the back row, as they say, with every gesture and musical phrase exaggerated, all nuances washed away. But this was a good night for them. Standing at the edge of the stage, I was close enough to field spittle from Jagger's freakishly oversized lips at one point. Which I would find completely disgusting now, of course, but at the time was kind of exciting in an idolizing adolescent sort of way.

Most exciting of all was the prospect of getting such potentially great footage of Jagger at close range, since he was practically standing over me at times. That meant a lot to me from an artistic standpoint.

Or at least I thought I was getting such great footage. When the film came back from the camera store that next week, I discovered I had used all of it up to shoot scenes of the two opening acts, Terry Reid and Chuck Berry—all of it, that is, except for just one frame of Jagger. One frame. I had no idea beforehand how little film the camera actually stored, and the noise of the concert drowned out the change in customary clickety-clack noises those old movie cameras normally made when they ran out of film.

As a result, whatever joy I felt having attended the concert was summarily dashed. This wasn't an earthshaking tragedy, of course, but for an artistically-minded, music-loving kid like me, it was deflating in the extreme. Just to make sure I didn't forget about that miscalculation of mine, Rick was careful to remind me about it every few months those next few years.

Decades later, when I became involved with astrology, it occurred to me to look at Jagger's horoscope to see if something might shed light on that early disappointment. By that time, I'd had enough experience with synastry—the study of planetary chemistry between two or more horoscopes—to know that even fleeting encounters between people reflect the alchemy of their combined planets, and this applies as much to interactions with celebrities as anyone else. This seemed like a good case for putting that idea to the test.

I discovered that Jagger's natal Saturn in Gemini wasn't all that far from the Sun in my horoscope. That explained quite a bit, I thought, because Saturn/Sun connections between charts can often result in frustration, especially for the person on the receiving end of the other person's Saturn.

But it got me thinking about two other disappointing encounters I had in my teens with well-known musical celebrities I admired. I wanted to see if there might be a similar dynamic at work with those as well, specifically involving strong Saturn interactions. If it held true for me and Jagger, might it also apply to these other cases too?

For example, a few years before my experience at the Stones concert, the brilliant folk-rock group The Byrds did a promotional tour for their first album, "Mr. Tambourine Man," and that included a string of personal appearances throughout the Chicagoland area at Sears department stores, of all places. I was a huge fan of the group's music, which had just reached number one on the musical charts, with "Mr. Tambourine Man"; but I especially admired the group's founder and lead singer, Jim (later "Roger") McGuinn. The nearest Sears store at the corner of Harlem and North Avenues was only a few blocks away from where my family lived, so I excitedly looked forward to riding my bike over there and seeing them in person that coming Saturday morning.

But as fate would have it, our family dog decided to run away early that day, inconsiderate mutt that he was, and I spent the better part of that morning looking for him. By the time I found him and rushed over to the store, the band members were getting into their limousines and driving away, leaving me feeling incredibly disappointed. It didn't help any to hear the other young fans lingering outside saying how cool it was seeing and hearing the band up close and personal like that.

Here as well, I decided to look back with the benefit of astro-hindsight decades later, and discovered that McGuinn's Saturn not only landed near my Sun, but was smack-dab on top of my Venus and Mercury as well. So far, so good—or bad, I should say.

An even bigger disappointment awaited me two years later, when I read in the teen music magazines about an up-and-coming guitarist named Jimi Hendrix, who had (quite literally) burned up the stage at the Monterey Pop Festival shortly before. He had no records out yet, but the word of mouth on him had already reached a fever-pitch. Having just started playing guitar the year before myself, I was eager to hear what this buzzed-about musician could do.

As a result, when I learned that Jimi was scheduled to be the opening act for the Monkees on their first national tour, I enlisted my friend Rick to join me in catching the show. But when the concert began, instead of Jimi coming out, some very mediocre band (whose name I've long since forgotten) opened for the Monkees. We were mystified, and terribly disappointed. Months later, we learned he'd been dropped from the tour shortly before Chicago, when his act proved just a bit too wild for the hordes of young girls in the audience (and their disapproving parents).

But that wasn't the real letdown; that was yet to come.

That came two years later, when Jimi roared into town and visited one of our local radio stations. As was customary for many rock performers on their promotional tours, he agreed to take phone calls from listeners. I'd taken advantage of those opportunities before and had been lucky enough to get through and speak with various band members occasionally, including

John Entwistle of The Who and Chris Hillman of—well, what do you know?—The Byrds. Funny how that one played out.

Anyway, the phone lines were completely tied up with callers trying to get through to Jimi, since he was a big star now. I heard nothing but busy signals for almost thirty minutes.

Finally, to my surprise, the busy signals stopped, and I heard the unmistakable sound of my call going through. "Wow! This could be it," I thought as I gulped hard and waited. I then heard the sound of someone picking up the phone—at which point I heard the disc jockey say, "Well, Jimi, I know you've got to be on your way, so I just want to thank you for coming down and speaking with us and the listeners"—followed by the click of the phone hanging up.

When I looked up Jimi Hendrix's horoscope decades later, I again discovered that Jimi's Saturn was indeed on my Sun, Mercury, and Venus. Bingo.

To be sure, these experiences with near-misses aren't precisely typical of what might happen when someone else's Saturn is on your Sun, but they certainly convey some of the flavor. Sometimes it can be very double-edged—on the one hand, granting you some great worldly thing, like my teenage self getting just a few feet away from the Stones in concert, while simultaneously denying you something important, like my failing to capture them on film. Or like my missing those other connections with The Byrds and Hendrix. Or like my experience with *Apocalypse Now,* when Saturn crossed over my Ascendant, which was terribly disappointing but an interesting and valuable experience nonetheless.

Saturn can be like that, whether in birth charts or in synastry between charts. It both gives and denies simultaneously. Sometimes, that denial can be dealt by someone very intentionally, such as when a prospective lover rejects you or a boss reprimands you for your performance. The element of respect is usually a big issue in those cases.

But sometimes the heavy hand of Saturn can be just the impersonal hand of fate at work, as with my client who fell madly in love with a soldier whose Saturn was on her Sun and then was shipped off to fight in Iraq; or the actress I knew who was thrilled to audition for a world-famous director, whose Saturn was likewise on her Sun, only to learn that the film project was canceled at the last minute. (At least she was able to brag that she'd met the fellow, so there's that.) In that same vein, Jagger didn't personally do anything to me, of course, he simply acted as the unwitting messenger of fate, the agent of Saturn's double-edged influence.[1]

The ringed lord giveth, the ringed lord taketh away. Sometimes it even giveth back later on unexpectedly, as happened for me with the Byrds and bass player Chris Hillman. (Notice, by the way, it wasn't McGuinn who resurfaced for me but his second-in-command. That's a bit Saturnian too.)

Make no mistake: there are times when one person's Saturn on another person's Sun can be an extremely productive force, as with a dance instructor training a young student, or a drill instructor putting a new inductee through the steps. Francis Ford Coppola's Saturn was on Marlon Brando's Sun, and he helped shape Brando's persona in ways that led to bravura performances in both *The Godfather* and *Apocalypse Now*.

But Saturn being Saturn, even these circumstances are never particularly easy, and certainly don't seem to make for warm and fuzzy relationships. Just ask Brando and Coppola. (Well, Coppola anyway, since Brando's since moved on to greener pastures.) After all, Saturn didn't acquire its reputation as the planetary taskmaster for nothing. It can lead to big rewards—presuming you're patient and willing to carry that extra weight.

CHAPTER 18

THE ASTROLOGY OF HOLLYWOOD'S
GOLDEN YEAR - 1939

Various years have been singled out by film critics as the "greatest" for film production, with some of the candidates proposed including 1962, 1972, or 1999.

But the general consensus among most cinephiles tends to focus on 1939 as Hollywood's most distinguished "Golden Year." Consider a few of the entries from that time: *Gone with the Wind, Stagecoach, The Wizard of Oz, Mr. Smith Goes to Washington, Hunchback of Notre Dame, The Women, Of Mice and Men,* and *Grapes of Wrath,* among others.

Several theories have been proposed to explain that impressive run, such as the fact that there was an improved economy taking shape after the Great Depression which gave people more disposable income for attending movies, while allowing for more investment to be poured into film productions. Another factor was the flood of creative refugees coming from Europe that energized the movie industry as fascism took hold overseas.

But I've long wondered what might account for this cinematic bumper crop from an astrological standpoint. For a long time I assumed it was probably due to the fact that transiting Uranus was forming a trine to Neptune throughout that period, roughly from 1938 up to 1944 (and which reached one of several peaks when that trine became exact and was joined by Jupiter in late April and early May of 1941—precisely when *Citizen Kane* premiered). But while that Uranus/Neptune trine was surely a factor, I always felt like there must be something more at work, something that was particularly strong in 1939.

And as it turns out, there was.

While looking through an ephemeris from that period, I realized that throughout the late 1930s and very early 1940s, the United States was in the midst of its first ever *Neptune return*—this being the planet of imagination, film, illusions, and mysticism. In the U.S. horoscope for 1776, Neptune was positioned at 22 degrees of Virgo, and from 1938 through to 1940 it was hovering around that zodiacal degree once again [1] In other words, America was waking up to the imaginal potentials of its own Neptune throughout this period. It was as if a channel had opened up to our national collective unconscious, prompting a rich flood of ideas to come pouring out, many of which have continued holding a place in the imaginations of movie-goers around the world. [2]

But there's another interesting cultural synchronicity I came across, which may not be entirely cinematic but nonetheless worth pointing out. The first U.S. Neptune return, as calculated by tropical standards,[1] fired precisely on Oct. 28 of 1938, and triggered exactly one more time on August 29, 1939—the *same week* as the premiere of *The Wizard of Oz* (and three days before the outbreak of WWII [3]).

121

It's easy to see how *The Wizard of Oz* would be an expression of America's Neptunian imagination being activated during that second trigger, with a timing that strikes me as nothing short of uncanny. But did anything of Neptunian importance happen close to the date of that *first* exact return?

As it turned out, it was just about 48 hours after that first Neptune return of Oct. 28, 1938 that a young Orson Welles performed his infamous "War of the Worlds" radio broadcast, in which millions of U.S. citizens were fooled into thinking we were being attacked by aliens from the planet Mars. One would be hard-pressed to find a more fitting example of Neptune's deceptive face than masses of people being fooled into believing something that was actually a complete illusion—an illusion about the planet Mars, no less, which Neptune closely squares in the natal U.S. horoscope! [4]

One final note. As of this writing, the U.S. is currently undergoing its Neptune *half*-return, as it transits across the zodiacal point 180 degrees away from its natal position in July of 1776. (By tropical standards, this one is in effect throughout 2021, but according to sidereal calculations will be exact throughout 2023.) There's been plenty of discussion about "lies" and "fake news" throughout this period, as well as major court cases involving opioid producers, surely both signs of the strong Neptune in play; but will this period likewise be looked back to by future historians as a similarly rich one for the cinematic medium? And if so, which films or TV shows and series will find their place on that esteemed list?

Time will tell!

CHAPTER 19

TRADE-OFFS

I t's not something anyone can prove, of course, but I've come to believe that for every major "gift" the universe gives you in life, there is a trade-off of sorts, a karmic balancing act that has to take place. Moreover, the greater the gift, the greater the trade-off or "pricc" to bc paid.

Let me explain what I mean.

When you look at any individual who has risen to the heights of success, wealth, creative brilliance, or even spiritual attainment, you usually (if not always) see some not-so-pleasant circumstance alongside those achievements or gifts which seems to counterbalance that success or achievement. This might take the form of a heavy burden that needs to be carried, such as a health problem or physical "flaw," the heartbreaking loss of one or more loved ones early in life, heavy responsibilities, sexual frustrations, or an emotional or physical wound from childhood. I've lost track of how many times I've seen someone who appeared on the surface to have it all, only to learn later on about the heavy personal struggles or sacrifices they endured in private, or sometimes even publicly.

This all came to mind for me several years ago while eating at a restaurant when I overheard a young woman in the next booth talking to her friend about the country singer Shania Twain. The woman said, "She has it all— beauty, talent, money...It really seems like some people get all the breaks."

It just so happened that earlier that day I'd seen an interview with Shania on morning TV where it was mentioned how both of her parents died in a car crash when she was young, forcing her to grow up exceptionally fast and raise her siblings in the process. I didn't interject myself into that conversation at the restaurant, of course, but I was tempted to lean over and ask that young woman, "Would you trade places with Shania Twain if it meant losing both your parents at that same young age?"

That got me thinking in turn about my own fantasies as a kid growing up, when I was swept up in my admiration of the Beatles and other creative figures, and thinking about how "lucky" Lennon and McCartney were to have experienced so much success, talent, and worldly good fortune. Yet the fact is, both of them lost their mothers at a young age. Would I have traded places with either of them if it meant also accepting that more unpleasant side of the bargain? Considering how much I loved (and still love) my late mother, I'd personally have to say no.

Or consider the lives of individuals like Joni Mitchell, Neil Young, and Francis Coppola—three of the most brilliant creative figures of the last half-century—all of whom contracted polio as children and underwent severe physical hardships and isolation as a result. Or take the case of actor Christopher Reeve, who found early success playing Superman in films, but then was paralyzed from the neck down as a result of a horse-riding accident. And then there is Beethoven, one of history's greatest composers, who went completely deaf and experienced a deeply frustrating love life. I also think of the spiritual teachers I've studied with, who inspired me in terms of their discipline, knowledge and wisdom, but who endured extreme hardships of their own.

The list goes on.

I'm not suggesting there is necessarily a metaphysical or moral principle involved in all of this—although there may well be. For example, many astrologers believe that worldly success or achievement is often indicated in the horoscope by "hard" aspects (90-degree relationships particularly, but sometimes 180-degree or even zero-degree relationships). These are what astrologers regard as high-energy, "manifestational" configurations. By comparison, a chart with nothing but so-called "easy" aspects, like trines or sextiles, usually show a relatively comfortable life but not one particularly driven toward worldly achievement or activity; these individuals may well *dream* of such things, but they're not likely to have the energy or motivation to work for them. The trade-off with hard aspects, however, is they usually come with *hard life-experiences*. The upshot here is that "successful" lives are often associated with some of the most difficult horoscopes—and in turn, the most difficult lives.

But astrology and metaphysics aside, even from a purely psychological standpoint it's safe to assume that high achievers are generally those fueled by emotional difficulties or insecurities in life, and that the greater the achievement and success, the greater the psychological *need* for achievement and success.

Either way, whether it be something metaphysical or strictly psychological, it's a phenomenon I've come across so many times I can't help but wonder if there isn't a very real principle or "law" at work. There truly does seem to be a curious ecology of counterbalances at work in our lives, *however* we choose to explain it.

So if you should happen to depart this world and find yourself up on the astral awaiting your next incarnation, with a burning desire to come in and make your own big mark on the world, ala' Oprah Winfrey, Steve Jobs, or Genghis Khan, just remember: a hefty trade-off will probably be involved!

CHAPTER 20

TWENTY-ONE THINGS WORTH KNOWING ABOUT THE AQUARIAN AGE

For many of us who grew up in the 1960s, our first exposure to the idea of an "Aquarian Age" was through a popular song from the musical "Hair," which included lyrics like these:

"When the moon is in the seventh house
And Jupiter aligns with Mars
Then peace will guide the planets
And love will steer the stars
This is the dawning of the Age of Aquarius
Age of Aquarius"

It certainly gave many of us the impression the coming era would be one of harmony, peace, and brotherhood, with lots of people holding hands and singing "Kumbaya." Needless to say, the truth of the matter will surely be more complex than that.

In 2002, I published a book exploring some of my ideas about how the emerging Great Age may already be impacting such areas as media, politics, technology, science, pop culture, and religion. Released in 2002, I titled it *The Dawn of Aquarius*, later changed by the publisher to *Signs of the Times*. In the years since then, I've entertained the idea of boiling down some of the more complex arguments in that book to a few basic "bullet point" statements that distill its broader themes. What follows is the result of that distillation, along with a few more thoughts I've considered over the intervening 20 years.

This is a profoundly important topic, I believe. The great stories which drive humanity are in the process of changing in ways with seismic implications not just for our lives but for the planet itself. Astrology gives us a chance to better understand those stories—what they've been in the past, what they are now, and where they may be heading—as well as how we, as individuals, fit into them. But it's a profoundly *complex* topic as well, with many nuances beyond simplistic notions of "good" or "bad," positive or negative. Hopefully this discussion will provide you with a better sense of those nuances.

1. Timing.
Probably the most commonly asked question about the Aquarian Age is, *When does it start?* A surprisingly wide range of dates have been proposed by astrologers, ranging from the 16th Century all the way up to 3573 CE (the latter date proposed by Rudolf Steiner). But it's far more likely that for something as glacial as a Great Age, the impact doesn't begin on a given day or even year but unfolds over far longer periods of time. By analogy, when does the tide come in? Is there a precise minute when it arrives? No, it comes in gradually over time. Likewise, the Aquarian Age has arguably been begun making its presence felt since *as least* the late 1700s, and will likely gain momentum during the centuries ahead. But while it may not be in full swing yet, there's little doubt it's already begun to make its presence felt.

2. The Wave Effect
Staying with the "tidal" analogy, an emerging Great Age seems to make its strongest impact in the form of certain pronounced "waves"—periods when the incoming forms, values, and institutions thrust forward into manifestation with special force. Just as the tide ebbs and flows, moving ever higher onto the shore, the same holds true for any Great Age. These waves can be propelled by any number of factors, such as major planetary conjunctions, eclipses, stelliums (when multiple planets come together in a tight grouping), or the spring equinox crossing over key stars

along the ecliptic (as suggested by both Carl Jung and astrologer Robert Hand). Each of these triggers introduces some new theme or nuance into the unfolding mix, similar to the way different melodic or harmonic passages contribute their own qualities to a larger unfolding symphony.

While there are many examples of such historical waves from recent history, I've generally singled out a few as being especially noteworthy: the years around the discovery of Uranus in 1781 (this planet being one of the co-rulers of Aquarius); the period around the conjunction of Uranus and Neptune in 1821; the years immediately leading up to and following the Pluto/Neptune conjunction of the 1890s; the Uranus/Pluto conjunction of the 1960s; and the Uranus/Neptune conjunction of the 1990s. Each of these time frames witnessed older forms of culture disappearing and a significant dawning of new, breakthrough ideas and trends associated with the incoming era.

3. Transitional Symbols.
When a Great Age ends, its effects don't simply disappear, to be replaced by an entirely different set of symbols and influences. There is always an overlapping of ages at the intersection of epochs, resulting in a series of "transitional symbols" that embody both the new and old paradigms at once. A simple example would be Christianity itself, which clearly blended the influences of Judaism from the Arian Age with those of the emerging Piscean Age. A more recent example would be televangelism, in which we see the Piscean influence of Christianity merging with the hi-tech media technologies of a more Aquarian sort. An allied example from recent years would be TV images of Middle Eastern fundamentalists using cell phones on the battlefield to communicate with each other as well as the larger world.

A literary example of transitional symbolism would be Herman Melville's classic work *Moby Dick*, portraying Ahab's battle against the great white whale. By comparison, some metaphysical writers through the years have suggested that the Biblical story of Moses rejecting the Israelites' worship of the golden calf can be read as symbolizing the shift from the Age of Taurus (the bull) to that of Aries (the ram). *Moby Dick* may well hold a similar transitional meaning for our own time, with Ahab's attack on the white whale reflecting the effort to cast aside the "watery and emotional" values of the Piscean Age for those of the "airy and rational" Aquarian Age.

4. The Rise of the Air Element

As all astrologers know, the twelve signs of the zodiac boil down to four archetypal modes of consciousness: Air, Earth Fire, and Water. Aquarius is an Air sign, which is a predominantly *mental* element, concerned with the mind, thinking, information, and communication. That suggests that the emerging era will be one where the mind and information reign supreme in our world, in contrast with the more emotional, religious, and ideological Piscean Age. A more exoteric expression of this shift, symbolically, has been the rise of air travel in our times, originally via lighter-than-air balloons (first inaugurated around the discovery of Uranus in the 1780s) and later through propeller and jet-powered aircrafts.

But critical to understanding Aquarius is realizing that there are actually three different Air signs: Gemini, Libra and Aquarius. This pertains to the fact that the "mind" principle expresses itself through three distinctly different—and increasingly broader—contexts. Whereas Gemini relates to mind in its most personalized form, such as you might employ when talking to family members or neighbors, Libra is more about the *inter*personal mind, such as when a teacher or lecturer speaks before a class or an audience. But Aquarius represents the broadest and most *impersonal* form of mind, such as you find at work in the life of a scientist, sociologist, or engineer.

Everyday human emotions and thoughts aren't as much of a concern for Aquarius as those truths or principles that apply *everywhere* and *everywhen*. Aquarius isn't simply concerned with ordinary ideas, in other words, as much as ideas and relationships that are more global or even universal in scope. An engineer or mathematician deals with abstract truths that would be just as valid on the surface of Mars or Venus as they are here on Earth. For that reason, Aquarius might well be described as the principle of *cosmic* rationality, of *cosmic* mind—the ability to perceive and make connections of the most abstract and universal sort. As a result, the Aquarian Age will likely be an era when science rather than religion is the dominant paradigm, and its scientists, inventors, and technicians become our new high priests.

That same impersonality and broad focus is making itself known in other ways. Consider how we are all involved now in social connections and networks that extend over vast distances across our planet, via technologies like the internet, radio or TV. These allow ordinary people around the world to communicate with one another, albeit in largely cerebral and detached ways. Thanks to our technologies, it's one of the paradoxes of our time that we can sometimes be more connected to someone on the other side of the planet than the person who lives next door, or sometimes even our own family members.

5. How Do the Great Ages "Work"?
Try talking to a non-astrologer about the topic of the Great Ages—or for that matter, any aspect of astrology—and the question may come up as to how all this is even possible. What mechanism causes the movement of the vernal point through the constellations to cause major developments down here on Earth?

In fact, it's not a "mechanism" at all, nor does it really *cause* anything. It has more to with synchronicity, or *meaningful coincidence*, in the spirit of the old esoteric axiom "As above, so below."

The phenomena of our world, both terrestrial and extraterrestrial, coalesce in a meaningful order, even across vast distances. As a result, when the vernal point shifts into the constellation of Aquarius, its influence on us isn't because of forces emanating down to Earth but rather due to a coinciding of cosmic and earthbound patterns in meaningful ways. Everything interlocks in a grand matrix of symbolic linkages —and the precession of the equinoxes represents one element in that cosmic fabric.

6. The "Gender" of the Aquarian Age

For centuries, astrologers have believed that zodiacal signs— much like numbers, according to the Pythagoreans—possess gender. Six of the twelve signs are considered "masculine," or more extraverted in focus (Aries, Gemini, Leo, Libra, Sagittarius, and Aquarius), while the alternate signs are considered "feminine," or comparatively introverted in nature (Taurus, Cancer, Virgo, Scorpio, Capricorn, and Pisces).

This same idea can be applied to the Great Ages. For example, the Piscean Age was more "feminine" in the sense that its broad focus was more on the inner, emotional lives of humans, and upon the awakening of *soul*. On the one hand, that gave us the glorious heights of inspiration and artistic brilliance of figures like Bach or Michelangelo, along with the insights of mystics like Meister Eckhardt, Rumi, and Hildegarde of Bingen. But on the other hand, it also gave us the turbulent depths of dogma, guilt, and self-denial cultivated by religious extremists throughout the era.

By contrast, the Aquarian Age is a decidedly more extraverted one, pointing to a greater focus on the *outer* world and its understanding. At its best, that could lead to an effort to unlock the spiritual and mystical dimensions of materiality itself, while at its worst it could result in an eclipsing of Spirit by material values altogether, as well as a loss of those sensitive soul-qualities acquired during the Piscean Age.

7. The Principle of Octaves

One of the unique properties of symbols is that they can manifest on different levels, both in their meaning and form. That's particularly true when it comes to astrology. Simply consider the example of Sun signs: is Pisces a good or a bad sign? That depends entirely on who is "wearing" it. The same Piscean energy that gave us Michelangelo and Edgar Cayce also gave us Rupert Murdoch and serial killer John Wayne Gacy. It's the same zodiacal principle, but resonating at vastly different levels of meaning and expression. Likewise, was the Age of Pisces a "good" or "bad" era? It's an essentially meaningless question, because we have seen a vast array of manifestations during the last two thousand years across a broad range of possibilities, rather than any one expression.

Which brings us to the Age of Aquarius. Will this be a time of brotherhood and enlightened science, as some believe, or a time of Orwellian group-think and overarching bureaucracies? It could well turn out to be *both*, just at different times and in different places.

8. The Highest Potentials of a Great Age are Limited to a Relative Few

One occasionally comes across the suggestion that the coming Great Age will be a time when all of humanity experiences a raising of consciousness to a higher level—"Hundredth Monkey," something, something. Sad to say, that's not likely to happen, at least not in the widespread or uniform way many are hoping for. Precisely because of the "octaves" principle we just saw, people vary enormously in how they respond to the potentials offered up by any Great Age. Humans have *always* co-existed at wildly varying levels of spiritual or mental development. Only a relative handful at any given time act out the very highest possibilities. Consequently, for every saint or creative genius that arose during the Piscean Age there were many more perfectly ordinary men and women living out their lives, not to mention quite a few decidedly non-saintly ones, like Vlad the Impaler or Torquemada the Inquisitor.

There's no reason to think things will be much different in the next age. As such, I'm sure we can expect to see great geniuses emerging in areas of social reform, in the manner of Martin Luther King Jr.; or in creative areas, like Orson Welles or Stanley Kubrick; or in science, like Marie Curie or Albert Einstein; or technology, like Steve Jobs; or in spiritual areas, like Sri Aurobindo. But for every one of those there could be many more spending their time glued to smart phones and TV screens, engaged in comparatively pedestrian pursuits, all reflecting the somewhat less-creative side of Aquarius. That's not meant as a criticism or judgment, simply a realistic assessment of what might unfold, based on past history. At any given time, during any Great Age, only a relative few have the inclination, talent, or discipline to strive for the proverbial mountain top.

9. The Forerunner Effect, Aka Apostles of Change
To quote the poet Ezra Pound, "Artists are the antennae of the race." Artists seem to be more sensitive in picking up on emerging values and trends. We saw earlier how the Beatles were an example of emerging Aquarian values. Another example was Ludwig von Beethoven, who championed values of universal brotherhood and freedom of thought through his music and political statements (and note that his iconic Ninth Symphony, which was his central statement on that aforementioned "brotherhood," was composed during one of the historic waves I mentioned, when Uranus conjoined with Neptune in the 1820s).

Nor does this apply just to artists or writers, since it can just as easily take the form of politicians (like Abraham Lincoln), psychologists (like Carl Jung), or scientists (like Charles Darwin or Albert Einstein). Apostles of change come in many shapes and sizes—and they don't necessarily foreshadow completely positive potentials.

Consider Walt Disney, who was born with his Sun conjunct Uranus (the same day and year as quantum scientist Werner Heisenberg, incidentally). He was clearly a forerunner of future trends not only through innovations in cinema and animation or futuristic creations like the Epcot Center in Disney World, but also with his sprawling mass media empire. But was that legacy of his a positive or negative one? That depends entirely on your perspective. Likewise, consider Mark Zuckerberg, who's clearly a forerunner of Aquarian trends, Facebook being an especially obvious example of Aquarian "group interconnectedness"; but here as well, the positive or negative aspect of his legacy is largely in the eye of the beholder.

10. The Aquarius/Leo Polarity

When a Great Age comes in, it activates not only one new sign, but an entirely new gestalt involving *all* the signs. But of those eleven other signs, it's the relationship with the zodiacal sign directly *opposite* that is most critical.

In the case of the Piscean Age, for instance, the opposing sign was Virgo—and fittingly, in this epoch the global rise of Christianity was accompanied by a corresponding devotion to the Virgin Mary, while also ushering in an emphasis on doctrinal hairsplitting. In the case of the Aquarian Age, the opposing sign is Leo. What does that portend? As I explored more fully in *Signs of the Times*, there are a multitude of implications, but for simplicity's sake I'll focus on just a few.

Leo represents the reigning, "monarchical" individual who shines before all in his or her uniqueness, while at the other end of the zodiac, Aquarius represents the masses—the common man or woman standing arm-in-arm among the multitude. As a result, the advent of the Aquarian Age has already been ushering in the dissolution of royal institutions, as well as governance from the top down, to be replaced by governance from the bottom up—in a word, *democracy.* Or, in two words, *people power.* That doesn't mean that strongly Leonine figures will simply cease to exist; rather, it's more likely we'll see repeated efforts here and there by such figures to seize the reins of power, to be met with continued pushback by the masses in a geopolitical version of whack-a-mole.

But there are other implications besides purely political ones. This polarity relates to the possibility of ordinary individuals finding the spark of "Leo" within themselves: cultivating their own inner "royalty," their own kingliness or queenliness. To my mind, a beautiful technological symbol of that dynamic is solar power, whereby the energies of the Sun are drawn down into practical application for everyday use. Psychologically, that offers a concise metaphor for the potentials of this polarity in terms of ordinary people tapping into their higher "solar" potentials and becoming more empowered to make their mark on the world. To be sure, that can just as easily lead to ordinary individuals rising out of modest circumstances into positions of great destructive power, as exemplified by Hitler or Mussolini, as it can to someone attaining the summits of spiritual or creative achievement. Either way, it points to a vastly different set opportunities open to individuals in modern society than has existed before.

On yet another level of symbolism, this zodiacal polarity is giving rise to what could be called the *democratization of celebrity.* Leo is the zodiacal sign most commonly associated with society's stars—and quite fittingly, since it's the only zodiacal sign governed by an actual star rather than a planet or moon. In older times, the "stars" of our world were generally political or religious leaders of one stripe or another. But with the advent of modern telecommunications and pop culture, we've witnessed a newfound democratization of celebrity, whereby ordinary people now have the opportunity to rise out of complete obscurity into positions of fame. The Beatles did it, but so have many others, especially through social media. Theoretically, at least, anyone can become an object of worship and attain their fifteen minutes of fame, as Andy Warhol described it. *Disposable deities* is how I've sometimes described it.

And since Leo rules all forms of pleasure and fun, this polarity is also expressing itself through the advent of mass electronic pleasures such as we've seen appearing across the world over the last century. Millions of people can now watch the same TV show at the same time or engage in interactional video games, all suitably impersonally, as befits the detached nature of Aquarius.

11. The "Jazz Band" Principle

If I were asked to sum up the difference between the Piscean and Aquarian Ages in simple terms, I'd point to the difference mentioned earlier between an old-time Gregorian choir and a modern jazz band. In a Gregorian choir, all the members surrender their personal creativity and individuality in service of the greater ideal, while in a jazz band each member is actually encouraged to express their individual creativity, in a way that not only maintains but enhances the vitality of the group.

Under the influence of Christianity and Islam over the last two thousand years, the role of the individual was seen as largely subservient to God or to religious authorities. During the emerging Aquarian Age, we're seeing a greater emphasis on personal worth and autonomy, with each person's voice in the cosmic choir seen as having an importance all its own. Here as well, we're seeing the influence of the Leo/Aquarius polarity at work, with the spark of Leonine creativity ignited throughout the collective. Both Pisces and Aquarius are "group" signs, relating to larger masses of people; but in the case of Aquarius, as with the jazz band, each individual is able to contribute something of worth to the collective, whether through creativity, politics or social activism.

Image: Shutterstock

But jazz isn't just the defining metaphor of democracy, it's also the essential dynamic underlying phenomena like the Internet, where separate individuals interact with one another like members of a jazz ensemble, each one offering their own personalized input and with no one person lording over those interactions. The jazz dynamic is also apparent in the model of employee-owned businesses, where each worker has a say in the running of a company, or in corporate think tanks, where individuals pool their ideas rather than everything being decided by a single innovator or leader. Thomas Edison's workshop was a perfect expression of the "jazz" dynamic. He essentially played the role of a band leader to a selected group of unique innovators, each of whom contributed their own ideas to the group's output.

We even see the jazz dynamic being played out in the rise of the "gig economy"—the word *gig* here referring not to anything tech or data-related, but to the notion of independent, short-term employment, such as when a musician says they're taking on a gig. In contrast with more conventional full-time jobs, such as when an employee works for the same company for years on end, a gig employee tends to be more independent and flexible, and working for various employers. In its own way, the emergence of a more gig-based independent workforce reflects the jazz dynamic of multiple individuals, each of whom pursues their own liveli-hoods in ways that are not only more decentralized than in con-ventional models, but also more improvisational. But here as well, it's debatable whether this development has been a constructive or destructive force.

12. An Age of Decentralization

A good deal of I've been saying thus far could be summed up in the word *decentralization*. As one way to think about it, consider the biological correspondences associated with the Leo/Aquarius polarity: for most astrologers, Leo rules the heart while Aquarius rules the arterial distribution of the blood. Said another way, *Leo governs centralization Aquarius rules decentralization.*

Besides manifesting through such forms as jazz, corpo-rate think tanks, networks, employee-owned business, and the Internet (what is the central address of the Internet, for example?), we see decentralization manifesting in the arts, as with the break-ing up of perspective in abstract art and cubism, as well as in cinema. As we'll come back to later, Orson Welles' masterwork *Citizen Kane* not only decentralized its central character by pre-senting him from multiple viewpoints but also decentralized the conventional narrative by fragmenting the timeline into a patch-work of moments from different eras and locales. Experimental filmmaker Stan Brakhage also spoke about the need to break free of the conventional dramatic structures that cinema inher-ited from theater, as well as from the one-pointed perspective it inherited from painting in favor of more open-ended expressions of film's potentials.

In fact, the history of science over recent centuries could be summarized as one long series of decentralizations, beginning with Copernicus dethroning our Earth from its previously central spot in the universe, up through Darwin (who decentralized humanity from its perch on the Great Chain of Being), to Freud (who dethroned the conscious ego), to Edwin Hubble (who decentralized our home galaxy), to Albert Einstein (whose theory of relativity decentralized the notion of a single preferred reference point in time or space).

It's safe to say there are more cosmic decentralizations yet to come, but what form will they take? I'd throw two nominations into the ring: humans learning we aren't the only intelligent species in the universe, or learning that our universe or dimension is just one of many.

13. The Chakra Connection.

As I touched on earlier (and in most of my previous books), some esotericists believe there is a close connection between the outer sky and the internal chakra system—the psycho-spiritual model of consciousness described by yogic philosophy.[1]

As we saw, that begins with the basic correlation between the seven classical planets of our solar system and the seven primary chakric centers. In turn, each of those chakras has certain peripheral manifestations as well, "masculine" and "feminine" in nature, equated with the twelve signs of the zodiac. According to that cross-correlational approach, simply spin the zodiac around so that Leo and Cancer are positioned at the top, and you'll find a perfect match between those signs and the various levels of consciousness along the spine.

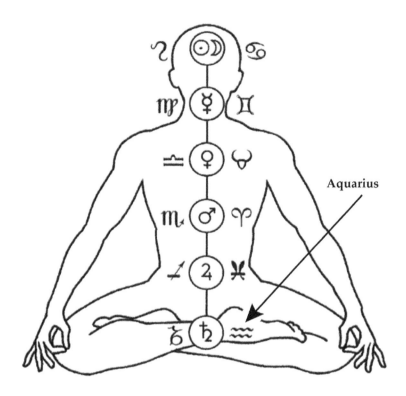

Aquarius

The Inner Zodiac

This leads to several important points for a deeper understanding of the Aquarian Age. The shifting of the Great Ages corresponds to a shifting of our collective awareness through different levels of consciousness over vast spans of time. In the case of the Aquarian Age, that leads to a curious blend of principles.

Simply put, *Aquarius is an Air (mental) sign superimposed onto a material-plane level of consciousness.*

All three Air signs are mental in nature, but since Aquarius is associated specifically with the root chakra, this means the coming era will heavily emphasize materiality but filtered through the *mind*. That's why Aquarius is so heavily associated with such fields as science, technology, electronics, media and engineering, all of which involve the practical world as modified and understood by human intelligence.

It's tempting to regard our collective movement into the root chakra as "bad," but that's far too simplistic. Every era has its place in the larger unfolding of consciousness. While this coming era may indeed wind up being a relatively materialistic one in some respects, that may simply mean, that we're entering into a more secular era—and already have, to a considerable extent. This doesn't necessarily mean we'll be discarding all our spiritual concerns or notions of God, but perhaps drawing a clearer line between church and state, where religious values no longer represent the dominant ones.

This also suggests the potential of a time when humanity learns to bring the higher values of spirit and light down into practical reality. We might even glean some clues from what I wrote about Chicago and the "earthiness" of its cultural contributions. The extraordinary impact of electrified Chicago blues on popular music the world over may reflect this broader shift taking place towards the worldly and secular in our global zeitgeist. This growing root chakra emphasis could also point to a time when science joins up with spiritual or occult principles in a way that sheds new light on our understanding of the world.

14. The U.S.A. ~ Forerunner of the Aquarian Age

Writer William Gibson once said, "The future is already here; it's just not evenly distributed." In much the same way that certain individuals are ahead of the curve in sensing future trends, the same can be said about certain countries. While it's true we catch early hints of the emerging Aquarian mythos in any number of cultures around the world, the United States appears to be at the head of the pack as the foremost national harbinger of Aquarian values —for better *or* worse.

To begin with, the U.S.A. was "born" near or even on the same year as the discovery of that very Aquarian planet, Uranus. While 1776 may have been this nation's "conception" date, the umbilical cord from England was severed with the defeat of Cornwallis at Yorktown in 1781. Some have suggested the "United States" as an entity was technically formed with the signing of the Perpetual Union Agreement under the Articles of Confederation, which was on March 1 of that year—just *twelve days* before the discovery of Uranus on March 13. Lastly, the Treaty of Paris was signed in 1783, which represented the final, *official* separation from England— the same year as the birth of aviation and the launching of the first hot air balloon by the Montgolfier brothers (a synchronicity I explore in far greater depth in *Signs of the Times*).

The symbolic connection between the United States' and the emerging Great Age is obvious in a variety of ways, such as this country's unparalleled involvement with technology, its emphasis on democracy, and its embrace of modern capitalism and the entrepreneurial spirit. (Synchronistically, Adam Smith's classic work *The Wealth of Nations* was published the same year as the Declaration of Independence, in 1776.) [2]

While the U.S. wasn't the first democratic society in history, it has become democracy's foremost symbol in modern times, armed with that most Aquarian of mottos, "We the People." Justly or unjustly, many people around the world have seen America as a beacon of freedom and the land of opportunity. I've spoken to immigrants through the years who told me that, despite their misgivings about the U.S., their dream since childhood had been to come to this country. What drew them here? In part, it's obviously this country's reputation for freedom and economic opportunity. But I also sense it involves a certain perception that this country rides at the cutting edge of change, and that coming here represents an act of leaving the "old world" and its values behind, and starting afresh.

Jazz has often been called the one truly American art form, and not surprisingly, the U.S.A. *is itself* based upon the jazz model, viewed symbolically. Think about it: the U.S. is a conglomeration of fifty states, all of which follow the same basic "sheet music" of the Constitution, yet those states are allowed a certain amount of creative leeway in improvising their own creative visions for their citizens. The President is to those fifty states and their governors what Louis Armstrong was to his jazz ensemble, spearheading their varied interests while allowing them their own contributions to the mix. That delicate tension between the federal government and individual states' rights reflects the same tension that exists in any jazz ensemble as well as within the sign of Aquarius itself, with its dance between individualism and "We the People" collectivism. I've sometimes been asked, "Does Aquarius rule groups, or the individual?" In truth, it's both.

By itself, "decentralization" is a neutral principle, and can be either a constructive or destructive force; it all depends on how it's applied. Another illustration of that principle in U.S. politics would be anti-trust laws, designed to prevent any one company from amassing too much influence. Then there is the tri-partite structure of the U.S. government; rather than allowing all power to reside in one autocratic leader or branch of government, it divvies up control between the executive, legislative, and judicial branches to provide checks and balances. While that poses its own set of problems, it's obviously a form of governance more closely in keeping with the will of the people than a dictatorship.

But you'll notice when I said the U.S. represents the emerging tip of the coming Great Age, I added, "for better or for worse." While there's much to be said about the virtues of the American experiment, there's clearly been a dark side to this development as well, as reflected in this nation's slide into root chakra materialism, its over-emphasis on technology and mass entertainments, undue corporate influence on policies, and still other problems.

Another fundamental challenge has been this country's afore-mentioned balancing act between individualism and collectivism. Some of its citizens blindly go along with the crowd, while others at the opposite end cling so tightly to personal rights and freedoms that they infringe on those of others.

Then there is this nation's tendency towards *superficiality*. That is a common problem with the Air element as well, truth be told. Years ago, I read an essay by a Russian journalist who spent time traveling through the U.S. He remarked that Americans seem to display a curiosity that is a mile wide but an inch-deep. By analogy, I think it's clear the Aquarian Age will be an exciting time for science, technology, and endless entertainments of many types—but we're obliged to ask what compromises that could mean in terms of our collective soul. Will our fascination with the outer world cause us to lose touch with certain emotional sensibilities inside us?

Last but not least, there's the unmistakable streak of violence which seems to percolate through the American soul, as reflected in the genocide and slavery upon which this nation was built, the many conflicts it's initiated or been party to around the world, and of course our nation's obsession with guns. That double-edged dynamic—between shiny superficiality on top and turbulent emotions down below—is also one of the potential problems of the Air element. Because of Air's general discomfort with feelings, emotions can easily wind up being denied outright, resulting in simmering undercurrents of unresolved energies that metastasize into something far more dangerous. With its need for rational order, Air can restrain and categorize the emotions. Over time, these may erupt into Air's rarefied world, as those emotions struggle to break free from that orderly straightjacket. This has been an ongoing problem with American society through the years, but it could prove to be a key challenge for life throughout the Aquarian Age as well.

15. The Spiral Effect

The Aquarian Age is part of a much larger cycle that lasts roughly 26,000 years and repeats over much vaster periods of time. There have been roughly forty Aquarian Ages during the last one million years, so it would be simplistic to think each one of these has played out in exactly the same way. "History doesn't repeat itself but it often rhymes," Mark Twain is reputed to have said, and that idea should be applied to the Great Ages as well. Because human consciousness is part of the equation, the Great Ages are not eternally fixed in their meanings and manifestations from one round to the next. They are more like cosmic triggers that activate the latent potentials of humanity at *whatever level it is currently at*—and these potentials can change radically over time.

Here's a simple analogy. A season like autumn will be experienced in a radically different way by a freshly planted apple seed than by a twenty-five-year-old apple tree. Though the season is in both cases the same, the response differs depending on the maturity of the life form involved, especially in terms of whether or not fruit will actually result. In much the same way, the Aquarian Age has a range of archetypal meanings which dispose us to think or act in certain ways, but it would be foolish to think that the Aquarian Age as experienced by Neanderthals was exactly the same as it will be for us now. A given Great Age bears whatever "fruit" is appropriate to the level of consciousness rising up to meet it. In short, the Great Ages do not *cause* us to act in particular ways so much as synchronize with the unfolding of our existing potentials.

16. The E.T. Question

The space race and our exploration of other planets and stars are certainly part and parcel of the emerging Aquarian mythos. It also seems likely that a key aspect of the coming millennia will involve actual contact with intelligences from other worlds, whether those be other solar systems, universes, time-frames, or even dimensions. Many of our modern pop mythologies—*Star Trek, Star Wars, Close Encounters*, and countless films or TV shows—already center around that possibility. It's worth mentioning, too, that in the primary mythic story associated with the constellation Aquarius, the human Ganymede is abducted into the heavens. While that may literally point to humanity's ascension into the "heavens" in literal ways, it could also symbolize our collective shift into the realm of Air—that is, heightened *mental* experience.

The impact of an encounter with beings from elsewhere would certainly be revolutionary, and as I have suggested, would also be a profound decentralization of our status in the universe. Such a meeting of the minds would surely open our psyches to new and more galactic ideas about religion, science, culture, and psychology. In later chapters we'll look briefly at how an exposure to such possibilities affected two unsuspecting individuals. Most intimately of all, this would force us to see *ourselves* in a new light, by facing us with forms of thought, life, and consciousness different from our own. Whether all this would be an enlightening or disruptive force for society remains an open question. One thing seems certain: the Aquarian Age is destined to bring about a dramatic change in our familiar conceptual frameworks, and our exploration of space will almost certainly play a major role in that intellectual revolution.

17. The Privacy Issue

As we've seen, the Aquarius/Leo polarity revolves around the dynamic between the group and the individual, between the system and the part. This has a wide range of implications, both constructive and destructive, all of which are amplified exponentially by modern media and telecommunications. On the one hand, these technologies have connected us not just to other individuals around the world but to other cultures, philosophies, and assorted global developments. It's nearly impossible now for anyone to remain insulated from what's happening outside of their community or small circle of acquaintances.

That development has come with a hefty price tag. In a time when each of us is now technologically plugged in to the world, there is also the possibility of the world plugged-into *us*, with our private lives now being scrutinized by many others beyond our private spheres. Although the "www" prefix on Internet URL's stands for "World Wide Web," it might just as well stand for the "The Whole World Is Watching"! What happened to celebrities like the Beatles is simply representative of what's happening to all of us now, to one extent or another.

There are undoubtedly benefits to these networking technologies, such as the need to monitor and apprehend criminals and enemies of the state, or in allowing each of us to become more aware of lifestyles and peoples besides our own. But what are the risks to our freedoms? There is a direct link between democracy and our right to privacy, as affirmed by the Constitution's Fourth Amendment. Tamper with the one and you necessarily affect the other, since no one who is subject to the prying eyes of neighbors, corporations, or the government can ever consider themselves completely free. In the Aquarian Age, we will all be interconnected. The question is, can we hang onto our hard-won liberties at the same time?

In an earlier chapter I mentioned the brilliant film *The Truman Show*, which dramatizes this problem with its tale of a man whose life has been the subject of media coverage since birth, unbeknownst to him. Every day and night, he's been watched by millions of TV viewers around the world, who follow his story like a soap opera. In a way, that's each of us now: we're all subject to the watchful eyes of the world.

But the film ultimately ends on a message of hope. As Truman ("true man") gradually becomes aware of his predicament, he struggles to break free from that media-permeated world, and finally escapes from its clutches to find his own personal freedom. The message? Perhaps it's this: while we all face these challenges posed by the modern interconnected world, we still possess the option of remaining true to ourselves and making sound decisions about how and where we allow ourselves to be plugged in.

18. The Changing Face of God

The emergence of a new Great Age invariably brings about a shift in the spiritual and religious sensibilities of humanity, which naturally reflects itself not just in the mythological themes of the time but in the very concept of God itself. During the Age of Aries, for instance, religions like Judaism described a God of wrath and anger, while in the Piscean Age, Christianity and Buddhism introduced more compassionate elements into the religio-mythic landscape.

How will the incoming Aquarian mythos shape our religious and spiritual perspectives? On one level, it's good to remember that Aquarius is, more than any other zodiacal sign, the one most associated with the *human*, making this incoming era what might be called the "Anthropocene Age." At its most extreme, that could mean humanity won't simply dominate all other life forms on the planet but could possibly even eclipse "God" entirely as it moves to elevate its own role in the cosmic order.

But I think there are subtler levels than that. A more mystical interpretation would be that this humanizing of the Divine has more to do with a recognition of the Divine within each person, not just located in some far-away heaven as has been the belief for much of humanity's history. We aren't simply God's children, but more akin to brothers or sisters. In *An Infinity of Gods*, I discuss how Shelly Trimmer proposed a distinctly Aquarian theology which suggested that the being we call "God" is actually one of an infinite number of godlike beings—ourselves included—but vastly more evolved than any of us. In a sense, that would be the ultimate democratization or decentralization of divinity, in which *every person* becomes a true God in his or her own right.

Alien as that idea may seem to some, this notion is already deeply embedded in the popular mythologies of our times—notably L. Frank Baum's *The Wizard of Oz*.

This tale features a classic "heroic" quest, with Dorothy and her companions setting out to find the answers to their pressing life-queries. One wants a heart; another a brain; another hopes to find courage; while Dorothy wants to just get home. They all travel together to the fabled city of Oz in the hope that the great and powerful Wizard might grant them these things.

Yet when they finally confront him, what they find instead is a great disillusionment—or a great gift. That's because the Wizard turns out to be an ordinary person rather than an all-powerful being. They also learn that what they had sought all along actually resides much closer to home: as the Good Witch says, "The answer to your journey has always been *within* you!" Symbolically, that's telling us that in our own spiritual journey, the external "Wizard" (i.e., God symbol) must be set aside in order to awaken the God *within*, to realize our role not just as God's children but as cocreators. Psychologist Carl Jung referred to this process as the "Christification of many." [3] In *Masks of God, Volume 4*, Joseph Campbell described it this way:

> Just as in the past each civilization was the vehicle of its own mythology, so in this modern world...each individual is the center of a mythology of his own, of which his own intelligible character is the Incarnate God, so to say, whom his empirically questing consciousness is to find. The aphorism of Delphi, "Know thyself," is the motto. And not Rome, not Mecca, not Jerusalem, Sinai, or Benares, but *each*

and every "thou" on earth is the center of this world.... (emphasis mine) [4]

The Wizard of Oz was also prophetic in pointing to a more jazz-style approach toward religion and spiritual community. Rather than merely suggesting the "answer lies within," it depicts a coordinating of diverse, highly different life-paths as well, reflecting a new group dynamic in play. As mentioned previously, the story doesn't simply depict one person setting out to realize his or her own heroic quest, or even a group setting out to find a common goal like the Holy Grail or Golden Fleece; instead we find in Baum's story is a *group of totally different beings, each seeking completely different goals.* Despite those differences, they are somehow able to harmonize their respective quests. It's the jazz model applied now to religion, in other words. In a previous chapter we saw that dynamic reflected in the work and lives of the Beatles, but we also see it in the modern "superhero" film craze, in movies like *Infinity Wars* or *Justice League.* Questions of artistic worth aside, these stories don't simply portray a conventional band of mortals following some god or hero on a great mission, but a group in which *every member* is either a god or possesses unique god-like powers.

19. The Defining Symbol of an Age
While any given Great Age manifests through a multitude of symbols and forms, there are generally one or two primary symbols which embody its essence. During the Piscean Age, the Christian image of crucifixion exemplified both the best and worst of that era. I say "best" in terms of the spirit of sacrifice, compassion, and the rescuing of others implied by Christ's final act, all of which are clearly Piscean in nature; "worst" in terms of the self-negation, persecution, and suffering also represented by that crucifixion, and which underscores the more problematic side of Pisces.

What will the "defining symbol" of the emerging Aquarian Age be? While it's too early to say definitely, I'd like to nominate a few possibilities.

The airplane (or rocketship. This is a technology that represents freedom from gravity and local boundaries, and the mastery of the Air element—i.e., the mental realm.

The Internet. Here is a technology that allows people from all walks of life and countries to connect in a very cerebral and detached way, while allowing each participant to offer their own input into the collective mindstream.

Neil Armstrong's first steps on the Moon. This was an epochal event in modern times not only in terms of representing a huge leap of our collective imagination, but of uniting millions of people across the planet in one-pointed focus through television and radio. Here too we also glimpse both the positive and negative implications of an emerging "hive mind" society.

The jazz band. As I've suggested, the jazz band represents a novel type of system in which all the parts interact while simultaneously retaining their own autonomy. This links it to many other emerging Aquarian manifestations, from the Internet and think tanks to democracy, employee-owned businesses and pluralistic religions.

20. The Environmental Challenge
In the end, it could turn out to be that humanity's relationship with the Earth will prove to be the most consequential result of the coming Great Age shift, with repercussions for millennia to come. For while Aquarius is fundamentally a root-chakra sign—meaning that it's heavily focused on material plane matters—that won't necessarily happen in the comparatively warm, heartfelt way you might find with some other signs, like Taurus or Cancer. With Aquarius, our relationship with nature is heavily mediated through mind and technology, and as a result can be rather cold

and technocratic (reflecting the Saturn co-rulership of the sign). At its most extreme, that's already visible in how vast tracts of land have been paved over to make way for expressways and smog-belching cities, or in the strip mining of wilderness areas for precious minerals, and in other such developments.

It's even possible that early clues of our current environmental crisis are subtly present in some of the ancient mythologies associated with Aquarius. In ancient Greece, the constellation of Aquarius was most famously associated with the image of Ganymede, the young prince who pours water out of a bucket. But another perspective links the sign Aquarius with Deucalion, king of Phthia and son of Prometheus. Sometimes called the Greek Noah, Deucalion built a great chest in which he and his family could survive the rising floodwaters Zeus sent to destroy humanity. Just as we find ourselves on the brink of a zodiacal age associated with images of a great flood, we are facing the threat of rising sea levels around the world.

Or we could look at those legends associated with the Greek sky god Ouranos, the mythic namesake of our planet Uranus, the modern ruler of Aquarius. In Greek legend, the sky god Ouranos was a cruel tyrant and was particularly abusive towards Gaia, the Earth goddess who was his mother and lover. Viewed archetypally, our growing environmental crisis seems to be acting out the dynamics of that mythic relationship on a global scale: just as Gaia was oppressed by Ouranos, so our own mother Earth, or Gaia, is being trampled underfoot by our modern-day Uranian consciousness, with its technology and mechanistic rationality.

But it doesn't have to end up that way. The same technology and science that threaten to destroy our environment could also be applied to help solve our problems, through the development of clean energy sources, environmentally-friendly living spaces, and the restoration of natural habitats. But that will require a commitment the likes of which we haven't begun to see yet.

21. The Great Ages as Psychological Stages

Finally, in a more cumulative way it's possible to see the advent of each new Great Age as contributing new abilities and skills to the evolving soul-development of humanity. For example, during the Age of Aries—a zodiacal sign associated with the core principle of *I AM*—there was a rudimentary awakening of individualism, self-awareness, and ego. In religion, that manifested as the displacement of polytheism by monotheism through figures like Akhenaten in Egypt and Moses in Judaism (who fittingly, actually met on Mount Sinai with a God named *I AM*). That Aries-like ego also revealed itself in the rise of great warlike empires around the world, as evident in areas like Egypt, China, and Rome. These empires concentrated resources and energy from their adjoining regions much as the ego concentrates the diverse mental and emotional energies of the personality into a core governing identity. But in the end, Aries represents a form of egoic awareness that is still relatively primitive and immature, with little internal reflectivity.

During the watery Age of Pisces, which is a more feminine and inwardly focused zodiacal sign, that sense of self-awareness was enhanced by a new sense of interiority, or what I have been calling an *awakening of soul*. Exoterically, this manifested in the rise of the dome shape in architecture, which conveyed a more distinctive sense of interiority and space than found in earlier temples and civic buildings. More psychologically, it was reflected in a newfound sense of *conscience*, whose flip side was a more corrosive sense of guilt and self-denial, reinforced by the globally expanding religion of Christianity.

But as I pointed out earlier, the Pisces Age was also an era of great mystics, like Meister Eckhart, Hildegard of Bingen, and Dogen, while the more aesthetic side of this Piscean influence is apparent in the works of great artists and musicians like Michelangelo, Bach, and Leonardo da Vinci. These and other creative spirits illuminated the profound emotional gifts to be called up from the watery depths of Pisces. It's entirely possible that future generations will look back on the last two thousand years as the preeminent era of great artists, musicians, and mystics.

So what role will the Age of Aquarius play in this ongoing process of collective soul growth?

My own sense is that it will build upon those previous layers by introducing a dramatically *new level of mind*. We see this already in the rise of modern psychology, with its highly analytical (and detached) approach to human behavior,[5] as well as with modern science and the complex theories of quantum mechanics, mirroring a mental life dramatically different from those of previous eras. In more mundane ways, we glimpse this emerging mentality in the myriad complexities of modern life, both obvious and hidden, as anyone knows who works with smart phones and computers, juggling diverse data points in ways that would have baffled most anyone looking on from older times.

Whereas the Piscean Age gave us great artistic and spiritual geniuses, geniuses of the Aquarian Age will more likely be of the scientific and technological sort.

But there's something else at work here, and it has to do with a newly defined form of *individualism* that is being introduced into the collective experience, made possible by this awakened rationality. The Age of Aries was individualistic in its own way, true, but with a crucial difference. In the case of Aries, that individualism was relatively rudimentary and more "me"-oriented, with no sophisticated understanding of itself in relation to the larger community.

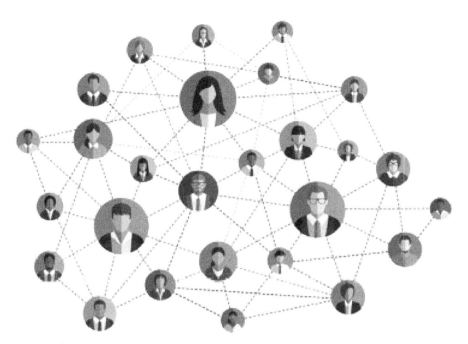

Image: Shutterstock

With the advent of Aquarius, our individuality is now learning to see itself in relation to *viewpoints beyond our own*. Philosopher Jean Gebser referred to this as an "aperspectival" shift—a movement beyond conventional, one-pointed perspectives and worldviews.[6] This makes for a dramatically new form of individualism, and the challenge of Aquarius will be negotiating the delicate balance between one's own perspective and those of several billion other people sharing our planet—possibly even perspectives from beyond this planet or dimension. [7]

Final Words

I hope this discussion has given you some idea of the complexity of the Aquarian Age and what that concept might actually imply. It's been largely depicted in pop culture in almost comic book terms, when in fact the truth of the matter will surely be more multifaceted than that. Rather than becoming a single monolithic reality, the coming Great Age will likely be a mosaic of possibilities, both constructive and destructive in nature.

Kind of like what we already see happening now, come to think of it.

CHAPTER 21

FRANK

Around 1980, when I'd just started trying my hand at writing, I knew I could meet authors I hoped to talk with at book signing events, and there were quite a few of those in downtown Chicago. I'd been a fan of the book *Dune* and heard that its author, Frank Herbert, was going to be signing books in the city, so I made a point of taking the train down there to see him.

It turned out to be a group-author affair, held in one of the city's big department stores. There were maybe twenty or twenty-five writers spread out around the room. Off to the one side were four very different individuals seated just a few feet from one another: Charles "Bermuda Triangle" Berlitz, political commentator Arnaud de Borchgrave, reformed con man Frank Abnagale (subject of Spielberg's movie *Catch Me If You Can*), and Frank Herbert. Quite a mixed crew.

But there were surprisingly few people there to meet with the authors, either because it hadn't been advertised very well or perhaps because people weren't interested in meeting with these particular authors. These weren't romance novelists or whodunit writers, after all. At any rate, Berlitz and de Borchgrave looked decidedly uncomfortable being there, especially being next to each other. Some of their discomfort may have had to do with the fact that almost no one was buying their new releases or asking them for autographs. But both Abnagale and Herbert seemed reasonably happy in their skins sitting there. Abnagale was holding forth with a couple of admirers about his past escapades, and looked fairly relaxed. I went up to Herbert with my dog-eared first edition paperback of *Dune* (published during that epic Uranus/Pluto conjunction in 1965, by the way). I handed it to him and he cheerfully signed it.

With no one else around, I was able to speak with him for about twenty minutes about an assortment of things. I asked him about the proposed movie version of *Dune*, which I'd been hearing rumors about. He said it was slated to go into production under director Alejandro Jodorowsky, with figures like Salvador Dali playing key roles, but the entire project fell apart before getting off the ground. As far as he knew, the producers were currently in talks with David Lynch about taking on the project. He didn't seem particularly concerned one way or another about the project, which surprised me.

When I told him I'd just started writing and asked about his own experience with the craft, he spoke about the enormous commitment and hard work involved but didn't express any particular angst or suffering about it. From what I could tell, he didn't strike me as a classic tortured artist, which was something of a contrast to the few other writers I'd either met or read about.

Before leaving, I asked him for his birth information, which he gladly provided (October 8, 1920, 7:18 a.m., Tacoma, Washington). He added that his wife practiced astrology and had done his horoscope for him. He didn't seem to know much if anything about the subject himself, but was obviously open to it. When I looked up his horoscope later that day, I saw that his Sun was positioned at 15 degrees of Libra—the same degree as my own Moon. That undoubtedly explains why I felt so comfortable talking to him, since Sun/Moon connections can be one of those synastry factors typically showing an easy flow between two people.

Just a few years later, I was surprised to learn that he passed away. Surprised, because he was only in his mid-sixties at the time. I still wish I had kept that copy of *Dune*, but I had to sell it on eBay some years later to help pay off some medical debts. At least I still have the memory of that meeting, which is worth a great deal more to me than a signed book.

CHAPTER 22

MY THEORY OF SLEEP

It's one of the great ongoing mysteries of biology. All humans need it, as do animals, possibly even plants.

But *why* do we all have this need to unplug and venture off into a decidedly different dimension through sleep?

Every few years I come across some new scientific explanation for the mystery of why we sleep, usually based on some reductionist model of the brain and consciousness. One of the most recent of those is by Matthew Walker Ph.D, author of the book *Why We Sleep*. He argues that sleeping enables the brain to produce neurochemical baths that enhance it, reinforce the immune system, and ward off sickness, among other health-related benefits. Like quite a few others, Walker also speaks to the problem-solving side of dreams. In short, there are certain very practical, evolutionary benefits to sleeping.

Without in any way denying those benefits, I have a different theory, which I'd sum it up this way.

We are essentially nonphysical beings, and exist in physical bodies much like the deep-sea diver who can stay underwater for a certain period of time—but only for a certain period of time. Sooner or later, the diver must surface and come up for air. If not, he or she will suffocate and drown.

In much the same way, we can only stay encased in materiality so long before we too have to "come up for air," and break free from our physical encasement long enough to breathe the air of unfettered consciousness, or what the yogis call *prana*. If we don't, then we too will drown—that is, we'll literally go crazy, we'll lose our minds. It's at that point, when our soul can't take it any longer, that we're forcibly catapulted into bodylessness.

Likewise at the moment of death, whatever the cause, we move into bodylessness—but this time once and for all.

There is a story Goswami Kriyananda once told which comes to mind here. As a young man during the early 1950s he was drafted into the Korean War, where he wound up serving as a medic on the battlefield. When not on the front lines, his job was to oversee the medical barracks with another soldier, where he monitored and took care of injured or sick soldiers.

One night, he noticed that of all the soldiers asleep in their beds, all had their astral bodies floating a few feet above their bodies, each connected by their ethereal cord—except for one, that is, where no astral double was visible. As a result, Kriyananda clairvoyantly knew this fellow had passed away. He mentioned this to his fellow medic, who didn't understand why he would make such a statement just from looking across the barracks. But that medic went over and discovered that the soldier Kriyananda pointed to had indeed died. That soldier's astral body would be returning to its physical sheath no longer.

So sleep indeed holds many benefits to our physical and emotional health, just as the pragmatically-minded researchers claim. But these are peripheral to an even more fundamental need to sleep, which is to be temporarily released from our encasement in matter.

Said another way, *our souls need to breathe.*

What then of dreams?

They are the linqua franca of that other dimension, or what the occultists call the astral plane. There, reality appears in more analog or metaphoric form than in our waking state. In fact, we're *continually* dreaming, even while awake in our physical bodies. During those waking hours, our dreaming persists as a symbolic sub-text to our rational thoughts and perceptions, periodically surfacing into visibility during moments of imagination or meta-phoric wordplay. But it's during sleep that we plunge more fully into that other dimension of being.

So there you have it. Sweet dreams, reader—and sweet waking life, too.

CHAPTER 23

HOW WIDE IS THE *NOW*?

"You live your life in the moment.
Miss the moment and you miss your life."

—*John Daido Loori*

I was back in college when I first came across Ram Dass's iconic book *Be Here Now*, a chronicle of his life that culminated in his studies with meditation, spirituality and spiritual teachers. The book's title derived from the words a young traveling companion of his in India kept repeating to him whenever he, Ram Dass, started reminiscing about one or another episode from his past, back when he went by his birth name, Richard Alpert, and worked as Timothy Leary's colleague at Harvard University.

The book got me thinking about an assortment of things over the ensuing years, and among them was this question:

Just how "wide" is the NOW?

Is it two seconds long? One second? Or some small fraction of a second? And just how far can we really drill down into this NOW?

I came across a news item recently which helped put this question into a new perspective for me. The shortest span of time described by scientists is something called a "zeptosecond," which is a trillionth of a billionth of a second (10^{21} seconds). I'm not very good at math, so I asked my much smarter friend, Jon Parks, to calculate what that means in real world terms.

"Said another way," he responded, "a zeptosecond is to a second, what a second is to 31,000 years (31.7098, to be precise)."

That's a lot, and of course the human mind can't really grasp numbers like that. But it surely gives us a different understanding of what the NOW is, and just how deep that rabbit hole must really go.

A hummingbird clearly has a very difference experience of the NOW than we do, as does an elephant or a tortoise. I've watched birds fly through complex tangles of tree and bush branches with ease, never so much as even brushing up against a single one of those branches. That made it obvious to me they see things with a far more detailed sense of time than we do.

But the idea I most carried away from learning what those scientists said was simply that this phenomenon we call the NOW is as vast and deep as the ocean itself. To some extent, we might well say that mystics make it their mission to explore that NOW and dive down deep into its depths, like those daring explorers who venture to the ocean's floor in their submersibles, or better yet, those "free divers" who descend unaided by any technology at all.

In a very different way, this is something I found myself compelled to do—quite unwittingly—as a result of an experience I had when I was young, and which gave me a different perspective on the NOW than I ever considered before. That will be the focus of our next chapter.

CHAPTER 24

DOWN THE RABBIT HOLE ~ A PSYCHEDELIC JOURNEY INTO THE HEART OF TIME

B y now, virtually everyone has heard of the classic "near death experience," or NDE, experienced by many of those teetering on the brink between life and death. The NDE often involves a light seen at the end of a tunnel, variously explained by mystics as a confrontation with one's own essential nature, or "higher Self," or possibly as an encounter with the radiant light of God, Jesus, Buddha, or some other deity or guide.

When I was nineteen, I had a psychedelic experience that shed new light on that concept for me.

I was a sophomore at the Art Institute of Chicago when a fellow classmate handed me a marijuana joint in the school cafeteria one afternoon with the cautionary comment, "This is powerful stuff, don't smoke it by yourself!" I'd heard that sort of hype before and never took it seriously. This time, though, the warning proved to be true.

I got together that night with my childhood friend Tom, and we proceeded to light up the joint, no pun intended. Before we'd even gotten past the first two puffs, the room began to swim wildly, like a Van Gogh painting come to life. For the next half hour or so—that's only a guess, since I still don't know how much time elapsed—the two of us struggled to keep our wits about us as the world seemed to career out of control. Looking back on the experience years later, I came to believe the marijuana was likely laced with DMT, or something equally powerful.

At one point my friend seemed to fall ill and stumbled to the bathroom while vomiting, mumbling along the way, "I think this was poisoned." I wasn't sure what to think myself. Unlike him, I didn't vomit, but a wave of anxiety flooded through me that was different from anything I'd experienced before. I began trembling and worrying about what might come next.

As deeply disturbing as this was becoming for me, the intensity of the experience so shattered the framework of my ordinary mental constructs that it allowed for certain insights to bleed through that I normally wouldn't have access to. Each of those insights unfolded organically out of the other, like stages of a rocket. I took great pains after my experience to chronicle as many of those insights as possible in writing, but I'll focus here on just one of those, which is directly related to my opening comments.

As the minutes went on, my mind became like a microscope whose magnifying powers were progressively amplifying, allowing me to peer ever more closely into the nature of time itself, *into the heart of the NOW.*

We normally experience the present moment as though it was a continuous, unbroken stream. But in that hyperaware state I saw that the NOW actually consists of thousands—possibly even millions—of finer "thought-moments." A crude analogy would be a second of movie film, which seems to the casual eye like a fluid motion, when it actually consists of twenty-four individual snapshots moving by so fast it only *seems* continuous. It's much the same with our experience of time, I realized: it also seems fluid but actually consists of many quicker, discrete thought-moments, but they're largely unnoticeable because they pass by so rapidly. The difference for me was that, rather than just twenty-four frames a second, this seemed to me more like hundreds if not thousands of frames a second.

Buried deep in the heart of those spaces between two thoughts wasn't simply darkness, as you might find between any two frames of film, but a light—a light at the end of the tunnel, I'm tempted to say—which I knew was actually the radiance of pure being itself. Each moment was like a stroboscopic flashing on and off rapidly, so rapid that we don't even notice the light in between those cracks.

That's a simple way of explaining it, anyway. Instead of my frames-per-second analogy of successive "on/off" moments, I could see that some of those frames were more obvious and gross, being closer to the surface of ordinary consciousness, while many more were extremely subtle, with the deepest and subtlest of those residing closer to that ground source of light. Our consciousness careens through this succession of thought-moments like a roller coaster each second, going up and down through the various levels of being, climaxing at the deepest point of that ride in the encounter with that luminous ground of being.

It was a while later that I came across Raymond Moody's famous accounts of NDE's, with their tales of individuals moving through a tunnel with a light at its end. That struck a chord for me, but in a far more immediate way than described in those accounts. Rather than occurring just once at the threshold of death, *this encounter with the Self actually occurs each and every moment, hundreds or perhaps even thousands of times each second.* We plunge into a naked confrontation with the source of being each and every moment

Said another way, we're dying and are being reborn constantly.

Other insights occurred to me that evening, but that was the one which left its greatest imprint on me. I wouldn't wish to ever relive the more unpleasant aspects of that night, which was the closest thing to a bad trip I ever experienced, but I can't deny how it shaped my understanding of the world, and of time itself.

Postscript: Several years later I discussed this experience with Shelly Trimmer. Knowing of his long background in meditation, I was anxious to get his feedback about what I had experienced. He essentially validated the experience, and I also couldn't help but notice how it related in some ways to something he taught about the nature of time as well. We're existing inside of God's memory banks, he suggested, and our perception of ordinary time actually consists of many minute "frames" within those memory banks, which we string together in our own consciousness to convey the illusion of movement.

But Shelly went on to suggest a slightly different analogy that he felt struck even closer to the mark. Instead of a movie film with its multiple frames per second, he likened the phenomenal changes of consciousness each moment to the fluctuations of frequency that occur in *music*. I had some idea what he was talking

about, since I'd long been fascinated by how a seemingly continuous sound, like a singer holding a single note for a long time,
could be encoded on the surface of a phonograph record as a multitude of minute peaks and valleys within the record grooves. As
a kid, I would sometimes fiddle around with my mother's record
player, manually moving the turntable by hand, and hearing how
that caused the sound to change. If I slowed the turntable down
far enough, I heard how the sound was composed of many subtler, quicker sounds—hundreds or thousands of beeps and pops
and clicks, rising and falling in pitch and duration. But because
our ordinary perception is so slow, we only hear the cumulative
effect of those frequencies strung together, with the result being
the fluid music we hear.

The conclusion I drew from both my experience and Shelly's
teaching? Simply, that we may talk about "altered states" as if
they're something special, but consciousness actually is *altering
all the time*.

CHAPTER 25

A BRUSH WITH KUNDALINI

In my modest experience with meditation through the decades, I've had a few moments of heightened clarity here and there, where I felt as though I was beginning to "wake up" just a little bit more. In my book *The Sky Stretched Out Before Me,* I wrote about the months I spent at a Zen monastery in upstate New York and described one of my more meaningful meditations there. But one experience from that time, not included in that book, touches on something commonly referred to as "kundalini," and I'd like to talk about that here.

To be clear, this wasn't a fully realized version of that state, but it was just realized enough for me to believe I gained some genuine insight into the phenomenon. There are a host of misconceptions around this subject, I've come to think, and what I'd like to relate here sheds a somewhat different light on it than what has generally been described.

My experience took place shortly before I was set to leave the monastery, during an event called *rohatsu,* an intensive seven-day silent meditation retreat conducted in the leadup to New Year's Eve. Every day of rohatsu, meditation sessions are progressively extended until the very last day, December 31, with that day being devoted almost entirely to sitting meditation (with short periodic breaks every forty minutes or so, devoted to silent walking meditations).

In the hours leading up to midnight on that final day of the year, I'd been doing my best to focus my attention as fully as possible on the technique at hand, which at that point was the sound *MU,* held silently. Eventually, I began to feel as though my mind was settling down, with the inner mental chatter that normally plagues me being nearly absent. I knew without a doubt that I was burrowing deeper into the moment, into the NOW.

At some point during this process I began noticing the energies throughout my body drawing into the middle of my spine, and slowly begin percolating upward. I say "percolating" because that comes close to describing what it felt like. It was an extremely pleasant sensation, and the analogy I came up with later to describe it was this:

Imagine a seven-story building stuffed with thousands of helium-filled balloons on all its floors, but with an empty elevator shaft in the very center of the building. Then imagine that all the doors to that elevator shaft begin opening, starting with the ground floor then continuing on up through the higher floors, with all the balloons now filling into that central shaft and gently floating up to the top of the building, culminating at the penthouse.

That comes close to describing how it felt to me. I was convinced that if I could simply sustain my focus on the meditation technique a bit longer, and move even more fully into the moment, that percolating energy would soon funnel up into my head and converge into the middle of my forehead—and then shoot out from there. This wasn't a conceptual notion; I somehow *knew* that's where this was heading, since the "I" observing all this was actually located up there. Everything was coming gradually to a point, and that point was up in my third eye, which is where *I* was.

But as it turned out, the bell signaling the end of the meditation period—and indeed, the entire seven-day *sesshin*—rang out from the end of the hall, thus bringing my burgeoning meditative experience to an abrupt end. I was disappointed, because I was convinced that with just ten more minutes I would have experienced what the teachings describe as "mind and body dropped," where all physical and mental perceptions fall away in pure awareness. But I was nevertheless grateful to have experienced it at all, since I felt that I learned some important things from it.

Perhaps the most important of those was the realization of just how *natural* this all was. The energy moving up my spine wasn't so much struggling to ascend as it was *returning to its source.* Another analogy would be a beach ball. If you've ever tried holding one underwater, you'd know that getting it to move up to the surface doesn't require you to force it upward so much as to *let it go.* Do that and it will naturally ascend upward. One might also think of a hot air balloon; one way to get it to ascend higher is to simply drop its ballast off the sides.

Likewise, the natural abode of consciousness is in those higher levels of being, so that consciousness naturally *wants* to ascend. Getting it to do so requires simply "dropping ballast"—letting go of heavy thoughts, emotions, and attachments. But while that may be a natural process, it doesn't necessarily come easy, in light of how fixated we can be on those *cognitive* sacks of ballast.

The common perception that kundalini is somehow coiled up at the base of the spine like a sleeping serpent, as some books describe it, seemed terribly misleading to me, as if to imply this energy was stored down below, when in fact its roots were much higher up. In the kundalini experience, all of reality is simply enfolding back into its source.

I came up with another analogy to describe this process: that of a movie projector. Your ordinary projector sends light and imagery out towards an external theater screen; but imagine if all of that light and imagery being projected outward could somehow retract back up into the projector, back into the light bulb itself. Rather than being "coiled up" in the theater screen somehow, the light is reverting back to its true source—the projector bulb. That's what happens in full-blown samadhi as well, I'd suggest, where all the varied phenomena of experience retract back into their seat and source within the third eye, or *ajna* chakra.

(To be clear, most mystics regard the raising of kundalini as being just one half of the overall awakening process, the other part being the bringing of that realization down into everyday life, and manifesting it through one's ordinary actions and relationships. After all, Moses didn't just ascend to the mountaintop, he came back down again!)

Since that experience, I've also realized how helpful moments of inspiration can be to furthering the process of meditation. I've developed the habit of starting off my own meditations by first conjuring up a memory of some inspiring experience—such as the memory of a crystalline starry night out in the desert, or the face of a beloved person or pet from my past—and using that as my foundation. Even when my meditations don't go deep, which is frankly most of the time, starting off that way never fails to trigger some subtle awareness of the energies in my spine. For that matter, I'm convinced that *any* time we experience a truly inspirational moment, those energies *automatically* begin centering and ascending upward through the spine.

This experience also gave me new insight into a meditation technique I learned in the Kriya Yoga system but with analogs in other meditative traditions—Coptic, Sufi, Taoist, and others. That is to imagine a current of light ascending and descending along the full length of the spine. (That's a simple description; various traditions add further nuances, such as coupling that visualization with a mantra or breathing technique, or imagining the current moving around the spine in a specific direction.) The point of these techniques isn't to force the energies up the spine as much as to *gently coax* them. Which is all the more reason why it can be helpful to begin one's meditation with an uplifting or inspiring visualization, prayer, piece of music, or loving memory, simply to help lift the energies.

I remember reading accounts of kundalini when I was young that made it seem like the experience was akin to a psychotic episode, or like sticking your finger into a wall socket and experiencing a shock. From the likes of those descriptions, it seemed potentially dangerous, and disturbing. To be clear, I *do* believe there are potential dangers to lifting the spinal energies too early or fast, especially if someone isn't grounded. In those cases, it does no good to awaken higher states of awareness, since it can cause even greater imbalances, or even to overloading or "frying" the subtle circuits.

I now believe those earlier accounts didn't describe actual kundalini but rather what happens when the energies veer off to the right or left sides of the spine. As Goswami Kriyananda and Shelly Trimmer sometimes suggested, kundalini is a purely balanced energy, whereas the "kundalini" experiences described in some books seem more like examples of *shakti*, which involves the more emotional and compulsive energies of those channels alongside the spine, known as *ida* and *pingala*. When I'm affected by something emotionally, whether positively or negatively, my body wants to move—that's shakti. But the sensation I experienced at the monastery felt extremely balanced and peaceful to me, with no compulsion or strong emotionality attached to it at all.

Since that time at the monastery, I've not had an experience like it again—and that's all right. I've come to believe if I can move through my days with just a bit more balance and equanimity, that's quite enough for no

CHAPTER 26

NAKED BEFORE ETERNITY ~ AN ESOTERIC MEDITATION ON SEX

Whether we contemplate the erotically spiritual writings of twelfth century mystic Bernard of Clairvaux, or the poetry of the Middle Eastern mystic Rumi, or gaze at Tibetan *yab yum* imagery depicting a man and woman seated in naked embrace, it's clear that the world's mystics have long regarded sexuality as a potent symbol for spiritual awakening.

What is it about the merging of two beings in sex that implies a deep mystical truth for so many? I'd like to suggest a few possibilities.

The Marriage of the Sun and Moon

On one level, the joining of lover and beloved echoes what yogis refer to as *samadhi*—that mystical state in which boundaries dissolve, and where "outer" and "inner," objective and subjective, are realized as one. Though we ordinarily see ourselves as separate from the surrounding world, the mystic recognizes that it's all part of a single reality, two aspects of the same consciousness.

That's led some to suggest that the closest most people come to that mystic realization is during sex. Why? This is because when engaged in a deep sense of communion with the partner, that sense of a division between self and world dissolves, and there awakens—however dimly—a realization of one's true nature.

Consider the example of Tom, a young man I knew in my childhood. At age eighteen he went off to college in a neighboring state, where his turbo-charged libido led him into a string of one-night-stands with various young women around the campus.

Eventually Tom came to Jesus and changed his ways, expressing sincere regret over his history of past excesses.

Of all the sexual encounters he had throughout that period, however, there was one during which something quite extraordinary happened. While in the midst of sex, he said, he was staring into the young woman's eyes and had a life-changing epiphany. "I'm not sure how to say this," he tried explaining it to me, "but I *became* her," shaking his head as if still mystified all those years later by what happened that night.

In that moment, the boundaries between self and other completely evaporated, as he and the young woman became one. Yogically speaking, what he experienced was a basic form of samadhi, or heightened consciousness. (I say "basic" because tangible phenomena were still involved—what some yogis call "samadhi within form"—so he was not yet at the level of what I described in the previous chapter as "mind and body dropped.")

Not only did Tom harbor no lingering regrets over that particular affair, he seemed genuinely grateful for having had the chance to glimpse something as profound and life-changing as that, in which his separate ego-self disappeared and he realized—however momentarily—a far greater truth.

Secrets Encoded in the Human Anatomy

Profound secrets about the significance of sex are also concealed within the human body itself, specifically in the male and female genitalia.

Consider the shape of the male and female organs. Whereas the penis is akin to a spear which comes forward into a point, the vagina is more of a receptacle, with these two constituting the proverbial "blade" and the "chalice" mentioned by some writers. That difference in actual form and shape says a great deal about the "male" and "female" states of consciousness—and by that I'm referring not so much to specific genders as to archetypal principles of consciousness, as experienced by *either* men or women.

In a "masculine" state of consciousness, for instance, the mind is pointed forward, actively moving towards its subject and directed sharply beyond itself; whereas in the "feminine" state of consciousness, the mind shifts into a more receptive mode, absorbing and integrating diverse impressions in a more holistic way. Again, while these may conventionally be more dominant in one sex than the other, both of these states can be experienced by either sex.

A simple example of that difference would be what happens during an ordinary conversation between two individuals. The one who is talking focuses awareness outwards toward "getting their point" across. The person listening is conventionally more receptive and focused on absorbing, on receiving the incoming data and processing before replying with a more active response.

In enlightenment, those two modes of consciousness come into equilibrium, where there is neither grasping outward nor a drawing inward, but rather a balancing of those polarities.

Sexuality is one expression of that merging of opposites, with the ecstasy and bliss associated with sex reflecting the bliss associated with samadhi itself.

Going Deeper

Yet there are still other insights concealed within the sexual organs of the two sexes, but to explain that we need to first look back briefly at that spiritual phenomenon I referred to in the last chapter as kundalini.

Yogic mysticism says there are three primary channels of energy in the subtle body, called *ida, pingala,* and *sushumna.* These are generally associated with the left side of the spine, the right side of the spine, and the center of the spine, respectively.

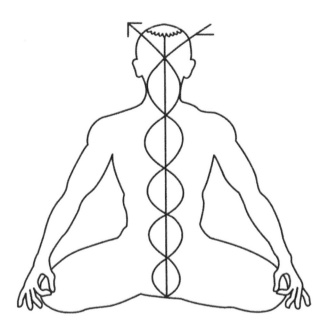

Each of these channels relates to a different mode of consciousness. The center channel of the spine, *sushumna,* is considered to be the path of balanced consciousness and spiritual freedom—the proverbial "straight and narrow path," or what Yogananda called the "highway to the infinite." (In Jewish Kaballistic mysticism, this central channel has its analogy in the "Tree of Life," as the fittingly titled *Pillar of Equilibrium.*) When the energies of *ida* (feminine) and *pingala* (*masculine*) on the sides of the spine collapse into that central channel, consciousness rises up in the form of *kundalini,* which is experienced as blissful, heightened awareness.

Different mystical traditions offer various techniques designed to help balance those energies and move them upward. These include visualizations, postures, or mantras aimed at drawing consciousness into the center and gently coaxing it upwards. (The classic image of a street fakir in India causing a snake to rise out of a basket using music naturally comes to mind here.) We might even say the repetitious nature of some of these techniques serves to gently pump the energies of consciousness upwards into higher and higher levels, culminating eventually in their escape out through the top of one's head in a fountain of spray.

How does all this relate to sexuality, and to the human genitalia?

Simply put, the erect penis is a microcosm of the spine in a state of heightened awareness. The upward flow of semen through the central channel mirrors the clear, whitish essence of spiritual consciousness associated with rising kundalini. Just as sperm flows up and out of the top of the penis at the moment of orgasm, so with a true awakening of kundalini—spiritual "orgasm," so to speak—there is a corresponding flow of blissful consciousness out of the head.

Ejaculation thus becomes what some might call a "lower-level" reflection of that higher-level transformation of consciousness, along with its corresponding end result, enlightenment.

A New Birth

"The birth of a child is a sacred phenomenon."

—Lailah Gifty Akita, *Pearls of Wisdom: Great Mind*

What about the *feminine* principle in all of this? The male anatomy and its symbolism are obviously just one-half of the overall process in play here. That's because the sex act is not simply about *ejaculation*. In conventional biology, sex between a man and a woman culminates in the journey of the sperm toward the female egg, which in turn results in pregnancy, and childbirth.

What does *that* signify, esoterically?

The female egg represents the cosmic feminine, the cosmic divine beyond one's personal spark of divinity. *The journey of the sperm towards the egg mirrors the journey of the personal divine towards the cosmic divine—the proverbial drop of water uniting with the ocean, the microcosm making contact with the macrocosm.* Just as the sperm seeks to pierce the egg, and as the man seeks to "pierce" the woman, so the personal consciousness seeks to pierce the mystery of the divine feminine, the macrocosmic Self. As Goethe wrote in the closing lines of *Faust*, "The eternal feminine draws us on high."

As the spermatozoa is transformed by its encounter with the egg, so the personal self is forever transformed by its encounter with the cosmic feminine. Physical sex results in the birth of a child, which shares in the characteristics of both father and

180

mother. Similarly, from enlightenment emerges a new being that is neither entirely human nor entirely divine, but a combination of the two.

The enlightened personality is thereafter a dweller in two worlds, personal and transpersonal, worldly and transcendental, living a dramatically different life from anything before, naked now before all eternity. In the words of the thirteenth-century German mystic, Mechtild of Magdeburg,

> *Lord, now I am a naked soul*
> *And you in yourself All-Glorious God.*
> *Our mutual intercourse*
> *Is eternal life without end.*

CHAPTER 27

LIFTING THE CHALICE

I first published the following short anecdote about Goswami Kriyananda in my book Urban Mystic, *and I've adapted it to illustrate the theme being explored here. —R.G.*

I recall the time Kriyananda spoke of attending a Catholic church service conducted by a priest he'd been friends with for a number of years. Occasionally, he explained, he'd sit in the back of a church and watch the energies of parishioners during the service to see how they were affected by the rituals.

Normally, whenever the priest would lift the chalice upwards at that key point in the communion ritual, Kriyananda would see the spinal currents of everyone raise upwards as well, as if in sympathetic resonance with the symbolism being enacted on the altar.

But one particular Sunday morning, the priest lifted the chalice upwards, and nothing happened in the spines of the parishioners; no subtle energies were stirred. Curious about the difference this time, he spoke to his priest friend after the service and inquired whether there was anything different about the ceremony this particular Sunday.

It turned out the church had run out of wine. The priest had substituted grape juice.

CHAPTER 28

WALT DISNEY'S "SORCERER'S APPRENTICE" ~ A CAUTIONARY TALE FOR OUR TIME

As those familiar with my writings will know, I often look to popular culture for important clues into the shifting astrological zeitgeist, but with a special emphasis on the imagery and narratives of cinema. To my mind, one of the most interesting examples of that can be found in the 1940 Walt Disney movie, *Fantasia*.

Disney's quasi-experimental film features a series of animated sequences illustrating various works of classical music, of which the most iconic—indeed, the one that's become emblematic for the Disney empire itself—is "The Sorcerer's Apprentice," set to Paul Dukas' music of the same name.

Spend time in any of Disney's theme parks, or surf the web for signs of Disney's impact on the world, and you'll inevitably come across the image of Mickey Mouse dressed in his apprentice garb, using his hands to direct the cosmic energies around him, almost like an orchestra conductor. The imagery in this short segment holds some intriguing insights into the shifting energies of our time, I'd suggest—specifically the potentials and dangers of the emerging Age of Aquarius, the sign of the water bearer.

First of all, as we saw earlier, Walt Disney's horoscope itself holds some clues along these lines, since he was born under the influence of a Sun/Uranus conjunction. At its most dramatic, that energy can indicate an attunement to futuristic or even revolutionary currents in society, as well as to technology and media in general. That's obvious enough in Disney's case, considering his impact on media and television across the world, as well as through the massively influential Disney empire, which ballooned to gargantuan proportions in his wake. But due to the connection between Uranus and the sign Aquarius, which this planet co-rules, that conjunction of his also implies a potential connection to the concerns of the Great Age emerging onto the world stage now at seemingly breakneck speed.

Although the link is subtle, it's also worth noting the stylistic synchronicity between the musical composition which accompanies Disney's "Sorcerer's Apprentice" and another musical work composed several decades after Dukas composed his. I'm referring to the "Uranus" suite from Gustav Holst's famed *The Planets*, a work characterized by unconventional time signatures and abrupt key changes (stylistic elements distinctly different from those of the other planetary suites in Holst's work). I once heard a musicologist claim there was no clear evidence Holst ever heard Dukas's work; but even if he had, it wouldn't really explain why Holst chose that particular style to represent the planetary qualities of Uranus. To my mind, that coincidence alone may hold a potential clue for us into the deeper nature of Uranus itself, and its powerful but potentially problematic energies.

Let's look deeper. In Disney's animated version of "Sorcerer's Apprentice," Mickey Mouse usurps the sorcerer's magical powers and taps into energies far beyond his understanding and, eventually, his control. In the process, he nearly brings destruction down upon both himself and the world around him.

In one sense, that's also a fitting description of the role Uranus has played in modern times in terms of the energies and technological capacities it's awakened for all of us. Curiously, in Disney's version of the story, that awakening of powers is accomplished largely by means of a magical cap with stars and planets emblazoned on it—yet another Aquarian touch, hinting at the cosmic and celestial knowledge associated with this archetypal principle. (If we also go with the association between Uranus and the Greek mythic figure Prometheus suggested by astrologers like Richard Tarnas and Stephen Arroyo, we even find a parallel between Disney's story with the *theft of fire* motif in that ancient tale, since Mickey is pilfering powers that are not rightly his.)

Here we encounter the familiar "man versus technology" motif so prevalent in the Western imagination. The broom that Mickey Mouse commands to perform his chores for him, carrying buckets of water, eventually splits into multiple copies of itself in a way that elicits images of assembly lines, and practically foreshadows *cloning*, curiously enough.

But note the symbolism of that task performed by those animated brooms: it's none other than that of *water-bearers!* They carry water for him, but then go too far with their appointed task and unleash a dangerous flood. As I mentioned in an earlier chapter, the symbolic figure most associated in the West with the sign of Aquarius is that of a water-bearer (Ganymede), a task which esoterically signifies the bringing forth of hidden energies into manifestation. The fact that Disney's tale—and indeed, his entire empire—specifically centers around this core image is itself a remarkable testament to its importance as a cipher to our changing times.

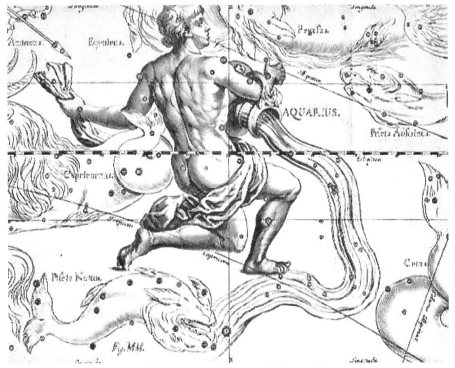

Engraved depiction of the constellation Aquarius
(from *Uranographia*, 1690)

In the end, I'd suggest that Disney's depiction of "The Sorcerer's Apprentice" can be read as a cautionary tale for humanity as we step into the Aquarian Age, implying both the perils and promises of our newly awakened capabilities (which first burst onto the global stage around the time Uranus was discovered in 1781—also the period of the Industrial Revolution). The technologies we've created to take over our tasks for us, from the menial to the momentous, from microwaving meals to atomically powering our energy grids, now threaten to undermine our existence.

And notice that as Mickey is being carried away by his fantasies of controlling the world, it is specifically an *environmental* disaster he sets into motion: flooding. In the film, the water keeps rising ever higher, while Mickey remains oblivious to the mounting dangers around him until he's practically drowning. As it so happens, one of today's most pressing environmental dangers is that of massive flooding, due to the melting of the world's ice caps resulting from a rise in global temperatures.

In Disney's animated version of the tale, Mickey desperately turns to his master's books for answers to his predicament; but by then it's almost too late. I say "almost" because at the last minute the master sorcerer appears and uses his magical powers to avert complete disaster.

Will we likewise be lucky enough to be saved at the last minute by some masterful "sorcerer" in the form of a technological genius like Nikola Tesla, or by divine intervention, or even some altruistic aliens riding to our rescue (ala Arthur C. Clarke's *Childhood's End*)? Nice as it would be to believe so, I think it's naïve to place our bets on someone other than ourselves to save us from the consequences of our own actions.

Either way, if there's one thing Disney's tale makes clear, it's that this isn't a child's game we're playing.

CHAPTER 29

RECONSIDERING THE HIGH WISDOM OF ANCIENT EGYPT ~ AN INTERVIEW WITH JOHN ANTHONY WEST

*D*uring the 1980s I came across an intriguing book titled Serpent in the Sky: The High Wisdom of Ancient Egypt *by independent scholar John Anthony West. Based on the research of the mathematician and orientalist, R.A. Schwaller de Lubicz (1891-1962), his book suggested there was a deep wisdom encoded in the art, mythology, and architecture of this ancient culture, which could be unlocked when viewed from a "symbolist" perspective.*

As I recounted in The Sky Stretched Out before Me, *it was several years later while working for Quest Books in Illinois, I learned West's book had gone out of print. At that point I contacted West and helped to secure the rights for a new edition. Thus in 1993 Quest Books came out with a new, updated version of John's book, almost precisely as John's work was reaching a worldwide audience through the TV special that John and his partner Boris Said produced for NBC, titled "Mystery of the Sphinx." It was hosted by actor Charlton Heston, garnered huge ratings, and coincided exactly with the Uranus/Neptune conjunction happening that year—a configuration that hadnt occurred since the 1820s.*

Two years before that, however, I conducted an interview with John for the winter 1991 issue of The Quest *magazine. Besides looking at the importance of ancient Egypt, we discussed the implications of his (and geologist Robert Schoch's) research on the Giza Plateau regarding the antiquity of the Sphinx. As John explained after we finished, this interview would essentially be breaking the story about their research on the weathering patterns both on and around the Sphinx. It proved to be one of the most widely circulated articles* The Quest *ran during the entire time I worked on the staff and was picked up by several other publications, including* Science of Mind *magazine. Here, then, is that interview with John.*

Ray Grasse: For a number of years you've argued that the Sphinx holds the key to a different understanding of ancient Egypt. Could you explain that?

John Anthony West: Yes. An observation made by R.A. Schwaller de Lubicz in one of his books, translated into English as *Sacred Science,* was that the Great Sphinx of Giza had been weathered by water and not by sand and wind as was generally and universally assumed. I realized that in principle it should be possible to prove that. This is a geological question, not an Egyptological or archeological one. And I realized that if you could prove that the Sphinx of Giza had been weathered by water it would upset virtually the entire historical applecart, not only regarding Egypt but everything that was accepted about ancient history and the evolution of human civilization.

Ray: Why is that?

JAW: First of all, I knew enough about the geology of Egypt—I'm not a geologist but I had done my homework—to realize that the conventional scenario held that the Sahara was a relatively recent desert. Before 15,000 BCE it was a fertile savanna, something like modern Kenya. Between 15,000 and 10,000 BCE there is a somewhat shadowy period, during which Egypt was subject to enormous rainfalls and periodic high floods. Following the cessation of the waters, Egypt became Sahara and has been Sahara ever since, becoming increasingly drier.

So I reasoned that if you could prove that the Sphinx had been weathered by water, it would have to mean that the Sphinx was there before the water was there. If that geological dating is correct, it would mean that the Sphinx dated from sometime before 10,000 BCE and probably before 15,000 BCE Now, the actual dating is still at issue, but the scenario is fairly iron-clad. In other words, the sequence of events is fertile savanna, long periods of rains, and then desert. So whenever or however that dating is revised or arranged, the Sphinx was there before the rain was there. This means that no matter how you slice it, the Sphinx is a great deal older than anything else in dynastic Egypt. And when I say the sphinx, I don't mean just the Sphinx itself, but other structures connected with it on the Giza plateau.

Ray: You've been back to Egypt several times recently to try and establish further corroborations for this theory, haven't you?

JAW: Yes. I've been back there on several excursions with a team of geologists and geophysicists, all of whom agree with me that absolutely, the Sphinx is weathered by water. It was not built by the pharaoh Chephren around 2,500 BCE, and it's a lot older than conventionally argued. Exactly *how* much older we can't yet determine, but that's the next big stage of research.

Ray: As you know, some theorists claim the erosion you are talking about could be due to other factors, such as ground water.

JAW: Yes, this is one of the current explanations, but none of those theorists who have suggested this are experts in stratigraphy or geomorphology, or in patterns of weathering. But the geologists with me are. My principle investigator, Dr. Robert Schoch of Boston University, is a stratigrapher, and the others are knowledgeable in these and other specialized areas, and all agree that groundwater weathering, or any other form of weathering, would not produce the weathering patterns that you see. They can *only* be produced by precipitation—that is to say, rainfall, lots of rainfall—over long periods of time.

Ray: I understand that part of your current research has involved seismic studies done around the Sphinx itself.

JAW: Yes, we went in there with seismographs, which are activated by hitting a metal plate with a sledge, which sends shock waves into the ground, when then go through the different materials underground and return, and are then read out by a computer. In other words, it's a way of looking for underground structures. Basically, we went looking to see if there were any possible chambers or cavities under the Sphinx which might corroborate, say, Edgar Cayce's readings, which suggested that there was a so-called "Hall of Records" under the Sphinx in which the whole history of mankind could be read out.

John Anthony West at the Temple of Kom-Ombo, Egypt

Ray: And did you find anything?

JAW: Well, we found some very interesting stuff. And the Japanese, who were working with, I believe, radar detection, also found sort of suspicious-looking cavities in front of the Sphinx and on either side. Our resolution is probably better than that of the Japanese, better than anything that has been done to date, and it's still not good enough to tell us precisely what it is. They could be what are called "karst" features, which are natural deformations in the bedrock. However, the way they come out, and the way they are sited, certainly makes it look provocative. The next step probably will be to go back there, now that we know what we are looking for, and go in with seismographs and do an even more detailed study. The Department of Antiquities is interested in this, and if we can tell them exactly where they ought to look, they probably would go through with a drill and one of those micro-cameras and see if they can photograph something.

Ray: As you know, your own work and theories have come up against some resistance in the academic community and among conventional Egyptologists in particular. To what do you attribute this?

JAW: Well, one of the features of the academic community is that they are notoriously resistant to new ideas in general, and in this case what's at stake is overturning the entire historical apple-cart—and these people make a living selling apples. So it's not surprising that you get this sort of resistance. It's unfortunate, because scholars and academics are supposed to be interested in the objective truth, which is not supposed to be associated with emotional reactions. The fact of the matter is that there is invariably an emotional reaction to *any* new idea, particular one as radical as this. It's a psychological rather than an academic problem.

Ray: Part of the problem seems to be over the fact that you are coming from outside the mainstream academic community?

JAW: Well, yes, and actually, in a sense, rightfully so. This is why I need my geologists and geophysicists to back me up. I'm *not* a geologist or a geophysicist. The fact of the matter is that until very recent times *most* of the important discoveries in archaeology were made by amateurs; Schliemann with Troy is perhaps the most dramatic example of this. But generally speaking, many of the most important discoveries were made by impassioned amateurs. And, actually, since I've been studying Egyptology and related subjects for some 20 to 25 years, I don't regard the lack of formal credentials as an impediment. In fact (laughing), I tend to regard it as an advantage, because my tenured neck is not on the line, and I'm not obliged to worry about the ruffled feelings of my colleagues.

Ray: How do you feel we can go about implementing or learning from the ancient Egyptian worldview? In other words, is this all just something of academic or intellectual interest to us, or is there something the ancient Egyptians actually have to teach those of us now in the twentieth century?

JAW: Well, we stand to learn a great deal. To begin with, it hinges upon understanding the difference between *progress* and *civilization*. What we now have we call progress—I call it a kind of shiny barbarism—and it has nothing to do with civilization. In a true civilization, human beings generally understand that we are on this Earth for a purpose, that our lives have a certain meaning. In Egypt, if we wanted to apply a single definition to the Egyptian esoteric doctrine, it would be the *transformation of the soul*; the possibility that we have to transform ourselves from the material beings that we are by birth to the spiritual beings that we are by birthright. And all of the Egyptian doctrine, all of their temples, all of their tombs, everything that they ever did, was directed towards that tremendous aim. And while we're not about to go rebuild temples or pyramids, or anything of that sort, we can certainly learn from the Egyptians how a true civilization functions when it understands this question of meaning and human destiny.

After all, it's now becoming quite clear what the results of progress are: we're living on a planet that's about to founder in its own landfills, the skies are polluted, the seas are polluted, the earth is polluted, all of this being a result, actually, of "progress" and the materialistic philosophy that backs it up—i.e., we have no destiny, our lives have no meaning, we might as well be comfortable as we can and produce as much rubbish as we can because this pleases us. We can see the results of progress unfolding in the headlines every daily newspaper.

So, with the model or example in front of us of a true civilization that functioned for thousands of years—it too went under in the end for a complex variety of reasons—those of us who have our wits still about us and are not blinded by the technological feats of progress, can in fact start to personally and collectively reestablish a civilization on this earth. That's the reason I personally lead my trips to Egypt, to let people see Egypt for themselves, through symbolist eyes, which in turn dramatizes as nothing else can this crucial and glaring difference between the progress of today and the civilization of the past.

Ray: But, practically speaking, how could one bring about such a state of civilized "sacred" values in today's world? In ancient times, it was possible for a certain set of values to be imposed on a society from the top down by the priests or pharaohs. But in a pluralistic, democratic society like ours, how would one even go about effecting such a change?

JAW: In one sense, you couldn't, but in another, I think it's a mistake to think that in ancient Egypt such things were imposed, as it were, "from the top down." It certainly *came* from the top down, but it's unlikely that it was *imposed*. We tend to think of these as tyrannical societies and that all of the slaves did what they were told. But it's quite clear when you look at what they produced that slaves don't produce that kind of work. They produce Yugos, and Russian guns, and junk. But slaves don't produce masterpieces of art. In other words, everything that works well works via hierarchy. The word "imposed" connotes that the system was a tyranny, and I don't think that a legitimate civilization works that way. It works because the people at the top are doing their job correctly, and everyone knows that.

Nevertheless, how do you get such a thing going? You get it going by starting with yourself, obviously; that's the only person you can work on. This is one of the reasons politics is so useless; it imagines that people who have never worked upon themselves can suddenly be changed. The only way to change anything is to start off by trying to civilize yourself. If enough people start doing this, suddenly you have the possibility of something approaching a civilization. And obviously, if a few people are trying to civilize themselves, and if they're getting anywhere, then you have a little organization.

So you don't start off trying to build a little pyramid or a Temple of Karnak, but maybe you start of trying to build a little school or a little farm, or something according to sacred principles. If a small group of people is behaving in some kind of civilized manner, they tend to have an influence outside their own sphere. Let's face it: this is how the great religions all got their start, because there was one Buddha or one Muhammad, or one Christ who had the sufficient inner authority to convince a lot of people that this was the way that they could live their lives. In modern history, these things have tended to function for a while relatively inefficiently, compared, let's say, with a tremendous civilization like ancient Egypt, particularly in the Old Kingdom. Nevertheless, you can see that the examples are there. And it can only start with individuals, understanding what is at stake—that we have the potential for the immortality of the soul, as the old doctrines taught. This is our birthright, and this is the promise held out to us by all the great religions and all of the great teachers.

Postscript: Shortly after this interview with West in 1991 a heated controversy erupted in both Egyptology and archaeology over his and Robert Schoch's hypothesis that the Sphinx is older than its conventional dating of 2500 BCE. One of the primary criticisms leveled at their work centered around the fact that no other evidence exists for the construction of large megalithic structures in the world as far back as West was suggesting for the Sphinx. That all changed with the discovery of a large megalithic site in Turkey called Göbekli Tepe, which dates back to around 10,000 BCE—much closer to the time frame West was suggesting for the construction of the Sphinx. While the precise age of the Great Sphinx remains an ongoing debate, West has clearly been vindicated on that one key point—that there were societies advanced and motivated enough during that earlier period to have constructed large megalithic structures.

John Anthony West passed away in 2018. I'd known him for over 30 years since our first meeting in early 1987 in upstate New York, and his insights and wit are greatly missed. I'd like to believe he's continuing to stir up mischief wherever he may be now.

CHAPTER 30

SOME PASSING THOUGHTS ON SACRED ARCHITECTURE

I magine building a house, and you're being especially careful during the blueprint stage to incorporate artistic or spiritual elements into its geometry and design. Then you pick the best astrological time for starting the construction, and take pains to infuse every board, brick and nail with your best energies, whether through chanting, prayer, singing or sheer focused intention. And while painting that house and any murals inside of it, you and your coworkers go to great lengths to infuse those colors and images with your best emotions, perhaps including uplifting or holy symbols into those murals as well. Then once it's completed, imagine how it might feel being inside such a structure, imbued with the most elevated energies you were capable of and aligned with the most harmonious energies the cosmos had to offer.

In truth, that pretty much sums up the ambience of cultures like ancient Egypt, where virtually every major temple and monument was built in much that way. (Forget the "slaves built them" theory, by the way; as John Anthony West noted in the previous chapter, the best research suggests that's a myth.) While some of that energy has undoubtedly dissipated from those structures over the millennia, since they're no longer being constantly reenergized by priestly ceremonies and such, one still feels some of that lingering ambience in those spaces today if you're fortunate enough to spend some time visiting them.[1]

One of the basic steps toward understanding sacred architecture is realizing that, in a certain sense, a building is essentially something *alive*; it has a personality of its own, and when you step into it you're entering into the body of a living entity.

Needless to say, not all buildings are created equal, and a structure's quality of aliveness or personality is a combination of the intentions put into it, the quality and vibrations of the building materials, the astrological period during which it was constructed, the beings who currently inhabit it, the energies of its history and past inhabitants, and even the region it's located in. True sacred architecture works to combine all of those factors in as harmonious and complete a way as possible.

These days we've largely lost that sense of the sacred in our approach to building, opting instead for functionality, speed and cost cutting. While it may not be realistic to expect the older ways to return anytime soon, there's no reason we couldn't resurrect them on a smaller scale in our own work with building homes, gardens, or personal shrines.

How about on a larger scale, as a goal for our civilization? I'm not so sure about that. But some of those formal principles from ancient times *have* been passed down into present times, albeit to a limited extent. I'm referring here of course to the mason's trade. When I shared my thoughts about architecture with my colleague David Whitlock, he replied with this observation:

> Along these lines of building temples and cathedrals, the Mason's symbolic wages were the consumables of corn, wine and oil. Also, at the dedication and during rituals the very same corn, wine and oil were used as offerings. The Masonic rituals stress that a Mason's body is a temple and should be seen as a dwelling place of their God. Likewise, the parallel temple being built is the dwelling place of the living God where the consumable oil, wine and oil is offered. *The Mason himself is a living stone and this fractal train of thought is continued endlessly as All is One without any bias of separation. The deductive reasoning is that you are God living in the temple of the living God.* (emphasis mine)

Whatever one's feelings may be towards modern-day Masonry (my father was a thirty-second degree Mason, incidentally, though I've never been particularly drawn to the movement myself), there's no denying that masons in general have often been the safekeepers of important bodies of knowledge through history.

Think of Europe in the thirteenth century, for instance, and you'll probably imagine a fairly primitive time characterized by peasants, beasts of burden, and dimly lit huts. But spend time inside any of the old great cathedrals from that period, like Chartres or Notre Dame, and you'll be struck by what it must have required to create those architectural masterpieces, not just physically but intellectually and spiritually. One can't help realize there was far more going on during that period than is generally appreciated now. If nothing else, it's abundantly clear that the masons of the time were among the foremost bearers of higher knowledge during that era.

Could we eventually create a deeply spiritual civilization similar to what John Anthony West claims thrived in ancient Egypt, where values of sacred architecture were amongst those infusing every aspect of the culture? I'd like to believe so, but it would have to take a very different form than it did in older times.

By way of illustration, I grew up in the northwest corner of Oak Park, Illinois, and lived near homes and buildings designed by the architect Frank Lloyd Wright. I was always impressed by the elegance and austere beauty of those private homes, but it was the more publicly accessible Unity Temple on Lake Street he designed that intrigued me most of all.

Late one evening I was able to spend some time alone in the central worship area of the structure. There had been a gathering of people elsewhere in the building, and I wandered off to spend some time exploring the structure on my own. The exterior of the building never did much for me, but the interior had a surprising impact on me, especially while standing in the dim light there by myself. But it was an impact dramatically different from the ones impressed on me by those European cathedrals or the temples of ancient Egypt. Among other things, Wright's temple reflects a distinctly modern, more "democratic" sensibility in its layout; in contrast with more traditional worship spaces where everyone faces in the same direction toward the officiant, Wright's design is such that everyone in the congregation enjoys relatively equal sight lines to everyone else. While I wouldn't suggest its power as a sacred space was exactly equal to what these older spaces held for me, I'd be dishonest to pretend that Wright's structure didn't possess a holiness all its own.

The Great Kiva, Chaco Canyon, New Mexico

Whether we prefer to draw our water from newer or older mystic tributaries, it's worth taking time to consider what does or doesn't constitute sacred space, and how to best actualize that in our own time. We give shape to our structures, and they in turn shape us.

Moreover, if we're truly on the brink of a new era, then our buildings won't simply play an important role in how we express those unfolding potentials but may even serve as vessels for passing on knowledge and teachings to future generations. In a perfect world, I'd like to believe our descendants would be inspired and educated by our structures just as we are by the sacred structures of our past. We occasionally hear someone talk about the importance of "paying it forward"—of giving to others down the line just as we have received from those who preceded us. That's not a bad philosophy for an entire society to hold in mind either, and architecture can be one of the tools we utilize for realizing that.

CHAPTER 31

THE GENIUS OF *CITIZEN KANE*, PART I ~ A WINDOW ON THE SOUL OF AMERICA

W hen *Citizen Kane* exploded onto the cinematic scene on May 1, 1941, it left some viewers agape at the originality and breadth of its vision. Writing for *Newsweek*, novelist John O'Hara stated that he thought the film was the "best picture he ever saw,"[1] while in the *New York World-Telegram*, critic William Boehnel declared that the film was "staggering and belongs at once among the greatest screen achievements."[2]

Since its release, countless essays have been written about Welles' film, discussing its technical and stylistic innovations, the relative contributions of cinematographer Gregg Toland and screenwriter Herman Mankewicz, and of course the controversy surrounding the film's real-life inspiration, William Randolph Hearst.

Here I'd like to approach the film from a slightly different direction—two of them, actually, one more socio-political in nature, the other more symbolic and esoteric. As I hope to make clear, these dual perspectives go hand-in-hand, and together have something important to say not only about our own times but quite possibly the one ahead of us too.[3]

Kane's Story Is America's Story

As I heard one commentator say long ago, *Citizen Kane* is, above all else, a distinctly *American* work of art. It drew on influences from European cinema, of course, but its dynamic energy, subject matter, and technical innovations make it clear that it arose out of the imagination of an artist born and bred in the twentieth-century U.S.A.

Photo: Paramount Pictures

Besides reflecting a distinctly American aesthetic, Welles' film has something important to tell us about the nature of the American experience itself. To explain what I mean, we need to briefly recap the underlying story of Charles Foster Kane's life in broad strokes.

The movie shows young Charlie being raised by poor parents under rustic circumstances in rural Colorado. His life dramatically changes when gold is discovered as a result of a mining deed belonging to Kane's mother, Mary. She hires a banker named Walter Parks Thatcher to establish a trust that will provide for young Kane's education and has him assume guardianship of the boy, at which point young Kane is whisked away to his new life in the big city.

By the time Kane gains control of that trust at age twenty-five, he's become one of the richest men in the world and uses it to take over control of a newspaper, the New York Inquirer. He starts out as an idealist with apparently humanitarian intentions. As his newspaper grows in circulation, Kane increasingly moves his newspaper into the direction of yellow, or tabloid, journalism. He eventually expands his media empire to the point where he exerts massive influence not only on public opinion but on broader political developments as well.

Kane's life is increasingly characterized by a pursuit of empty pleasures, failed relationships, and a compulsive acquisition of things. He eventually builds an extravagant, sprawling castle, a "pleasure palace" called Xanadu, where he pursues his empty life, in the end basically dying alone, a spent soul whose final moments center around memories of a long-lost childhood.

Let's take a moment now to consider the similarity of these stages in Kane's life to those of the American experience:

- Welles' film depicts Kane as having come from relative poverty and rustic circumstances, rather like the early settlers on the American continent, who confronted an undeveloped natural wilderness.
- Like Kane, the early American nation became massively wealthy as a result of valuable natural resources uncovered on its land, catapulting it from a backwater country to the wealthiest nation on the planet.
- Kane was adopted from a young age by a bank. As its own wealth grew, the young American nation was taken over by banking and corporate interests as well.
- Kane's life became focused on developing a media empire. As the United States expanded into the nineteenth and twentieth centuries, it also became a major force in

telecommunications and media technologies, exemplified by its TV networks, movie industry, and the sprawling Disney empire. To a certain extent, American culture and politics have been inextricably entwined with American media—newspapers, TV, movies—which in turn has exerted a profound impact on global culture.

- Over time, Kane's media empire became increasingly debased, pandering to mass tastes and manipulating popular opinion—like American media.
- Kane is originally depicted as an idealist who sets out to fight for the little man, even creating a "Declaration of Principles," paralleling the U.S.A. and its Declaration of Independence.
- In the end, Kane's life is depicted as a sad tale of empty materialism, selfishness and unhappiness. Here as well, it's easy to seeing an analogy to what the American empire has to some extent become, with its original idealism having been largely replaced by materialism and a seemingly insatiable consumerism. Xanadu, the extravagant castle Kane dies in, becomes a metaphor for America itself: its diverse elements and kitschy influences even present a close analog to Walt Disney's mega-playgrounds Disneyland and Disney World (the last actually being in Florida, like the movie's Xanadu).

I'd add one other element to that list. Kane is shown as having essentially had no childhood: it's cut short when he is whisked away into his new life in the big city. That reflects Welles' own life, since his parents both died while he was young, throwing him into a world of adult concerns. But that's also the story of the American nation itself, since it too had very little "childhood." As I pointed out in *Signs of the Times*, America was different from most other countries around the world, with their long histories of cultural development spanning centuries or even millennia. Modern American culture didn't experience that same slow development, being the product of European culture grafted onto North American soil. That growth resulted in a kind of stunted development, an indisputable technological and scientific superiority atop an emotional immaturity and lack of sophistication.

On the one hand, that's given the U.S. certain clear advantages. Unbound by many of the traditional values and customs that weighed down earlier cultures, America has been the great innovator, the proverbial child genius bursting with ideas and inventions—like Welles himself. On the other hand, a lack of the emotional grounding that comes from a normal childhood has led to a certain superficiality in the America psyche, a lack of emotional depth that's reflected in our seemingly tireless pursuit of glitzy entertainments and prime-time pleasures, among other things.

In short, the story of Charles Foster Kane is, in microcosm, the story of the United States itself. Interestingly, the original title of the movie's script was simply *American*. On some level, Welles and Mankiewicz seemed to have sensed the deep relevance of their story to our experience as a nation. In fact, Welles' own horoscope may give us some hints of that attunement, since his Moon was aligned with that of the United States (using the nation's July 4 birth date). And as suggested earlier, the United States may well be a portent of what lies ahead of us, as the cutting edge of the emerging Aquarian Age.

In that vein, I'll be taking this discussion one step further in the next chapter, with a look at what Welles' movie may also be saying about our future, not simply as a nation but as a global culture.

CHAPTER 32

THE GENIUS OF CITIZEN KANE, PART II ~ A WINDOW INTO THE SOUL OF OUR FUTURE

I've come to believe that great works of art not only tap into a deeper stratum of the human psyche, but in some cases even reach layers of the collective unconscious that extend out into both the past and future. In part I of this article, we saw something of that backward-looking aspect of *Citizen Kane* as it relates to the grand arc of American history; in that sense, Kane's story is a microcosm of the American story.

In this installment, I'd like to look at how the film points forward in some ways to our collective future—not just America's but that of the world. Viewed symbolically, it is a cinematic Rosetta Stone, a cipher of trends and themes not just of recent or current times but possibly the next Great Age.

Photo: Paramount Pictures

Stylistic and Technical Innovations

It's often been noted how *Citizen Kane* foreshadowed filmmaking techniques that became commonplace during the following decades. That includes such things as deep-focus cinematography, nonlinear narrative, jump cuts, high contrast imagery, fisheye lens shots, cinema verité, overlapping dialog, visible ceilings, point-of-view imagery, long takes, artfully crafted dissolves, contrapuntal sound editing, and film-within-a-film sequences. While many of these had already been utilized in earlier films, Welles perfected and combined them in ways that made them uniquely his own.

When someone says, "Welles didn't do anything that hadn't been done before," one might as well respond, "All the notes of the scale existed before Beethoven, so he didn't really do anything all that novel either."

In his essay "Citizen Kane," David Bordwell describes Welles as the ancestor of Godard, Bergman, Fellini, Bresson, and Antonioni, among others.[1] But that list should also include Tarantino, Kubrick, Scorsese, and countless other directors from the last seventy-five years, all of whom owe a debt of gratitude to *Kane*. So simply on technical and aesthetic levels, it foreshadowed what was going to cinematically unfold in later decades.

The Aquarian Dimensions

From a more esoteric standpoint, *Citizen Kane* also foreshadowed some of the defining themes of the emerging Aquarian era in very subtle ways.

It's worth mentioning again Welles' own horoscope and the role that Aquarius and Uranus play in it. In addition to being born with a Uranus/Moon conjunction in Aquarius near the top of his chart, his 24-degree Gemini ascendant is precisely aligned with the discovery degree for Uranus; factors like these strongly suggest he was strongly attuned to futuristic trends. As I've also pointed out in various articles and books, *Citizen Kane's* world premiere on May 1, 1941, took place during an extremely rare aspect involving Uranus, when it conjoined with Jupiter and both of them exactly trined Neptune around the same time—a remarkable combination of innovative and creative energies.

One theme I'm referring to revolves around the dangers of materialism. Just as Kane's materialism reflects that of America, it also points forward to one of the potential dangers of the greater Aquarian Age. This may be a strongly mental (Air) zodiacal sign, but as I've already observed, it's transposed *onto the lowest level of the spine, onto the root chakra.* Just as Kane was essentially adopted by a bank, we run the risk of having our civilization hijacked by corporate and banking interests and by worldly values based on wealth, prestige, and technological distractions.

The Power of Media

In some ways the most explicitly Aquarian aspect of the film—and one that's strangely overlooked in many critical discussions—is the all-important role played by the media in it, with all its potentials for either good or ill.

In the beginning, Kane is depicted as an idealistic humanitarian intent on using his media influence to combat injustice and fight for the little man or woman. Clearly, that highlights the more constructive potentials of the Aquarian media in action. But as he grows older and progressively rudderless morally, we see Kane using the media to influence and inform the masses in very nonhumanitarian ways, to foment scandal, spread lies, and take down opponents.

Eventually the media becomes, in his hands, a tool of mass manipulation. In the newsreel footage which opens the film, the narrator utters the descriptive line "Kane . . . molder of mass opinion though he was . . ." Later on, Kane himself makes such revealing comments as, "I'm something of an *expert* on what people will think" (since he will shape their thinking himself). And this: "If the headlines are big enough, the *news* is big enough." This mirrors the very real danger posed by mass media when it falls into the wrong hands (which it usually does). It also says something important about the dangers of the mass mind in the coming era. Noam Chomsky coined the term "manufacturing consent" to describe how people's tastes and opinions can be molded by those in power. How easy is it for us to get swept up in groupthink? All too easy, it seems, when the media machine becomes involved.

The Privacy Problem
The film slyly portrays another danger associated with mass media, in hinting at that precarious balance between the group and the individual, which is the dynamic associated with the Aquarius/Leo polarity. I'm referring here to the problem of privacy. As the purveyor of tabloid journalism, Kane is not only an instigator of intrusion into our personal lives but ironically also its subject. (Note also the coincidental similarity of his paper's name with that of our present-day tabloid the *National Enquirer*.) That is established at the film's opening, with its "News on the March" newsreel, which is focused on uncovering the most intimate secrets of Kane's life.

Welles adds an interesting touch here: the face of the investigative reporter sent out to get to the heart of what "Rosebud" means is *never directly shown*. In every scene of the movie where he's involved, he's either shown from the back or in shadow, but never from the front. That element of anonymity says something about the anonymity of the Aquarian media as well. Mass media is more of a vast faceless machine than it is the expression of any one individual, and recalls the iconic line from Bob Dylan's song "Masters of War": "The executioner's face is always well hidden."

The Paradox of Mass Connectedness and Personal Isolation

The "privacy" problem touches on another facet of the Aquarius/ Leo axis, and a somewhat paradoxical one at that. Note that Kane is connected to massive numbers of people via his media empire, yet is himself increasingly isolated, essentially dying alone without family members or loved ones nearby (his first wife and child having been killed in an auto accident, and his second wife having left him).

To my mind, this speaks to how our modern Aquarian media allows us to be connected to countless others via news outlets, social media, and telecommunications, while also making it possible for us to remain isolated in our own little shells, walled off from other humans. It's a mode of "interconnectedness," yes, but a somewhat false one, since it's very cerebral and impersonal. This points up some of the problems of Aquarian energies at their most extreme. The character Linus in Charles Schulz's *Peanuts* strip summed it up pretty well: "I love mankind; it's people I can't stand."

A Decentralized Life

Finally, and perhaps most subtly, the movie touches on a particularly important facet of Aquarius, that being the principle of *decentralization*.

As we saw earlier, Leo governs the heart, the organ where all the blood of the body is "centralized," whereas Aquarius is the distribution of the blood throughout the body—hence, the principle of decentralization. *Citizen Kane* expresses this principle in several dramatic ways, to the degree that Argentinian writer Jorge Luis Borges once even referred to the film as a "centerless labyrinth."

Photo: Paramount Pictures

Rather than showcasing Charles Foster Kane from a single omniscient perspective, or what is sometimes referred to as the "God's-eye viewpoint," the film presents him from a *variety* of perspectives, as described by the various people he knew in life. In short, it decentralizes his identity. Which of those perspectives about him is the right one? That's left up to the viewer. (Welles returned to this motif even more explicitly with his fun house sequence at the end of *The Lady from Shanghai*, where the lead characters are reflected many times over in a series of mirrors.)

That splitting up of a single, dominant viewpoint is paralleled by a more temporal or chronological splitting, since *Citizen Kane* breaks up the conventional linear narrative by hopscotching all over Kane's life. It presents a smorgasbord of scenes from old age, childhood, and middle age, all scrambled together in seeming defiance of conventional A-to-B-to-C storytelling. It's a decentralization of time, in other words.

On both of these fronts, it's a brilliant *tour de force* of filmmaking, one that's been copied so often that the originality of its vision is difficult to appreciate now. In any event, that decentralized viewpoint reflects the multifaceted, aperspectival reality now taking shape as the Aquarian Age starts to settle in. We see evidence of this not only in an increasingly pluralistic society but in our multifaceted sense of reality itself, as various ideologies and philosophies compete for our attention, as well as in our scientific theories, as we ponder the possibility of multiple universes and dimensions.

At its best, that decentralizing of reality offers us a richer and more complex understanding of the world, while at its worse can give rise to what I've called the "Frankenstein" (or "fractured spectrum") principle, where wildly disparate elements are patched together in a chaotic and disjointed way. If you want an example of that, just spend a few days in Las Vegas, or for that matter Disneyland—or simply take a few hours to flip through channels on your TV set or smart phone. Compared to the life that your great grandmother Mabel lived out on the farm, our existence has already become decentralized in a wide range of ways.

These, then, are a few of the many ideas contained in Welles' film. It's a unique work that bears multiple viewings, but also has something important to tell us about our time in history, as well as the one looming before us, too.

CHAPTER 33

ASTROLOGY AND THE HEALING POWER OF LABELS

I could pontificate at length about all the ways our human-made labels can cause us problems in life, not only by walling us off from the world with layers of concepts, but also as a source of prejudice and bigotry in our relationships with others. Like when we dismiss someone out of hand because of their religion or political persuasion, or when someone labors under the burden of being called stupid or fat while young and then has trouble shaking loose from those connotations decades later.

I've even seen the problems that labels can cause in the practice of astrology, like the time I watched a teacher criticize a student's answer to a question he posed, saying to her, "Well, you *would* say that; you're a Scorpio!" Naturally, she felt hurt and resentful being labeled in such a simplistic way. But after all, she *was* a Scorpio. (Oh, wait . . .)

But there are times when labels can be an enlightening and healing force in our lives. I remember years ago watching a TV interview with actress Patty Duke in which she opened up about her struggle with mental illness. She explained how throughout much of her life, she was greatly disturbed about her seemingly mysterious condition, which led her to endure disorienting mood swings from depressive lows to manic highs. But the worst part of it, she said, was feeling she was not only a flawed person but completely alone with her problem. That sense of isolation convinced her she couldn't talk to anyone about it, and as a result it metastasized into a horrifying secret that remained bottled up inside her.

That all changed one day when she finally decided to see a psychiatrist, who formally diagnosed her as being bipolar. Simply hearing that diagnosis proved to be hugely liberating, conferring a great sense of freedom and healing. Why? Because she realized a problem she thought was unique to her was experienced by many people around the world, and it could be treated. Hearing that diagnosis also made her feel there was an underlying reason for what she had gone through; it wasn't just a random fluke of the universe but a real condition with neurological roots. Having a label attached to her condition changed everything.

I've encountered much the same situation when talking with some friends over the years about their own struggles. Recently a friend told me how her problems with reading comprehension back in grade school and high school caused her to feel stupid from an early age, leading to an inferiority complex that left scars well into adulthood. It was only when she started reading about dyslexia that it all started to make sense. As it had been for Patty Duke, it was a huge relief to learn this was a common problem for many people, and it had a name.

I thought of both those situations while working with a new astrological client recently. A young woman came to me in the midst of a painful time, having just been rejected by a boyfriend of many years. I didn't know that romantic backstory when she came to me, but when I saw her horoscope, I knew there were serious problems afoot. She was born close to a new Moon in Taurus, with the Sun and Moon separated only by a degree, and now Saturn was squaring both of them at the same time. Saturn in hard aspect to *either* the Sun or Moon can be challenging—but both at the same time? That's a heavy load.

I gently began describing the extreme challenges this pattern was probably posing for my client and how it might involve a difficult work or romantic situation, possibly both. I made sure to mention some of the constructive potentials these energies could bring, but I didn't want to sugarcoat things either, so I was abundantly clear about the possibility for depression and feelings of rejection that might come up.

But I also added, importantly, that if she *did* have those feelings, it would be quite understandable for anyone in the midst of those transits, and wouldn't simply be the result of her own inadequacies or imperfections. I was careful not to lay the astrological jargon on too heavily, but I knew she had done a little reading on the subject so I explained how it was specifically a Saturn energy affecting her chart.

Simply hearing all this was liberating for her, as if a huge weight had been lifted off her shoulders. Why? For much the same reason as Patty Duke described: hearing a label attached to her experience, hearing it given a *name*. It suddenly made her realize this wasn't all just in her head, and that she wasn't a defective person; there was actually a cosmic reason for it. For her to be experiencing difficult feelings in response to those transits wasn't just possible, it was to some extent normal, even expected. Maybe she wasn't such a failure after all!

There are many valuable things about astrology, but this strikes me as an especially important one. By realizing that a challenging emotion or circumstance we're going through has a name, and may actually be connected to cosmic forces far beyond ourselves, those emotions and circumstances take on a very different importance, and their impact hopefully becomes lightened.

CHAPTER 34

A TWO-TIERED APPROACH TOWARDS HISTORY ~ PLANETARY CYCLES AND THE GREAT AGES DOCTRINE

Among the various branches of astrology is a discipline known as *mundane astrology*, from the Latin *mundus*, meaning *world*. Mundane astrology deals with developments of a broad sociopolitical nature—the fortunes of nations, weather patterns, disasters, cultural trends, and so on.

As its tools, mundane astrology focuses on such phenomena as planetary cycles, eclipses, and national horoscopes, and explores how they are related to historical developments. For instance, I have briefly mentioned how the turbulent changes of the 1960s could be chalked up in large part to the Uranus/Pluto alignment that climaxed during the middle of that decade.

A somewhat broader approach to mundane interpretation hinges on the Great Ages. This approach is concerned less with planetary cycles and configurations, or with snapshot horoscopes for singular moments in time, than it is with the broader stages of history demarcated by the precession of the equinoxes, with each Great Age lasting roughly 2100 years. You might call this version of astrology the view from 30,000 feet, since it offers a broader perspective on what's happening than what can be gleaned through the snapshot approach that uses cycles and transits.

Each of these approaches offers something uniquely different, one more microscopic, the other more macroscopic, and each complements the other in important ways. Either one can be practiced entirely on its own, but there are times when both are necessary for a fuller grasp of the picture.

For instance, suppose you want to know what life was like in the year 2500 BCE using only astrology. You could study the outer planet cycles, eclipses, and stelliums of that period until you're blue in the face, but that's only going to tell you so much about life during that era. That's because those transitory planetary cycles won't reveal much if anything about the broader context in which those patterns were unfolding. It would be a bit like only hearing a select bit of dialogue from *King Lear* without knowing the larger story surrounding it.

In astrology, the concept of the Great Ages provides just such a context for the cycles and alignments that unfold from century to century. As a result, a Uranus/Pluto conjunction that took place in the Age of Taurus will not be the same as the one which happened more recently in the mid-1960s. The archetypal dynamics may be similar, but the sociocultural "clothing" will be very different. A Uranus/Pluto conjunction during the Age of Taurus 5,000 years ago would have surely triggered a certain amount of unrest and revolutionary fervor amongst the populace, no doubt, but not a flourishing of rock music or space exploration!

On the other hand, focusing solely on the Great Ages has its own limitations, like knowing the overall thrust of Shakespeare's play without grasping the subtler nuances ("Well, Shakespeare's play is about a king and his daughters. . ."). Planetary cycles and alignments are analogous to subthemes, subplots, and dialogues within a larger drama and which serve to drive the story forward.

Let me give a few real-world examples from history as to how these two approaches inform one another, and where focusing on just one or the other can give you a limited perspective.

For starters, consider the emergence of the United States as an independent nation. We can of course look to the chart for July 4, 1776, and study that horoscope's patterns, which will give us some useful clues. But as we saw in an earlier chapter, a far broader significance emerges when you take a step back to glimpse how it fits into the shifting Great Ages.[1] In a wide number of ways, America has been the virtual spearhead of the Aquarian paradigm, particularly with its emphasis on "We the People" democracy and its preoccupation with technology, media, and outer space. We could cite many precursors of the coming era, to be sure, but the United States is clearly one of the most significant of those in political, cultural, and technological terms—and that won't be revealed by a single horoscope constructed for a single moment in time.

Much the same can be said about the U.S. Civil War. As one possible approach, you could erect a horoscope for April 12, 1861, when Confederate troops fired on Fort Sumter, as signifying the start of the conflict. Or one can look at how in the 1860s, Uranus was returning to the position it occupied during the signing of the Declaration of Independence back in 1776, adding yet another level of meaning as to why the country struggled to realize the ideals encoded in its founding charters. But one could also look at the Civil War as representing one of several key transition points between the Piscean and Aquarian Ages, with slavery representing a vestigial holdover of the fading Piscean mythos, and emancipation expressing Aquarian values. In fact, slavery of various types was being abolished or lessened in different countries during the 1800s; for example, serfdom was abolished in Russia in 1861, the same year of the outbreak of the Civil War. That broader trend across the planet clearly reflected the fading influence of the Piscean Age and its associated values.

Yet another example of this dual approach would be the first manned Moon landing in 1969, when Neil Armstrong set foot onto the lunar surface. Strictly using the planetary cycles approach, we could draw up a horoscope for that moment in time and learn there was an alignment of the planets Uranus and Jupiter when it took place (and which punctuated the broader Uranus/Pluto conjunction affecting that entire decade). This combination of archetypal energies typically accompanies cultural breakthroughs of a scientific, technological, or cultural sort. For instance, Charles Lindberg's pioneering solo flight across the Atlantic in 1927 took place during an alignment between Uranus and Jupiter; and as we have already seen, *Citizen Kane* was released under a conjunction of those bodies in 1941. In that same vein, the Jupiter/Uranus conjunction was climaxing almost exactly as those astronauts made their descent to the lunar surface.

Neil Armstrong stepping on the Moon in 1969

But there is a broader way to see this event, within a far longer time frame, and which gives it a far broader significance. The context of the shifting Great Ages makes it possible to see the Moon landing as a significant transition point in our movement into the next Great Age. It represented a quantum leap in our technological and cultural imagination, signifying a clear demarcation between old and new. This was clearly an Aquarian development of the most conspicuous sort—and surprisingly enough, even Neil Armstrong interpreted the event that way. In a speech to Congress in late 1969, he said:

> We came in peace for all mankind whose nineteen hundred and sixty-nine years had constituted the majority of the age of Pisces—a twelfth of the Great Year that is measured by the thousand generations the precession of the earth's axis requires to scribe a giant circle in the heavens. In the next twenty centuries, the age of Aquarius of the Great Year, the age for which our young people have such high hopes, humanity may begin to understand its most baffling mystery—where are we going? [2]

Then there is the contentious debate in modern times over abortion rights. What horoscope could we possibly use to analyze that development, considering that it's unfolded over many decades, if not centuries? Do we look to the final court decision over *Roe v. Wade* in 1973? Not very likely, considering that was just one event in a long and complicated history.

On the other hand, we could also look to this debate in the context of the Great Ages. On the one hand, we have the prolife, antiabortion forces, ostensibly representing a very Piscean (and largely Christian) concern for the rights of the unborn, while on the other hand there are the prochoice forces, representing the more secular principles of personal freedom and autonomy. As a result, in that cultural struggle we aren't simply witnessing a conflict between two ideological factions, but the tectonic clashing of two Great Ages, and the meeting of two fundamentally different zodiacal paradigms.

It naturally raises the question: which side in the abortion debate will win out in the end? Some could take the Great Ages perspective to assume that the prochoice, Aquarian side of things will triumph, but it's not necessarily that simple. More likely is the possibility that we'll see a diminishing influence of the prolife movement, but not necessarily its disappearance. By analogy, consider how Judaism, a religion distinctly born of the Aries Age, was eclipsed in its influence by Christianity while itself never actually disappearing (and itself became considerably more "Piscean" after the sack of the Temple in Jerusalem in AD 70, when animal sacrifice was discontinued). As a religion, Judaism is still with us today, and in its own way quite influential. Likewise, it's probable that prolife forces will continue to exert an influence on public discourse long into the future, even if they no longer act as the dominant voice in the debate.

Finally, let's consider the tragic events of 9/11. In the minds of most astrologers, the precipitating trigger for the tragedy was the powerful Pluto/Saturn opposition which was coming to a head at that time. This is a celestial combo archetypally associated with the death and dissolution of old structures and a collective struggle with shadow forces, and sometimes even accompanies the outbreaks of wars. The official account of that day claims that it was an attack by nineteen Islamic terrorists against our modern, secular, imperialistic society. Whether one fully accepts that explanation or not, the symbolism of that narrative is fascinating to consider. Viewed in light of the transition between Great Ages, it speaks to the forces of a dying hyperreligious era violently resisting the values of a new, incoming one. Seen that way, the tragedy takes on a considerably different—and broader—significance than simply reflecting the transitory energies of a single moment in history.

I could use many other examples to demonstrate this two-tiered approach—the birth of the atomic age, the UFO phenomenon, the rise of the Internet, the feminist movement, the history of aviation, the debate over evolution, and so on, all of which can properly be viewed in either of these contexts. In the end, the transits and cycles approach and that of the Great Ages are complementary, since each one fleshes out nuances often absent from the other when taken by itself. I hope this essay has provided some insight into the values of a cross-pollination between these two.

CHAPTER 35

"MIDNIGHT MASS," THE TV SERIES ~ ELEGY FOR A DYING AGE

I n late September 2021, Netflix premiered a seven-part series titled *Midnight Mass*, directed by Mike Flanagan (known for his previous Netflix series *Haunting of Hill House* and *Haunting of Bly Manor*, as well as films like *Doctor Sleep*). Out of consideration for those who haven't seen the series yet, I don't wish to give too much away, so I'll just offer a few basic descriptions of the story, with a couple of very mild spoilers, and encourage those unfamiliar with the series to tune in and perhaps revisit my comments later on.

In simplest terms, the story centers around a fishing village on a small island in what appears to be either Canada or the Northeastern U.S. coast, and is set in contemporary times. The series looks at how a community becomes progressively embroiled in a supernatural drama involving a priest who comes to the island and who turns out to be someone other than what they first thought. From there, it gets stranger and stranger, culminating in a fiery (and bloody) climax.

But there's much more to it than that. Although the series ostensibly falls into the horror category, describing it that way is a bit like calling *Moby Dick* a story about fishing. It's a complex and multileveled work, incorporating themes of addiction, religious fanaticism, forgiveness, redemption, mass manipulation, and the herd mentality. In terms of cinematography and directing, it operates on a level beyond most television dramas, even beyond most theatrical film releases.

Director Mike Flanagan takes huge risks by tossing out cryptic allusions in early episodes that initially make little or no sense, and which in the hands of a lesser director would cause most viewers to tune out early. But as with his other Netflix series, all the pieces eventually come together in an intricate way towards the end. For reasons like these, I've gone out on a limb to call it the *Citizen Kane* of horror films. Is it perfect? No. But then neither is *Citizen Kane*. ("Rosebud," anyone?)

But my primary interest here is more astrological in nature, since the series offers yet another illustration of how a cultural work can be understood on both the micro and macro levels, as we saw in the last chapter.

On the micro level, it's notable that the series premiered on the eve of a Pluto station point, when that planet was essentially standing still and branding its influence into our collective psyches. (The planet changed directions on October 6, 2021, but its influence extended easily from late September up through the middle of October, which is precisely when the series reached peak viewership). That Pluto emphasis is especially obvious in the way the film's story hinges so heavily on themes of death and resurrection.

But it's the macro level I'm more interested in discussing here. I believe the series (however unwittingly on the director's part) makes a powerful statement about the conclusion of the Great Age slowly disintegrating all around us, making the series a potent transitional symbol in the shift between epochs.

The Piscean imagery is obvious enough, not only in the story's heavy emphasis on Christianity, churches, and Holy Communion, but in the fact that it's all set in a fishing village, bounded on all sides by water. In addition, there is the story's intertwined motifs of addiction, alcoholism, and Alcoholics Anonymous—all heavily Piscean in nature.

Viewed on that level, the chaos and apocalyptic struggles depicted in the series mirror those our own civilization is facing now as we contend with the darker legacies of the last 2,000 years. Look around these days, and you'll see a world nearly gone mad in heavily Piscean ways: major conflicts involving religious fundamentalism in both East and West; scandals in religious institutions; and a society struggling to break its addiction not only to religious and political ideologies but to oil and fossil fuel. In the end, that legacy has left us with a world in turmoil as humanity tries reconciling the outdated value systems of the past with the very different ones of the future.

Sentinels of the New Order
Yet in the face of all that, *Midnight Mass* has a more hopeful side as well.

In an especially powerful scene in the final episode (here as well, I'll refrain from saying too much), actor Henry Thomas, as the character Ed Flynn, meets his wife on the road following a horrific scene that's disrupted the community. He explains to her how he's chosen to resist the affliction so many others have succumbed to. It's a brilliant moment, which says something powerful about how we as individuals can likewise choose not to succumb to the lures of the dark side, whether that take the form of political ideologies, out-of-control escapism, violent impulses, or religious cultism and fundamentalism. It also mirrors the Alcoholics Anonymous motif that recurs throughout the series. On a broader level, his monologue may symbolize how humanity is itself slowly waking up from the hypnotic spell that the lingering Piscean mythos has cast on us for the last two millennia. Some of us, anyway.

Other figures in the series stand out as harbingers of the new order, like the village's female doctor, who is extremely rational and scientific in temperament, unlike some others in her community. She also turns out to be the daughter of certain key figures in the story who represent the old order, so that she symbolizes the next generation of thinking beyond the old era.

Then there is the lead female character in the story, Erin, who proves to be a major agent of change in the drama, albeit an unfortunate one. As my friend Barbara Keller pointed out, Erin plays a particularly critical role in clipping the wings of the dark force that's befallen her community and thus helps to ward off the more direful influences of the fading order.

Finally, there are the two children sitting in the boat at the series' end, who represent a message of hope in more ways than one.

For the most part, disability has been used in films and TV show to horrify viewers or elicit pity, but not in *Midnight Mass*. We see a disabled young woman, Leeza, living a good life despite her infirmities. She then undergoes an apparent healing, and the audience is initially led to believe this is a good and inspiring thing. But by the last episode, we realize there is more to the story than we realized, and her healing was not the entirely righteous event it first appeared to be.

In the movie's concluding moments, Leeza experiences a relapse—yet, amazingly, it's not presented in the film as a fail-ure. Her almost flip acceptance of her reversed condition is easy to miss, but as reviewer and journalist Rosie Knight insightfully noted, "To end the show on this line feels radical. To recognize that a disabled person can be content or even happy with their life in the face of the horrors they've faced is huge."[1]

To my mind, that scene embodies the brighter side of the Piscean legacy. Leeza isn't healed by high-tech Aquarian tech-nology or by some positive thinking program. A healing occurs, but it results from a surrender of the highest Piscean sort: an acceptance born of equanimity, rather than a resignation driven by defeat—a recognition that despite all one's best efforts, there will still be problems to contend with, and the best response may simply be to reach down and draw from deeper wellsprings than merely intellectual, technological, or physical ones. She and her friend become the seeds of the new order, but bearing a gift from the old one as well.

CHAPTER 36

WAS THERE A SECOND "ROSWELL INCIDENT"?
THE STRANGE STORY OF IRWIN FORTMAN

"And we looked down and saw these things and I said to myself—it just didn't register to me. And then all of the sudden I realized what we had seen and I just couldn't believe it, you know, like it was not happening. And yet it was happening, like it was a dream." —Irwin Fortman

It's probably the most discussed UFO event of our time and has been a source of controversy even amongst UFO researchers. But is it possible the now famous incident at the Roswell Air Force Base in July 1947, where witnesses claimed to have encountered the wreckage of one or more crashed UFOs in the New Mexico desert, was followed by a similar incident just a few months later? As unlikely as that might seem, I'd simply you to consider the following story before making up your mind.

First, a little background about how I became involved with this story. As mentioned in an earlier chapter, I spent some time during the 1980s at a Buddhist center in upstate New York—Zen Mountain Monastery—where I came to know a young man from Manhattan. He was a computer programmer who seemed both intelligent and informed. After I left the monastery, we kept in touch. Several months later, I received a phone call in which he told me he had something interesting to talk about.

While at a family reunion in Tucson late in 1987, he wound up talking with an older relative from California he hadn't seen in years, whom he called "Tiny." As the two began conversing about astronomy and space, Tiny finally divulged he had an unusual experience while stationed at the Roswell Air

Force Base back in the late 1940s. For fear of reprisals, he hadn't spoken with anyone about this experience—not his wife, not even well-known UFO researcher Jim Lorenzen, who played in a traveling jazz band with him for years afterwards. But now that he was getting older, the pent-up frustration of holding this story inside himself for so long finally got the better of him, and he figured his young relative would be a sympathetic listener.

According to my friend, Tiny's story involved a late-night retrieval of alien bodies from a crashed UFO out in the desert, after which he was sworn to secrecy by high-level government officials, who threatened him if he ever spoke about it.

On hearing this story, I was intrigued enough to want to get in touch with the man and find out more about his experience. Psychologically, I was also intrigued about learning how a historic event like this might affect someone's mindset. But my friend said that Tiny probably wouldn't want to speak with anyone outside the family and discouraged me from getting my hopes up. I continued to press him periodically about it over the next year, though, and my friend finally said he would give it a try and let me know what Tiny said.

After several attempts, and repeated assurances that I could be trusted, Tiny finally relented and agreed to talk with me. Several months later, I had my first telephone conversation with him. His legal name was Irwin Fortman. He ran a hardware story in Culver City, California, and struck me as a meat-and-potatoes kind of guy with a thick New York accent.

One thing was obvious: Tiny didn't want any publicity or financial compensation for his story. He simply wanted a sympathetic listener to hear his tale and record it for posterity. I assured him I wouldn't go public with any details of his account while he was still alive; if I did, it would only be with his permission.

We had four conversations altogether, all of them conducted by phone. Tiny hadn't followed developments in the UFO field beyond what appeared in the daily newspapers, so he was pleasantly surprised to learn there had already been a fair amount of discussion about the Roswell incident in recent years, with several witnesses coming forward who also claimed knowledge of the event. In fact, the first of my conversations with him took place shortly before the now famous episode of TV's *Unsolved Mysteries*, which catapulted the Roswell incident into worldwide attention during the fall of 1989. I told him about the upcoming show, which he eagerly watched. But when we spoke about it afterwards, he seemed vaguely disturbed about some of its details.

In particular, the timing of the famed July incident didn't jibe with his own. That's because he arrived at the base in the *autumn* of 1947 and was emphatic about the fact that his dramatic experience occurred in the dead of winter, *not* in the middle of summer.

Before long, it was clear to me he was describing a distinctly different event from the more famous one discussed in the media.

After hearing his account in full, a colleague recommended that I get in touch with well-known researcher Stanton Friedman, who was featured on the *Unsolved Mysteries* episode. I wanted to get his opinion, and perhaps even put these two figures in touch with each other. After talking it over with both of them, Stanton eventually met with Tiny at his home in California and later said he was impressed by his story and sincerity. But he chose to hold off on publishing anything about it until he could obtain either more evidence or a corroborating witness. He hadn't heard anything before about a second Roswell event, so he wanted to be cautious about going public with the information before it was validated. Using the 1947 Roswell yearbook, though, he could verify that Tiny was indeed stationed at the base the year he said he was. That was a start.

For some years now, I've considered the Roswell incident to be one of those important "transition events," not just because of its potential extraterrestrial (or non-human) nature but because of its timing. In 1947, Uranus had just completed its second full revolution from where it was upon its discovery in 1781. (In fact, the July incident occurred within days of that return, though its effect was strong throughout that entire year and the next.) With that planet's connection to the sign Aquarius, the events around each of its returns to that discovery point (first in the 1860s, then in 1947, and still to come in 2031), strike me as potentially holding a key to what might lie ahead for humanity, in terms both of technology and of our contact with life forms beyond our own.

I put my work with Tiny's story on the back burner in order to pursue other projects and didn't give it much more thought until twenty years later, when another well-known researcher in the UFO field, Anthony Bragalia, heard about it through the grapevine and contacted me for more details. Through him, I learned that Tiny died not long after my last conversation with him in the early 1990s. It was also through Anthony that I was able to obtain a copy of his photo in the 1947 Roswell yearbook, shown above.

What follows is a transcript of two of the four talks I had with Tiny in late 1989 and early 1990. I very much wanted to record the first two conversations but out of respect chose not to, because he hadn't yet granted me permission. As a result, I only recorded our third and fourth conversations; the transcript here is drawn from those recordings.

I should add that it became obvious as we spoke that Tiny hadn't given much thought to some of the finer details I pressed him about, as he struggled at times to recall certain events. But since forty years had passed since the incident, that was hardly surprising.

This is a composite of those last two talks, and I've pooled material from both into those sections where it seemed most relevant. Because of the age and condition of the tapes from which I transcribed this interview, some moments are inaudible, and I've marked those accordingly. (My thanks here to Anthony Bragalia and his associate Tom Carey for producing a cleaner version of these recordings, from which I drew much of this transcript.)

Ray: First of all, let me begin by asking you to describe what took place on the night this all came down, starting with how you were approached by the lead officer.

Irwin: Well, it seems like we'd just gone to sleep, and then—boom! We had been out late, you know, and they woke myself up and this other guy, and a couple other guys in the barracks, told us to get dressed, and meet us in what they called their "preop room," away from everything else, basically. They had coffee for us and they sat there and started talking to us, you know, just enough to wake us up and make sure we were mentally—that we didn't run the ambulance off the road or things like that.

Ray: So this was pretty late at night?

Irwin: Oh yeah, they woke us up out of a sound sleep. To me it felt like two o'clock in the morning.

Ray: And at this point they weren't acting like anything was out of the ordinary?

Irwin: No. Until we got in the ambulance and—you know that gate, the north gate? When we hit that, he was waiting there for us. And *then* they told us: "You are to keep your mouth shut! You don't repeat (inaudible)!"

And then after that, after we'd picked the bodies and the pieces there, we got back and then they *really* gave it to us, I mean they laid down the law. (Author's note: in an earlier conversation Tiny related how the officer in charge said something to the effect that, "If you breathe a word of this to anyone, they'll be picking your bones out of the desert, along with the bones of all your family members, too.")

235

Ray: I'm curious, here you were, seventeen or eighteen years old and . . .

Irwin: Eighteen, yeah; I wasn't nineteen yet.

Ray: It had to have been a startling experience. What was your reaction upon arriving at the site?

Irwin: I was so completely stunned, and I was half-asleep, and it was ice-cold out, I remember this, and we looked down and saw these things and I said to myself—it just didn't register to me. And then all of the sudden I realized what we had seen and I just couldn't believe it, you know, like it was not happening. And yet it *was* happening, like it was a dream. You know, how often do you see things like that?

THE BODIES

Ray: What did you think these things were once it finally dawned on you? Did you automatically assume that they must be from somewhere else?

Irwin: Definitely. I don't know what it was, they looked oriental-type, but you know, they were very small. And I knew that the Japanese weren't *that* small. And I couldn't think of any other countries, maybe Bali or something, you know, maybe they were very small there, but . . .

Ray: But the heads were very large?

Irwin: *Very* large, sort of like . . . Well, they were completely out of proportion to the body. I mean, to a point where it was like, if your head was about one and a half times what it is now, that's about how big it was.

Ray: And was there anything unusual about the features?

Irwin: (Pause) No hair on the head.

Ray: How about the eyes, nose or mouth?

Irwin: (Long pause) I saw nostrils . . . but as for a nose itself? If there was, it was very, very small. And the lips—wait a second, I don't know if it had lips, but I saw *teeth*, at least I think I did. Ears? Jeez, if there were, they were very, very small. I don't remember about ears.

Ray: What about the color of the skin?

Irwin: Ahh . . . yellow-like, but a very pale yellow. It looked very parchmentlike, a lot of wrinkles.

Ray: And you said something about how one of the bodies didn't have a helmet, but there was one complete body?

Irwin: Yes, that was the one we picked up.

Ray: And that one didn't have a helmet on?

Irwin: No, it didn't have a helmet on.

Ray: What was your reaction to that when you saw it?

Irwin: The only thing I can think of is that someone who helped me—I'm not sure if that was Tommy—said, "He must have taken his helmet off and come (kneeling?) out of whatever it was, the device." Because everybody else, their heads were in the helmets. Well, I didn't actually see that, but I *assumed* the heads were in the helmets, you know. The whole bodies were shattered, in pieces.

But this one that we picked up, he was completely whole. Now we didn't take his clothes off, so we didn't know if he was torn up *inside*: they wouldn't let us do that. They just said, "Put 'em in the bags." We didn't even put them, the bags, into the big plane that they took them off on, the transport planes.

Ray: What did you say to me a few weeks ago about the suits on these beings, how there was a fabric?

Irwin: There was a fabric, but it was like aluminum, or something. It wasn't something I had ever seen before. I've seen something like this lately, you know like a metal type fabric they're showing that the women wear . . .

Ray: On commercials or in fashion shows?

Irwin: Right.

Ray: Do you remember if the hands and the feet were enclosed? Or were they exposed? Do you remember anything about the hands and the feet at all?

Irwin: The feet had some kind of shoes on, something. The hands? They weren't shaped like ours.

Ray: In terms of the shape, or the number of digits? Or both?

Irwin: Both. Now the only thing I could think of when I saw it was, you know, that cold air and everything else from lying there, it got (inaudible) up or something. They just didn't look human.

Ray: And when you say they weren't shaped like those of humans, do you remember if they were larger or smaller than human hands?

Irwin: Smaller, [but] they were proportionate to the bodies. In other words, they weren't large hands, large feet. The feet itself were in a heavy shoe, like a boot. It seemed like it wasn't a leather boot; it was like a cloth boot.

Ray: And I think you said the eyes were closed?

Irwin: Yes.

Ray: But you could still see the shape of the eyes?

Irwin: It looked like a little old oriental (unintelligible).

Ray: How heavy were the bodies?

Irwin: Hmm . . . In those days I was stronger than an ox. . .

Ray: But they were light, though, right?

Irwin: Oh yeah, they were light—70–80 pounds, if they were that much. We both picked it up, but to me it felt like, uh, less than 100 pounds, like a sack of potatoes, you know?

Ray: And yours was the only complete body on top of that, right?

Irwin: Right, but these guys were throwing, I think they were trying to throw, you know, what they felt was one complete body . . . pieces. I don't think they just indiscriminately threw heads or (arms or) other things . . . They *could* have, but I thought they were trying to keep what they felt belonged to each other. How they did, I don't know. They spent more time looking for things like that than we did. We just went over and got the . . . they just pointed out what they wanted *us* to do, you know.

Ray: And you were there how long? Was it five minutes, or a half hour?

Irwin: I would say fifteen to twenty minutes. And the reason it took us that long is because we had to wait for the officers, the ones who were running the show, to show up.

Ray: So you couldn't act until they showed up?

Irwin: That's right. And we weren't allowed to shine the lights until we got there. And the only way we knew that we were there was we had somebody in a Jeep before us, and they came over and told us what to do, as far as parking the car (in?) the shape of, the U-shape. He told us not even to use the high lights, I remember that, just use your low beams.

Ray: So they were that secretive about it then?

Irwin: No, no, I think it was that they felt the high beams would be too high up in the air, because, you know, with those ambulances, the lights hit up so high. And I remember they said something about the low beams. And we had one little spotlight on each; they said to leave those off, just to use the low beams on the car. Now that, you know, it was still, about four or five ambulances, the way I could figure it out.

Ray: And each vehicle took a body, or set of pieces?

Irwin: Yeah. Oh, I'm just guessing that way, but I would say . . . or maybe they picked up pieces that they felt were critical and put them in the back too, you know. I can't tell you, because I don't know.

Ray: And when this happened, how many officials were standing around when you were taken to that site late at night?

Irwin: Well, I know there were quite a few officers there. In other words, when I say field grade officers or better, which would be majors or better. Now whether they were with the Washington group with the generals, or what, I have no idea. Because they just told us to get those bodies and get going. So we didn't have much time to turn around and look at people. And the lights, the way they hit . . . they were standing in like, they made like a semicircle (inaudible), the ambulances. You know what I mean? And some other cars were there. And we couldn't see too well. Except for what was on the ground. But as for what the facial features were, as far as the officers, go, I didn't catch that too much.

Ray: I seem to recall you saying something about how you could vaguely overhear some of the officers talking, and then they kind of backed away because they didn't want you to hear. Did I misunderstand that?

Irwin: I could overhear somebody talking, but you know, they were talking back and forth, but whether it was the high-ranking officers, I don't know. I was so excited about seeing a thing like this that the conversation wasn't that important to me. Looking down and seeing these things, and Tommy and I looking at each other, rather than listening to conversations that were about 25–30 feet away.

THE REMAINS OF THE CRAFT

Ray: Now what about the craft? Was there a craft, or were there pieces, or what exactly?

Irwin: There were metal pieces all around, I mean, big pieces, as big as a coffee table (inaudible). And the only thing I could figure out is the outline on the ground, you know, and so I knew it was in a circle. But there were pieces laying all over, outer (inaudible) circle, too, you know. There was quite a bit of metal shattered up.

Ray: And that was over how wide of an area? Was it the size of a football field?

Irwin: Oh, no, no. This was like, I would say, a good third of a football field. At least that big.

Ray: And you weren't able to pick up any pieces, were you?

Irwin: No, they were watching us pretty closely. They told us to wear these surgical gloves. In fact, I think we wore two pair, one was on top of the other.

Ray: Oh, really?

Irwin: Yeah. It was like, you know, "Be careful; don't pick up any sharp objects and cut yourself." Because they didn't know, according to the way I felt at the time, they didn't know what was going on as far as the biological. So that was why they told us to put on those rubber gloves, and two pair. In fact we had to help each other put the second pair on.

Ray: Now you and the others took away the bodies, but it didn't look as though they had taken away any of the metal yet?

Irwin: Well, yes and no. It looked like there was quite a bit of metal. And yet it didn't quite . . . look as though there was enough metal to . . . (long pause)

Ray: Make up a whole craft?

Irwin: Right. And yet you could see that it was a circle.

Ray: Apart from the pieces of metal, could you make out any distinctive items from the crash site, like chairs, consoles, or wires?

Irwin: Not really. Wait a second . . . there may have been something like crystals . . . but that may have been from the cold weather; they could have been ice crystals; I don't know.

Ray: And did you notice a crater? Was it your impression that this thing had plowed into the ground, or that it had exploded above the ground?

Irwin: The only thing I can think of, now you that mention that, was maybe there was a crater farther away, and this stuff was the stuff that bounced off of it, and it just, you know . . . that's the only thing I can think of. But I didn't see any real crater. I saw an impression on the ground, of these big pieces, you know. I don't know *why* I had the impression it was a circle.

Ray: Did you handle any of the metal?

Irwin: No. They wouldn't let us. First of all, because of the rubber gloves, I guess. I noticed that most of the stuff had sharp edges, though.

Ray: I thought you mentioned once before how there was something unusual about those edges. Was there some peculiar quality about the metal, far as you could tell?

Irwin: Well I tell you it looked like aluminum, but it sure didn't waver in the wind, or anything.

Ray: So it was thin?

Irwin: Oh yeah, it was thin!

Ray: So it wasn't like heavy metal beams or anything like that?

Irwin: Oh, no, no, no. It wasn't big heavy pieces, no, no.

Ray: So it was almost like shredded sheet metal, or something?

Irwin: Well, more like . . . I don't know . . . I can't figure it out. I've never seen anything like it. It was like somebody took and threw pieces of metal around; that's the only thing I can think of. You know, odd-shaped. As far as the edges are concerned, I don't remember talking about that.

AFTERMATH

Ray: An interesting detail from our earlier conversation a few weeks ago was your saying how when they first briefed you before heading out to the site, it sounded like they had their rap down pretty well, almost as if they had rehearsed this all carefully or had done it before, like this wasn't the first time. Do I remember that correctly?

Irwin: Yeah. To me it sounded like they knew *exactly* what was (inaudible). And then after that, after we'd picked the bodies, the pieces there, we got back, and then they really gave it to us. I mean they *laid down the law.*

Ray: So whatever happened to the bodies? They were taken off somewhere?

Irwin: Oh yeah, they were taken off somewhere, I'm almost sure they were, because we never heard about them again. Nobody mentioned them.

Ray: Colonel Blanchard never said another word about them?

Irwin: Nothing, no, no. In fact, he was very cool about the whole thing, and the general that was there—he was a three-star or a four-star general—disappeared that same night too. That I saw, anyway. Maybe he was staying around the base. But we didn't have to pull duty the next day, I remember that. They just let us stay around the barracks. They told us to stay around the barracks, and they just used the excuse that in case something else happened, they needed us. So we laid around the barracks.

Ray: And did you talk about it amongst each other?

Irwin: Well, Tommy—I keep mentioning Tommy because that must have been his name; I think it was Tommy. He and I talked about it when we were shaving the [next] morning, or in the afternoon. We slept all morning. We got back, we ate breakfast, and then we went to bed.

Ray: You never heard anything about the where the wreckage or the bodies might have been transported?

Irwin: No, I have no idea. I don't even know what kind of airplane the transporter was, whether it was it a small one, you know, or the big one, like the A-26's, which were part of the first ATU up there. (inaudible) They even had a couple of converted B-29s that were made into transports. That was the first ATU, they did all the schlupping for the, you know, bomber group, (inaudible) transport arm for the atomic bomb group.

Ray: I'm curious how you even wound up on this mission. In other words, how did you get clearance as an eighteen-year-old to go on a mission like this?

Irwin: I don't know. I had clearance to go right into the atomic area. They checked on my family and everything else.

Ray: You mean before the incident, you had clearance?

Irwin: Oh yeah, I had clearance before. We all did, to be able to get through those areas. Because that's where they started the atomic bomb. It was on the north end of the field. In other words, on every crew that stayed on the ambulance or the flight line, at least one guy had to have clearance through the north gate. But he would have to drive, and the other guys, I don't know, we never had any incidents where we had to go *through* the north gate. I did have to go down one time. We had a couple of fellas got burns, radiation burns, and we had to pick them up.

THE EARLIER INCIDENT

Ray: Now I'd like to talk a bit about the seeming discrepancy between the incident you're talking about and the one generally talked about back in July. You told me the incident you were witness to happened between New Year's and Christmas—or was it before then?

Irwin: I know it was not *before* Christmas.

Ray: And not after New Year's?

Irwin: It could have been, maybe a day or two. The base itself was pretty quiet.

Ray: I seem to remember your saying that the reason the base was comparatively quiet was because of the holidays, and you had given up your own holiday leave because you were Jewish, which allowed others to go off.

Irwin: That's right, and I figured I could always go away for Passover. It didn't make any difference for me to be there for Christmas. And the other guys who were there on the excursion (i.e., the crash retrieval mission) had basically just arrived at the base, so that's why they were there.

Ray: You said that you had heard something about the earlier Roswell case when you first arrived at the base in August or September.

Irwin: The guys who were still here from that group, that were there and witnessed it, they always talked about it. They talked about how they made this one guy, this civilian, sound like he was a moron, you know, the rancher or the farmer, they made him sound like he was . . . these guys knew that he *wasn't* crazy, you know.

Ray: But the official line was to make him look like he was a moron?

Irwin: Yeah, you know—stupid. Nothing was written about it in the papers by the time I got there, but some of the guys would talk about it. They'd sit there late at night when we got through with a late shift or something, drinking coffee, and they'd say, "Oh jeez, I wonder what's happening about the UFO?"

Ray: And these conversations took place before or after your own incident?

Irwin: Oh, it was *before!* The second time, *nobody* talked. The only ones who ever talked about it was me and this friend of mine, and we only talked about it in such a short conversation that if you didn't know what was going on, you wouldn't know what we were talking about. Look, when a three-star or a four-star general tells you, if you open your mouth, he's going to get you and your family, what do you think?

Ray: So why then do you suppose those other guys from the earlier incident spoke about it the way they did? Was there not as much pressure on them?

Irwin: I think it was open. You know, it was something that happened, and the government didn't clamp down on it until after a while, when they realized what was going on. That's the only thing I can think of. But the second time—man! They kept quiet about it! They probably got these guys down and just really . . . we all sat there and I tell you, most of the guys in the ambulances were young guys, eighteen, nineteen years old.

Ray: But what did you think when you first heard these stories about the earlier incident?

Irwin: I never did pay that much attention to it, because that was before we got involved with that other thing ourselves. So I never really did let it absorb into me that the guy said that, because I wasn't really interested, unless I had seen it myself, you know. I was interested in it as a curiosity rather than as a UFO, because I thought it was just something the guys made up. And then I realized they *hadn't* made it up. You know, some of the guys, I don't know if they were *all* there (at the first site), but as for why they spoke like (that), they knew it was really true. The first one, you know.

Ray: So when you saw a crash site yourself, you automatically drew a connection in your mind to the earlier one?

Irwin: Right.

PERSONAL IMPACT

Ray: In the long run, I can't imagine something like this happening without it having a pretty profound impact on someone's views. Has this had any kind of impact on your personal ideas or philosophy?

Irwin: The impact it's had on me is that I now believe in UFOs. (Author's note: during our first, unrecorded conversation, he spoke at greater length about the shock this experience held for him, and how he hadn't ever given any thought to things beyond our planet before, but in the blink of an eye, all that changed, and he was forced to realize we truly weren't alone.) And even when Jim was working with me . . .

Ray: Jim Lorenzen? (Author's note: Jim Lorenzen was an early pioneer in the UFO research field, and involved with the group APRO.)

Irwin: Yeah, you know, I kept thinking about the promise I made to the government that I would keep my mouth shut. And yet I was very interested, but I stayed away from it. Like when Jim called me the night before he made that trip to White Sands, New Mexico—we had a steady engagement at the old El Dorado lodge; I had a band there for seventeen years, and Jim was playing bass with my group—and Jim said to me, "I've got to go up to White Sands. They've spotted a UFO up there, and they've got quite a bit of information." I said, "Look Jim, that's no problem. I'll just get somebody else to fill in." In other words, if I was really just a stranger to the whole subject, I would have just said, "Well, Jim, you know, if you *really* believe in that kind of thing . . ." But I knew I couldn't tell him how much I believed in it myself.

Ray: But you did eventually tell him what happened, didn't you?

Irwin: Oh, no, no! I wouldn't take a chance. Because Jim had that magazine there, and he was a very open guy. If somebody gave him information, and he felt it was something that should be repeated—which I know this would have been—I would have felt that I'd be jeopardizing my family.

Ray: Considering how he was one of the foremost researchers on UFOs at the time, I imagine that must have been frustrating for you not to talk about it.

Irwin: Right, it sure was.

FINAL THOUGHTS

In the end, we're essentially left with this fact: Tiny was stationed at the base in 1947, just as he said, although there is yet no firm documentation as to precisely when he arrived. It's been suggested that Tiny might have actually witnessed the July incident, not one in late December, and simply misremembered when he came to the base. But throughout our four conversations he was adamant about the fact that he shipped into the base *after* July 1947, something especially apparent in his recollections of stories he heard from other servicemen about the earlier incident.

Regardless of when this particular incident occurred, Tiny's story is important, because there are so few firsthand testimonies from military eyewitnesses to the crash sites that year. (I even heard someone claim on a television show not long ago how there weren't any.) As for his trustworthiness, it bears repeating that Tiny sought no profit or attention for his story; in fact, quite the opposite. Which raises the question, why would anyone make up a story like this when it would probably do little more than subject him to ridicule?

Personally, I have no doubt he experienced *something* unusual, and that he struggled with conflicting emotions for years as a result, having been ordered to keep quiet about such a profound event. In fact, as our conversations progressed, I sensed relief on his part, as though he felt a weight lifting off his shoulders, now that he could finally talk about what happened back in the desert on that cold night.

While I agreed with both Stanton and Anthony that there's been no corroborating proof yet for his story, it's for precisely that reason that I felt it helpful to get Tiny's account out there, in hope that it might flush out any other surviving witnesses (or more realistically, surviving family members of witnesses).

Despite its controversial nature, this entire subject is an important one. I sometimes hear scientists say that the discovery of intelligent life beyond Earth would be the most important and paradigm-changing event in human history. But what if that discovery has already taken place? If stories like Tiny's are to be believed, then those wheels of change may have already been set into motion.

Postscript: Since first publishing this interview in 2010 on Greg Taylor's website, www.dailygrail.com, Stanton Friedman has passed away, and I've not heard anything further about other witnesses to the December event that Tiny described. However, shortly after my article was first posted, Tiny's widow got in touch with me to say she had read it and wanted to correct a few of the minor biographical details in the story (which I've since done). She also was able to provide me with Tiny's birth date (though without an exact time of birth, unfortunately): February 12, 1928.

Perhaps the most notable feature in his chart relative to his Roswell experience is the fact that he was an Aquarius with that sign's co-ruler, Uranus, aligned with Jupiter. This could be read as indicating unusual opportunities in life, possibly of a technological or futuristic nature. Also, during the general period of his experience in Roswell in 1947, transiting Uranus was forming a trine to his Sun, likewise showing some unusual experiences at the time, and perhaps an opening of his mind to unconventional ideas and viewpoints.

As I suggested in my book *StarGates*, I've long believed that powerful anomalous experiences invariably happen to people during times of important planetary triggers in their horoscope, and in turn, when deep transformative energies are taking shape *within* them. That certainly seemed to be the case with Tiny as well.

Maybe where he's now, he's found some answers to his questions about what really happened out there in the New Mexico desert that cold night.

CHAPTER 37

IS ASTROLOGY REALLY NOTHING MORE THAN "DIVINATION"?

S ometime during the mid-1990s, I first heard about a new book that hit the shelves, which at least one of my colleagues was calling an instant classic. Naturally, I had to pick up a copy and see for myself. It was called *The Moment of Astrology* and written by English author and astrologer Geoffrey Cornelius.

I found it extremely well-written and was intrigued by the book's central thesis, which could be summed up this way: Cornelius suggested that the efficacy of astrology relies less on the specificity of actual birth times, or on the objective mechanics of the universe, than it does on the "divinational" dynamics or *daemon* ("genius") of the astrologer working in the moment.

To paraphrase a bit, Cornelius seemed to suggest that astrology was more akin to practices like tea leaf reading or crystal ball gazing than to a purely objective system based on hard astronomical calculations. He used two chief examples to illustrate this point.

One of those was the uncanny way astrologers will sometimes be given the wrong birth time for a person, or simply miscalculate the time when preparing the horoscope, and yet somehow the reading will still turn out to be accurate. How is that possible if astrology truly hinges on the time of birth being the defining factor in decoding someone's life?

The other example he used involved the practice of horary astrology, where one calculates a chart for the moment someone asks a question about something, rather than a chart for the *actual situation in question*. Suppose you lost your gold watch on a Thursday; you might go to a horary astrologer the following

Sunday and say, "What happened to my watch?" By studying the horoscope for the moment that question was uttered, the horary astrologer tries to discern what happened to the timepiece.

Horary astrology poses such a striking challenge to conventional astrological theory because it dramatically differs from most other forms, which emphasize the moment of someone's (or something's) birth. Throughout much of history, astrologers have tried to explain astrology in terms of the classic "doctrine of origins," which is the idea that the seeds of the unfoldment of something are encoded in its beginning. You want to know what someone's life is really about? Look to the positions of the planets when they were born. You want to know how a new business will work out? Erect a horoscope for the moment it was started. That sort of thing.

When it comes to horary astrology, however, a chart might be erected for a question about something that happened long before the question was posed. For example, a person might inquire about that gold watch they misplaced two weeks earlier, but the astrologer will erect a horoscope for the time *that question is posed,* not for when the watch was actually lost. That's strikingly different from the notion of "origins," since the timing of the horary chart can be seriously displaced from the time when the event in question occurred. It focuses instead on the *moment of interaction between the client and the astrologer.*

From all this, Cornelius concludes that the participatory involvement of the astrologer is vital to the process. He takes the extra step of suggesting that this is the case not only with horary astrology but quite possibly for *all* forms of astrology. By this theory, the efficacy of astrology relies less on the objective workings of the universe than on the participatory experience of the astrologer. There seems to be an element of inspiration, genius, daemon— call it whatever you like—that involves the astrologer in ways not fully explained by more "mechanistic" theories of astrology.

To quote from the book: "There is, after all, no music without a musician, no language without a speaker, and no astrology without an astrologer."[1]

All right, so there is no astrology without an astrologer. It's a dramatic claim, and Cornelius states it probably better than I've seen it expressed anywhere else. But while there's clearly an important truth to that claim, I think it would be a big mistake to carry it too far, and I'll use two examples to illustrate why.

Take Cornelius's example of astrologers who somehow come up with accurate chart readings for clients, even though they have the wrong birth data to work with. Many of us working in the field have had that experience, and it's an uncanny one, to be sure. But it can be chalked up to various possibilities. Furthermore, it often doesn't work out that way.

I'm thinking particularly of an experiment conducted by archskeptic Michael Shermer involving Vedic astrologer Jeffrey Armstrong, presently available on YouTube. Unwitting test subjects were deliberately given the wrong horoscopes, but without either the test subjects or the astrologer knowing of the switch.[2] Clearly, the skeptics conducting the test fully expected the subjects to automatically agree with the vague generalizations provided by the astrologers. Once that was revealed, their gullibility would be exposed to the bright light of day, showing up astrology to be nothing but bunk. Very straightforward, very simple—and also very wrong.

When the subjects were finally asked whether the personality and life descriptions provided by the astrologers felt accurate to them, they said no. At that point, they were handed the "right" horoscopes by the skeptics, which actually struck them as being far more accurate. Instead of disproving astrology, the test wound up being supportive of it. So while it is true that in some cases a wrongly calculated chart can lead to accurate insights, that isn't always the case. It could well be in those cases when it *does* happen, the astrologer genuinely had insight into the lives and personalities of the subjects in a truly divinatory sense, as Cornelius suggests. Or it could just be the result of pure coincidence, or perhaps even that the comments by the astrologer were so vague that the readings only *seemed* accurate to the client. Whatever the answer, there are other possibilities than the one suggested by Cornelius.

The point here is that if the astrology-as-divination theory were rigidly true, Jeffrey Armstrong would have come up with at least reasonably accurate readings for the two test individuals, even though he was working with wrong birth times, due to that divinatory intuition Cornelius describes. In fact, the readings fell flat in those mismatched cases.

There's another example which point up the shortcomings of the astrology-as-divination argument even more critically, and it draws from the field of mundane (sociopolitical) astrology.

Consider the fact we can now use our computers to calculate major configurations involving the outer planets going back many millennia. That means we can chronicle the conjunctions, oppositions, and squares of distant Uranus, Neptune, and Pluto, which accompanied major events throughout history.

A particularly dramatic example of that involves the great triple conjunction of the outer planets in the sixth century BCE. Writers like Richard Tarnas, author of *Cosmos and Psyche*, have called that period one of the most important in recorded history, because so many important religious and political developments began or flowered then. As Tarnas wrote,

> These decades constituted the very heart of the axial age that brought forth the birth of many of the world's principal religions and spiritual traditions. This was the age of Buddha, bringing the birth of Buddhism in India, of Mahavira and Jainism in India, of Lao-Tsu and the birth of Taoism in China, which was followed a decade later by the birth of Confucius, Lao-Tsu's younger contemporary. This same epoch coincided with that sudden wave of major prophets in ancient Israel, Jeremiah, Ezekiel, and the second Isaiah, through whom a deep transformation in the Judaic image of the divine and understanding of human history was forged, one that is still evolving. In this same era the Hebrew scriptures were first compiled and redacted. The traditional dating for the immensely influential Zoroaster and the birth of Zoroastrianism in Persia, though still elusive to historians, has long centered on the sixth century. [3]

Why is this so relevant to evaluating Cornelius's thesis? Because the outer planets *weren't even known about at the time*: Uranus was discovered in the year 1781, Neptune in 1846, and Pluto in 1930. That means that whatever cultural changes occurred in association with those planets prior to those discovery dates took place entirely without the conscious participation of any astrologers living then. Therefore one can't possibly credit the divinatory or participatory involvement of astrologers for the huge impact of those configurations. If there is indeed "no astrology without astrologers," as Cornelius claims, how did the planets affect people on Earth so profoundly back in the sixth century BCE?

Another dramatic example of this point would be the French Revolution of 1793, which by virtually all astrologers' accounts corresponded to the powerhouse opposition between Uranus and Pluto unfolding at the time. Although Uranus was known at that point, having been discovered the previous decade by William Herschel, Pluto wouldn't be discovered for another 137 years. As a result, we can't very well attribute the bourgeois uprising that set France aflame to any conscious knowledge on the part of astrologers back then.

In short, as important as the intuitive and participatory component may be for some facets of astrology—a point I've argued for myself at times [4]—it isn't absolutely necessary in every instance. Astrology clearly incorporates daemonic elements, especially in systems like horary astrology or ordinary consulting, but it does so to a lesser degree than divinatory systems like crystal ball gazing or tea leaf reading, let alone mediumship or trance channeling.

In the end, astrological "influence" seems to involve a *combination* of objective and subjective (divinatory) factors in varying proportions, and it would be a mistake to tip the balance too far in either direction. As the historical record makes clear, the influence of the celestial bodies on our lives seems to operate quite effectively, even when astrologers aren't involved at all, thank you very much.

This article first appeared in The Astrological Journal, September/ October 2021.

CHAPTER 38

THE SON ALSO RISES

I first heard about psychologist James Hillman through my astrology professor Maureen Cleary, who spoke about teaching with him at the University of Chicago several years earlier (when she still went by the name Maureen Bates). I had no idea who he was at the time and only got around to purchasing his books later on. I was intrigued enough by what I read to search him out whenever I heard he was in town to give lectures or workshops.

I once heard someone refer to Hillman as the possible heir to Carl Jung himself, but whereas he seemed to draw from much the same archetypal well as Jung, James clearly put his own spin on things. He was a fascinating figure with a razor-sharp mind, that was obvious. I sometimes had trouble understanding his writings, since they were frequently couched in poetic or ambiguous language. But whether I understood them perfectly or not, something about Hillman's ideas kept pulling me back in to ponder their implications.

At some of the book conventions I attended while working for Quest Books at the Theosophical Society, I'd find Hillman manning the booth for his own publishing company, Spring Publications, and would stop to talk with him. I felt nervous approaching him at first, but he was always gracious and friendly towards me. The one time I went out on a limb to ask what his birth sign was, he responded, "What sign do you think I am?" Looking over that wiry frame of his, I took a stab and replied, "Capricorn?" "No, Aries." I didn't realize it, but the evidence had been staring me in the face. He held up one of Spring Publications' volumes from the nearby table, which displayed his company's logo on its cover: two rams butting heads.

I couldn't help but wonder what he really thought of my question, though. I knew he was smart and obviously steeped in Jung, but what did he really think of astrology? It would be a while before I'd have the answer to that.

Laurence

A year or two after that conversation, in 1994, I was invited to speak at a gathering of astrologers in the San Francisco area. It was my first astrology conference, so this was an important event for me. The woman organizing the affair, Barbara Morgan, asked if I wouldn't mind sharing a hotel room with another astrologer—Laurence Hillman, son of James. I told her that I'd be delighted to.

There was definitely something karmic taking place, I felt, because from the first moment we met, it was almost like long-lost brothers reuniting after a long separation. I'd only experienced something like that once before, with my college friend, Bill Hogan. This was Laurence's first astrological conference too, and we wound up spending our free time together over that weekend.

He was nine years younger than me, clearly intelligent, and just as clearly sensitive. There was a vague similarity between our ancestries, since we both had Scandinavian roots on our mother's side and Germanic roots on our father's (my father's family having originally hailed from the south of France, but resettled in Germany, courtesy of Napoleon's army). Laurence explained over wine and tiramisu that first night how he was raised in Switzerland and later emigrated to St. Louis, where he studied architecture and business. Unlike me, he was multilingual, spoke five languages, but he was also fluent in the language of the stars, which is where we connected.

That conference took place during a turning point in both of our lives. I was finishing up my first book and would be heading

to Egypt for the first time in just a few days, and Laurence's second daughter had been born a few days before the conference.
(Childbirth = a portent of new beginnings?) Over the next few
years, we'd spend countless hours at his home in St. Louis, discussing astrology, watching movies, going for walks, and mulling
over our various victories and heartbreaks. I was impressed at
how talented he was in so many areas where I definitely wasn't,
like cooking, carpentry, computers, business, and last but definitely not least, marriage. His home in St. Louis, nestled amongst
trees and enlivened with mythical statues on his property, always
felt a bit like an archetypal world all of its own to me.

Father and Son

He explained how his mother introduced him to an astrologer when he was a teenager, and from there began studying the subject with a nearly obsessive interest.

But I was also surprised by how much James himself seemed to know about the subject. On one occasion, Laurence called to ask if I would speak with the two of them about a horoscope they were studying. Rather than have to dumb down complexities in order to be understood, I could tell James understood everything I said, no matter how subtle or obscure. He obviously knew more about the topic than he let on in books or public lectures and interviews, and I felt sure that his psychological theories, like Carl Jung's, were more than a little influenced by astrology. That was particularly clear when it came to his "polytheistic" approach to psychology, which looks at the psyche as being populated by an inner pantheon of gods and goddesses, not unlike the role played by planets in an ordinary horoscope.

But just as obviously to me, Laurence's knowledge of astrology went considerably further than his, and I sensed that influenced James in certain ways. One example was his understanding of "calling," that inner sense of a larger purpose or meaning that draws one forward in life towards fulfillment or wholeness, as is indicated in certain ways by the horoscope. Were James Hillman's famous writings about the "soul's code" somehow influenced by Laurence's thoughts about calling? I thought it was more than likely.

During those early years of our friendship, Laurence lived a double life of sorts, cultivating his interest in astrology while simultaneously working as an environmental inspector, monitoring buildings and private homes for toxins. Though he was good at that, it didn't feed his soul like astrology. I could tell he was chomping at the bit, eager to pursue his passion for the stars full-time. It was several more years before he crossed that proverbial

Rubicon, but jump he did. Being a triple Capricorn (Sun, Moon, and Ascendant), he knew that to make any real change in the world, it required reaching those in positions of power and influence, since they are the ones steering the ships of state these days. As a result, he eventually expanded his practice from working strictly with individual clients to working with corporations and CEOs, some of them in very high places.

Like many children of famous parents, Laurence worked hard to climb out from beneath his father's shadow. In a light-hearted moment, Laurence and his close friend Richard Olivier, son of actor Laurence Olivier, hilariously discussed starting up an informal group they christened *The Son Also Rises*. The two of them eventually pooled their talents and began constructing programs for businesses and business leaders, incorporating elements from astrology but without using astrological jargon or terminology. I've heard the term "stealth agents of change" used on occasion, and that seemed a fitting way to describe what both Laurence and Richard were doing now.

Toward a More Holistic Astrology
Both philosophically and spiritually, the differences between Laurence and his father were considerable. Though they shared a deeply psychological outlook on things, James was clearly more agnostic about spiritual matters, whereas Laurence was more mystical and openly accepting of ideas like God and the afterlife. In a certain way, I respected that about James, since I knew from his workshops how careful he was to rein in attendees from speculating too casually about matters beyond their direct experience.

But I also saw how much Laurence, like me, had in common with his father's thinking. That hit home for me while talking with Laurence one day as he prepared to deliver a lecture at a conference dedicated to his father's work. Unlike some traditional schools of psychology, which regard patients as having "problems" that need curing, all in service of creating a more "well-adjusted" personality, James took a more holistic and nonjudgmental view, which honored all the aspects of the personality. This includes listening to the seemingly problematic or darker impulses of our nature for what they might have to tell us.

It dawned on me that was essentially the same approach Laurence and I used when interpreting horoscopes. In older astrological texts, one sometimes finds simplistic interpretations for certain patterns such that Saturn/Mars contacts are "bad" or "evil," say, while Jupiter/Venus contacts are "good," and so on. Very black-or-white, very cut-and-dried. But in more recent times, a growing number of astrologers have moved towards a more nonjudgmental approach, trying to view even the most seemingly negative energies in someone's horoscope as playing some role in their life and deserving their own place at the table. As a result, it's not so much a matter of simply curing a client's problems as it is of helping them better understand their inner cast of characters and perhaps redirecting their energies in more constructive or holistic ways.

Here's an example. Imagine if early in his career, film director Ingmar Bergman had gone to an astrologer trained in the more black-and-white, "curative" approach of some earlier schools. The astrologer might well have looked at the difficult energies in Bergman's horoscope and suggested ways of "fixing" them in order to make Bergman a more positive, well-adjusted individual. The astrologer might have even suggested that the director devote his energies toward making brighter, sunnier films! Unfortunately, that approach would probably have deprived Bergman of the depth that eventually made his movies the great studies into human nature and life they are, like *The Seventh Seal*. There were valuable ores to be mined from those seemingly dark veins in Bergman's imaginal landscape.

In other words, what initially seems to be negative or unpleasant in someone's personality may actually hold great gifts when understood properly. That doesn't mean there aren't improvements to be made, of course, simply that this shouldn't mean overlooking or even denying the potential talents or strengths that lie buried in those seeming faults. As an astrologer, I've come to see how vital it is to look at *all* the elements in someone's horoscope in as balanced and holistic a way as possible, to better understand what role they might play in that individual's life and growth.

This holistic perspective is precisely the one both Laurence and I take when studying horoscopes. Besides us, though, it represents a profound sea change in how many astrologers are approaching their craft nowadays. This way of thinking is encapsulated in a quote from the poet Rainer Maria Rilke that Laurence often uses in his letters and lectures, and which I often use myself:

"If my devils are to leave me, I am afraid my angels will take flight as well."

CHAPTER 39

EVERY MOMENT ~ AROUND THE WORLD IN NINETY DAYS

In the fall of 1982, I traveled around the world for three months, armed with whatever I could fit into a backpack or wear on my body. I had just turned thirty, and as I described in *The Sky Stretched Out Before Me*, this period had been one of profound anxiety for me, when I was desperate to find some direction and meaning in my life. I'd experienced repeated failures trying to get my life off the ground, both personally and professionally, and hoped that traveling might somehow open me up to new possibilities or ideas, or at least pull me out of the rut I was in. I'd done some extensive traveling through the American Southwest earlier that same year (described in my earlier book) and was now set to tackle an even broader journey. I'd saved up for these trips but also received a sum of money from a recently deceased relative and decided to use it up on traveling that year.

I was at the tail end of my first Saturn return, and now Uranus was moving in to shake up my horoscope in an unsettling way as well. But in addition to my own planetary energies, there was the heavy-handed Pluto/Saturn conjunction pressing its heavy boot down on the entire planet that year. That one concerned me, since it would be climaxing while I was on the road. Though I knew it could have some positive effects, I was well aware that combo could be a tough one, no doubt about it. Did it indicate serious problems or possibly even dangers cropping up for me during the trip? I asked a colleague knowledgeable about astrology for his objective opinion. He replied, "Well, it may simply mean the trip could be a bit grueling for you, or there may be a few obstacles along the way. But I wouldn't worry about it too much." I decided to take his advice.

My plan was to stay in the cheapest lodgings I could find in each area I visited, or perhaps even sleep under the stars, if necessary (which only happened two nights out of the entire trip, it turned out). I'd fly from place to place, or use trains and busses. I settled on the specific destinations I chose by looking through various "alternative" travel brochures or that I'd read about in books, and planned my itinerary around the most dramatic natural or historic sites I could find in each country.

The trip, not surprisingly, didn't achieve everything I hoped for in that quest for meaning, but it was nonetheless a profound experience, especially in widening my perspective on both the world and myself. There's a line from Emerson to the effect that "the mind, once stretched by a new idea, never returns to its original dimensions." This trip stretched my mind in quite a few ways. But some of the perspective I gained was of a different sort altogether, for which I owe a debt of gratitude to an elderly Japanese artist I'd cross paths with in Kyoto.

England

September 1982

As the jet began its descent, I could just make out the rolling green contours of the countryside below through a thin veil of fog. I'd been overseas before, but never to England. There's a unique feeling which courses through your bones the first time you enter a new country, and I had that sensation coming into England. In this case, I felt it as a blend of the pastoral and the Celtic, infused with an unmistakable sense of antiquity.

I took the long train ride into London and followed the crowds out onto its streets. Making my way around the city, I was intrigued by the subtle differences between American and English society—the language, the subtle mannerisms, and of course the ambience of history throughout the region and its architecture. It felt a bit like moving through a parallel dimension of sorts, with little details here and there different from what I knew back in the States.

I frequented some of the conventional tourist stops, but after a few days was compelled to venture out to other parts of the country, visiting sites I'd long heard about. After a brief stop at Stonehenge, which was far smaller than I expected, I traveled by bus to Glastonbury. This was a spot I dreamt of visiting, not only because it was a focal point for some important legends but because of something Goswami Kriyananda said to me before I left the U.S. He'd traveled a great deal during his life, and I asked him what places he'd most recommend in the countries I said I'd be visiting. When it came to England, he quickly answered, "Glastonbury," saying it had a "very unique vibration." I wanted to check it out for myself.

The Glastonbury "Tor," England.

I was put off by the encroaching commercialism of the small town, but I was entranced by the adjoining landscape and its monuments, especially Glastonbury Tor. This is a hill on the outskirts of town atop which sits the remnants of an ancient stone tower. As dark approached and the winds gathered strength, I climbed up the grassy sides to the top of the hill, where I stood completely alone, looking out over the surrounding countryside. Whatever the source or the reason, there was indeed an energy about this spot which left me feeling almost like I was straddling dimensions.

From there I made my way by train over to Hastings, site of the great battle of 1066 between the invading Normans and the resident Anglo-Saxons—a conflict that decided the future of Western civilization in some ways. The site was out of the way for me, but I decided to visit it because of a surprising synchronicity that happened several weeks earlier, which I recounted in *The Sky Stretched Out before Me.*

I'd been standing in line at my local bank, debating silently whether to add Hastings to my itinerary, when I suddenly noticed the address on the check in the hand of the man in line before me, which I could see while he scratched the back of his head. The number was 1066. That was surprising enough, but no less astonishing was the name emblazoned across the check: Norman Wave.

To my surprise, the battlefield exuded a sense of peace and quiet, which made it hard picturing the vast carnage that took place here at one time. Later on, I explored the ruins of a castle near the ocean, and decided to lie down and rest for a bit. For a brief moment, I faded in and out of sleep, when I unexpectedly heard a voice speaking as if out of nowhere: "Fear of Saxon power." That was all. I have no idea whether this was simply an impression picked up from the environment or just a fantasy. What I do know is, it was loud, and uttered in a voice I didn't recognize at all.

India

A few days later, on September 8, I caught a flight out of England and headed towards Asia. After England, India offered a tidal wave of exotic new impressions, from the brightly colored fabrics and powders displayed in the marketplaces to the disfigured faces of beggar children coming up to me on the streets. I heard an American once describe this as a "dirty" country because of all the garbage, dust, and grime, yet in some ways those elements imbue this country with more life and authenticity than many comparatively antiseptic communities back in the U.S. In a word, it felt *real*.

I spent a month in India altogether, and while it was a remarkable experience, it also tested my patience more than I expected. Especially difficult was the frustration I experienced dealing with the merchants and vendors in the larger cities. I learned that lesson the hard way my first night stepping off the plane, when the taxi driver I hailed charged me roughly ten times what I should have rightly paid, and I was just too tired to tell the difference. One has to be on one's toes and very tough simply to survive here, I could tell, and it led me to write a friend back home saying that "India is a crash course in assertiveness training."

Yet the more time I spent away from the big cities and in the rural areas, I more I noticed that the people seemed gentler and kinder. When I mentioned that to an Indian immigrant back in the U.S. several months later, he laughed and said, "Do you think it's really any different for foreigners in America when they to come to big cities like Chicago or New York?" Point well taken. Large cities everywhere can be rough-and-tumble for the sensitive soul.

The Taj Mahal

I found the historic sites, from Fatehpur Sikri and the Taj Mahal to Bodh Gaya, astonishing in their scale and beauty. The wealth and opulence that characterized this country in earlier times is hard to envision now. I found the swarming masses of people in these areas invigorating. Wandering the side streets at dusk felt magical to me, with everything slightly aglow in shades of leathery brown and gray, with the smell of food and wood-burning stoves heavy in the air. Wherever I went, I gravitated toward the older parts of towns, with their shops and colorful bazaars tucked away from more modernized quarters. On several nights, I stumbled onto impromptu performances being acted out on side streets, with locals playing parts in one religious tale or another.

Conversing with some of the locals, I found it interesting to learn how many in this country viewed America as a kind of utopia, a fantasy land where dreams naturally come true—an impression surely gathered from our TV shows and movies. But I spoke with one fellow who had traveled to the U.S., and he made a comment that caught my attention: he said he thought that Americans were somewhat "selfish." When I asked him to explain, he said, "In America you can't just drop in on people unannounced. They feel it's an imposition to arrive that way. But in India, you do that all the time, and it's no problem."

In Calcutta I walked the streets for hours, simply taking in the sights and marveling at the astonishing poverty. While walking through one fairly dilapidated marketplace, I noticed a curious thing. I came upon a street vendor selling paperback books, most of them in English. Only about forty titles in all were displayed, yet four of those were by authors from my small home town back in Illinois—Oak Park. Ernest Hemingway, Edgar Rice Burroughs, Richard Bach, and Andrew Greeley. That seemed odd, considering that such a small community would be so disproportionately represented on a bookstand thousands of miles away.

I knew that Calcutta was the home of Mother Teresa's mission, and it wasn't hard to find. Though I knew it might be difficult to meet the grand old lady herself, I decided to go inside anyway and speak to one of the representatives. I was escorted to a room with a somewhat intimidating nun in a habit sitting behind a desk, who looked up at me over lowered glasses with a slightly skeptical gaze. I said that I admired the work they did there, and if they needed a hand with anything, I would be happy to lend my assistance. She was very curt in her response, stating that if I really wanted to help, I should just take a walk on the streets outside for a few hours and look around.

I was taken aback at how abrupt she was, but thinking about it later, I realized how naive I was walking in there as I did. She had clearly grown weary of traveling Westerners dropping in and offering their help for a day or two, probably for no reason other than the prestige of having done service at Mother Theresa's center in Calcutta. *Humanitarian chic,* you might call it. A year or two after this trip, I happened to spot a photo in a Chicago newspaper of former California governor Jerry Brown helping out at this same Calcutta mission, which showed him carrying a dying person from one bed to another. There was talk of him considering a run for the presidency around that time, and there was something slightly disturbing to me about this very high-profile display of service. After all, how was it that someone just happened to be there at that moment to photograph that scene? Since then, I've tended to be considerably more impressed by acts of selflessness performed away from the spotlight.

I spent time in Benares visiting my friend Scott, whom I knew from back in Illinois. He'd been in India for two years by this point, completing his PhD in Sanskrit, and had married a beautiful local woman named Roma, an accomplished classical singer and dancer. They lived in a small apartment in the heart of the city, and over the course of a week he showd me to numerous sites both in and around Benares. At one point he took me to see a couple of home-grown Indian movies, one of which was a conventional Bollywood romance, the other a four-hour depiction of the Hindu epic the *Bhagavad Gita.*

Scott's own field of academic study was in comparative religion. Before walking into the theater, we spoke about the differences between world religions and their various mythologies, rather than their similarities, as Joseph Campbell tended to emphasize. That point became clear to me while watching the movie version of the *Bhagavad Gita,* which depicted Krishna as a sort of self-assured playboy, capable of great acts of violence. Whenever he killed one of his enemies, the audience cheered its approval. This was all quite different from the image of Jesus

I'd grown up with as a child—although it wasn't quite so different from the Old Testament stories I was taught back in grade school (stories born during the same Aries Age that gave us the *Bhagavad Gita*, as a matter of fact).

Unlike many other Westerners coming to India, I wasn't drawn there to find a spiritual teacher, since I felt I already had some formidable ones back home. By the time I arrived, I'd been studying for ten years with teachers in the Kriya Yoga lineage, which is a branch of spiritual philosophy and meditation practices brought to the U.S. by Paramahansa Yogananda. One of the key teachers in that lineage (and Yogananda's guru's guru) was a fellow named Lahiri Mahasaya, who lived in this city back during the late 1800s and whose home still stands there. That house was the site of a few stories in Yogananda's famous book *Autobiography of a Yogi*, so I was interested in seeing it, if possible.

Scott had visited there once himself, and spent some time talking with the current owner, the grandson of that original guru. One evening Scott decided to take me there. After we'd gotten lost on the dark side streets and alleyways of Benares, a patriarchal-looking gentleman sporting a white robe and beard stepped out from the shadows of a doorway saying, "Can I help you?" When Scott explained who we were looking for, the man causally said, "Oh, yes, that is me you are looking for. You're welcome to come to my house." It turned out he had seen us wandering aimlessly down those side streets and decided to follow us and see if we were indeed searching for his grandfather's home.

We sat in the courtyard at the center of his house and spoke for three hours about a wide range of spiritual matters. He certainly fit the mold of a classical guru, and seemed both highly intelligent and sincere in his demeanor. When Scott informed him that I'd never taken on a guru myself, he seemed much impressed by that. He himself had been an active practitioner of Kriya Yoga since childhood, and made a number of interesting comments about spiritual disciplines in general. Among them was the idea that while techniques have their place, they aren't as important as one's underlying sincerity. "Open yourself to God, if that works for you," he said; "that's what really counts."

His most controversial comments involved the legacy of Yogananda and the organization he founded in California, called Self-Realization Fellowship, or SRF. To my surprise, he was critical of Yogananda and the fact that Yogananda went public in forming a large center. His own grandfather, Lahiri, laid down strict guidelines regarding the precepts of Kriya Yoga if one hoped to become an initiate. These included such things as meditating six hours a day—three in the morning, three at night. Also, one should never accept money for spiritual teachings, never seek fame, and never, *ever* announce your spiritual path publicly.

By Lahiri's standards, Yogananda struck out on all of those counts. The grandson suggested that Yogananda diluted the techniques of Kriya Yoga when he brought them to the West. He was clearly bothered by the way SRF touted itself as the only authorized outlet for Kriya Yoga teachings anywhere in the world. In fact, he pointed out, there were *many* legitimate teachers and heirs to this tradition, who are in no way affiliated with that organization. That was actually something I already knew through my own teachers, Goswami Kriyananda and Shelly Trimmer, who were not affiliated with SRF.

I sympathized with him on some of these points, especially the last one, but I came away thinking he was probably a bit too severe in his judgments. By analogy, I'm sure the Buddha's teachers were none too happy when he broke away from traditional Hinduism to forge his own religious path, but that doesn't mean he was necessarily bastardizing the teachings. The teachings evolve and change through time, and must adapt to new environments. In that vein, Yogananda did what may well have been necessary to bring Kriya Yoga to the West. The fact that he changed some things along the way was not, in itself, necessarily a bad thing, I thought.

Throughout our conversation, Lahiri's grandson seemed calm and down-to-earth. His compassion was obvious, and before we left I offered to give him some money, which he refused. Before leaving, he showed us around the house, specifically the areas mentioned in Yogananda's autobiography, such as Lahiri's meditation room.

The next morning, I went down before dawn to the Ganges to watch devotees perform their rituals in the river's shallows, while bodies burned on funeral pyres further downstream.

Ladakh

Technically this region is part of India now, but its remote location in the Himalayas makes it seem like a world unto itself, both in culture and geography. It looks exactly as I would expect Tibet to look, and the two countries are in fact closely related in every way, although separated by an imposed political border between India and China.

The flight up to Ladakh was frightening at times, with our prop plane rising 11,000 feet in just forty-five minutes and the turbulence growing worse the higher we ascended. We finally swooped down between craggy mountain peaks and hit the runway, the plane landing with such force that all the oxygen masks dropped down from their compartments. One of the passengers behind me started vomiting.

Mother and child, Ladakh

Stepping out of the plane felt like heading back in time to a world unlike any I'd seen before. This area had only been opened to tourists for a couple of years, so it still enjoyed traditional clothing and customs dating back hundreds, perhaps even thousands of years. I wanted to come here before it changed with the inevitable onslaught of tourism—which is pretty much what happened in the years that followed.

This had been a largely agrarian culture, with minimal exposure to outside cultures or technologies, and the pace of life seemed extremely slow. The locals were dressed in the type of colorful medieval garb one associates with classical Tibetans, right down to their unique hats with upturned side flaps. It was all unspeakably exotic to me; but then, I'm sure the culture of the United States would seem exotic to the men and women of this area.

Tiksey Monastery, Ladakh

The surrounding area looked almost like moonscape, indescribably barren yet beautiful in its own stark way, all set against the deepest blue sky I'd ever seen. I spent the first few hours climbing around on rocks and hills near the main hub of town, called Leh. In retrospect, it was probably nothing short of miraculous I didn't come down with the same altitude sickness several others who flew in with me did, and whom I heard moaning and vomiting in adjoining rooms throughout the night.

I spent the next several days heading out by bus to various monasteries and temples located in the outlying regions, generally built into the sides of hills and rocky outcrops. Tiksey Monastery was especially striking to me in the ambience of its design and surrounding landscape. The monks seemed somewhat savvy to the emerging tourist game, and I sensed they were gearing up their chants just as two or three of us from the bus began wandering up the dirt path to the main entrance. One year later I recognized the inside of that monastery in the Bill Murray film *The Razor's Edge*, which was partly shot in this region.

The austere landscape of this region evoked something profound in me. At one point while walking across the lush carpet of green grass in one valley between neighboring monasteries, I actually fell to my knees and cried in sheer gratitude over the chance to experience such beauty as this. That evening I lay on my bed in the lodge back in Leh, the windows wide open, the soft mountain breeze blowing through as stars began to glisten in the sky. I could hear the sound of local farmers singing as they returned home from the fields, cowbells clanging softly. I felt in awe of life and its incomprehensible richness.

Inside Tiksey Monstery

The Road to Shangri-La

I wanted to go from Ladakh to Kashmir, and had the option of either flying on a prop plane or traveling overland by bus. On learning it took a full two days by bus versus one hour by plane,

I decided to take the overland route so that I could truly experience the area up close. I was told by a fellow traveler that the bus ride was more spectacular, but considerably more dangerous.

The bus was crowded with locals and other young travelers like myself. The Muslim driver prayed extensively before we departed, triggering some nervous jokes amongst the Westerners on board. As the bus made its slow, wheezing ascent up the winding road out of Leh, the scenery became even more stark and craggy than before. The road became so narrow at times that there was barely enough room for the wheels of the bus to fit. I remarked to the young Aussie seated next to me how treacherous this all looked. Having traveled this route before, he replied, "Oh, this is nothing. Wait until tomorrow!"

We spent the night in a small village called Kargil, and the next day my Aussie compatriot's prediction turned out to be right. The unpaved road became so bad at points, with large potholes strewn along it, that the bus slowly teetered from side to side, allowing passengers to stare out the windows straight down a few thousand feet into the gaping valley below.

It was at that point that nervous laughter gave way to genuinely frightened silence, as I overheard someone remark that at least six tourist busses are lost each year on this road. I hoped he might be exaggerating, but just moments later we came upon the broken wreckage of another bus that had plummeted from a point higher up on the mountainside. We all got out and silently examined the pieces of twisted metal and broken wood that littered the road and extended all the way down the side of the valley thousands of feet. It looked fresh, but there were no bodies, and the driver said they must have retrieved them during the previous days.

Examining bus wreckage on the road between
Ladakh and Kashmir, India

When we finally made it through the most dangerous parts of the pass, there was much joking and jubilation amongst the passengers, though the driver seemed unfazed by it all. The scenery changed radically as we drew closer to Kashmir, as the barren moonscape morphed into Swiss alpine–like vistas, streaming with beautiful rivers and valleys. Even the locals looked radically different than in Ladakh, dressed in distinctly Muslim-style garb.

We arrived finally at the capital or Kashmir, Srinigar. Some writers have suggested that the name *Shangri-La* may have well come from this very route we had traveled on, as an abbreviation of *Srinigar-Leh* (with the name Shangri-La itself having come from James Hilton's 1933 novel *Lost Horizon*). It's easy to understand why that might be so, judging from the sheer beauty and remoteness of the region. To my surprise, the city of Srinigar was extremely polluted, but there was an oasis of beauty nestled in its midst. In the heart of the city there is an exquisite spot called Dal Lake, with lotus paddies blanketing the water and mountains as a backdrop. Upon arriving at the water's edge, I could see innumerable houseboats with ornate decorations lined up in the water. I finally settled on one of the houseboats, roughly the size of a mobile home, and paid for a two-night stay.

The view from Dal Lake, Kashmir

The next morning I awoke to the dreamlike sound of thousands of chanting voices cascading throughout the predawn darkness. At first, I was confused, but eventually realized it was Muslim worshippers in all their houseboats sending out morning prayers across the waters.

That day I explored the city and surrounding area, and eventually paid a taxi to drive me up to an outlying region, a considerable distance from the city. There I went by horseback into the mountains along the Pakistan border, led by a local guide that I hired.

Yet the longer I stayed in this area, the more I found the locals to be even more aggressive than the city merchants of Delhi, so I was only too happy after two days to leave the area and continue on with my trip.

Nepal

Flying into Kathmandu, I could see the white-capped Himalayan peaks coming into view through the airplane windows. Kathmandu is the capital of Nepal, and displays a unique blend of cultural influences from both Asia and Europe, a sort of "Amsterdam of the East." I came here to hike through the outlying foothills and mountains of the region, which I had fantasized about for years since seeing images of it in magazines while just a teenager.

After exploring Kathmandu for several days and then procuring a trekking permit, I caught a bus and a taxi to the small town of Pokhara, from which some of the major hikes originated. At stops along the way, local children rushed up to the car and try to sell us vegetables or trinkets.

Having arrived at Pokhara, I decided to travel solo through the mountains rather than hire a Sherpa to carry my backpack, since I wanted the solitude to be alone with my thoughts along the way. I spent the next thirteen days making my way through the valleys and hills adjoining the Himalayas, in the region of the Annapurna mountain range.

I was surprised to discover how much of the country consisted of green valleys and humid junglelike terrain rather than the rugged mountain ranges I'd seen in pictures. The hiking trails weave up and down through the green valleys and hills directly adjacent to the towering Himalayas, and the contrast between the two geographies was dramatic—the lush greenery set against the stark black and blue whiteness of the Annapurnas.

I was lucky coming here when I did, because on my first day of hiking, the sky cleared and the monsoon season abruptly came to an end. As I was hiking in on that first leg of the trail, I crossed paths with two Englishmen on their way out who had just finished a thirty-day trek and were lamenting how disappointed they were. Why? Because the region had been blanketed in heavy clouds throughout their entire trip—until this, their very last day of trekking. They hadn't caught even a glimpse of the towering mountains until their trip was essentially over.

Each day I made my way up and down the narrow trails, sometimes over rocks and boulders, and at night I slept in one of the rustic huts situated along the pathways, where the locals rent out extra beds to travelers. The sights were breathtaking, from the terraced valleys and hidden waterfalls to the brilliant white snows of the Annapurnas. Sunrises and sunsets were spectacular. But the hiking was difficult: if one doesn't schedule departure times in this region carefully, one runs the risk of hiking up the steep valley grades in direct sunlight, which makes for tortuous trekking in the heat and humidity.

Along the trekking path, Nepal

At various stops along the way I engaged in conversations with other travelers. There was a Japanese climber who had previously been part of an expedition up Mt. Everest, which was beset by bad weather and killed nine of his fellow expedition members. Then there was the twenty-four-year-old German girl I met who at that age had already hitchhiked her way through South America, the U.S. (including Alaska), Canada, India, and Europe. I met more than a few like her on my trip, and it effectively absolved me of any illusions I might have regarding how adventurous my own trip really was. By their standards, my meager three-month journey seemed timid.

Then there were the local villagers, who were miserably poor and presented a sobering contrast to the comparatively wealthy Westerners hiking through their small hamlets. Some of the children were obviously sick, and a few were even disfigured from one disease or another. At one point an earnest young man told me they didn't have doctors in most of these villages and asked if I would send a specific general aid medical text to him when I returned to America. I promised I would, and made good on that promise several months later.

On the last few days of my trek, I began to feel unusually weak. Then one morning, while sleeping in a village called Dhampus, I awoke with a sense of unease in my stomach that became severe. I felt an overpowering urge to relieve myself and dashed outside in a state of near panic, giving my bowels free rein behind some bushes. I felt ill and dizzy, and began to wonder how I was going to make it down out of the mountains.

I packed up my things and began stumbling down the path that led back to Pokhara. Two young Germans passed me on the way; their names were Rainer and Frederich, and they could clearly see from my staggered walk I wasn't well. Rainer kindly offered to carry my pack by placing it atop his own, which was a huge help. But I grew dizzier as time went by, and we needed to stop frequently so I could catch my breath or run off into the bushes to relieve myself.

The two young Germans who helped me make my way down out of the mountains, with Rainer (closest to the camera) carrying my backpack atop his own.

To help take my mind off of my body, they engaged me in discussions about politics, travel, even philosophy. I happened to mention that I'd just starting working on a book about synchronicity and coincidence (which became *The Waking Dream*). Rainer, the older of the two young men, said he was skeptical of the notion that coincidences might have any real significance. Yet after talking for a bit longer, he admitted to experiencing some strange things himself over the years. When I asked him for an example, he related the following astonishing story.

One day a colleague of his unexpectedly asked if he wanted to accompany him on a trip to America for a week's stay in L.A. His friend's girlfriend had suddenly backed out of a trip they had planned, and he figured he'd let someone else use the ticket to keep him company, so he asked Rainer.

The two of them flew to Los Angeles, where they stayed at the home of a colleague who had moved to the U.S. One afternoon, while Rainer was hanging out in this upscale house by himself, the doorbell rang. He went to the door and opened it to find one of his closest friends from back in Germany standing there. They stared at each other in shock. It turned out neither one of them knew the other was traveling to the United States; his friend also had an unexpected opportunity to travel to the U.S., also to Los Angeles, just like Rainer. While driving around the city one afternoon, that friend became lost and out of desperation decided to go up to a random house and ask for directions—only to discover his old friend Rainer answering the door. As they say, you can't make this sort of thing up.

Rainer and Frederick helped me make my way back down to Pokhara, and from there I traveled back to Kathmandu. At a medical center in town, I had a cursory medical test, which proved inconclusive. The doctor told me I could obtain a more thorough diagnosis in Calcutta, back in India.

Once in Calcutta, I went to a hospital and waited along with hundreds of locals to receive attention. I won't forget the sight there: a sea of faces all quietly awaiting help for their ailments or for their children's ailments. I felt extremely uncomfortable being given preferential treatment by the doctors, who ushered me to the front of the line, visiting foreigner that I was, but I was simply too weak to negotiate or protest the point with anyone. The doctor there determined that I had giardia, a parasite that afflicts many campers and hikers, usually contracted from water that's insufficiently boiled and loaded with bugs passed down through animal urine deposited upstream. He gave me some medicine in the form of black pellets that resembled rabbit droppings, but it didn't help. The condition plagued me the rest of my trip, and for much of the following year.

The Philippines

I was determined to visit China as part of my trip, but it had only been opened to tourists for a short while. I heard that getting around on one's own could be very difficult, so before leaving on my trip I decided to book passage on a three-week tour that would cover the key locations I wanted to visit in that large country. But I'd have to meet up with the tour group in the Philippines, and from there we would depart to Beijing.

I flew to Manila and spent several days exploring the city while waiting for the rest of my group to arrive. My time there was uneventful, except for one episode where I made a foolish decision that could have had serious consequences.

While walking through one of the parks near the hotel, I bumped into a young boy. Speaking in fractured English, he kept trying to tell me about his sister, who was married to an American. They lived nearby, he said, and perhaps I would like to meet them? They'd be honored to have me as a guest, since they get so few Americans dropping by.

It went on like this for two days, and each time I crossed paths with him, I politely declined. But the third time I bumped into him, his older, more mature-looking cousin happened to walk by. The cousin seemed reasonably sane, and he too extended an invitation to come to their family's home. Even though I was slightly skeptical about the setup, I was intrigued by the possibility of getting away from the downtown area and seeing how some of the locals lived. After a few moments of deliberation, I decided to take a chance and go along with them.

The older fellow hailed a taxi, and we proceeded to drive considerably further than I expected through a maze of congested side streets and crowded housing developments. Our promised destination wasn't nearly as close as I'd been led to believe, and after thirty minutes we finally came to a nondescript, square dwelling set tightly amidst many other anonymous homes.

We went inside. I saw no "sister" or "husband" anywhere in sight. Instead, the young man and boy introduced me to another Filipino fellow, as the two disappeared entirely from sight, leaving me alone with this stranger. After some small talk over a cup of tea, he proceeded to describe a scheme he concocted that involved bilking money from a casino in the city, where he now worked as a manager. It entailed a system of hand signals on the part of a dealer he worked with, whereby a lot of money could be made with the help of a willing tourist. Would I be interested, he asked? "You and me—we can be *fartners!*" he said in mangled English. "You would be gone from here the next day with your tour group, so there would be no risk to you. So what do you say? *Do you want to be fartners?*"

The situation quickly felt ominous, since I knew that if I conveyed any sense of worry or disapproval towards his scheme, it could turn ugly. I decided that the best tack would be to show a modicum of interest, politely decline, and then hopefully leave without incident. I said that I simply needed to hear more before I could reach any decision, at which point he let out a loud whistle, and a retractable staircase lowered down from the ceiling.

Descending down its stairs came a thin, sleezy looking man with a pockmarked face and cigarette dangling from his lips. He eyed me cautiously, then sat down with us, as the two of them proceeded to explain the entire operation to me in detail. It specifically involved games of blackjack, and they said that if I wanted to take part, I could walk away with 25 percent of the take.

I didn't want them to think I would go to the authorities about their scheme, so I decided to call their bluff and pray that they didn't take the bait. I said, "I would need to get at least 50 percent of the take; otherwise it just wouldn't be worth the risk."

They were slightly taken aback, and even a little upset by my counteroffer, but eventually upped their proposed percentage to 40 percent. I maintained my stance on percentages, seriously hoping they wouldn't agree to it. After going back and forth about this for several minutes, they became exasperated, or at least acted as like they were, and we finally agreed to disagree. They gave each other a very piercing look, and curtly showed me the door.

Whereupon I found myself back out on the street, with no idea whatsoever where I was or how to get back to the hotel. There was no one nearby who could speak English, but I eventually found someone about a half mile away who gave me garbled instructions for bus routes back to the center of the city, and two hours later I finally arrived at the hotel. There I met up with the rest of my tour group I'd be joining for our China excursion.

China

At thirty, I was easily the youngest member of this tour group, which consisted primarily of elderly American couples and various second or third-generation Chinese-Americans hoping to visit their ancestral homeland at least once in their lifetimes. I was feeling weak from my lingering illness, and as we flew into Beijing I was more exhausted than excited over the prospect of traveling this country I'd dreamt about for years. Our itinerary was to include a wide range of cities, including Beijing, Xian, Guangzhou, Suzhou, Guilin, Canton, Shanghai, and Hong Kong. It was an extraordinary constellation of locations, yet I felt overwhelmed by the enormity of it all, and wasn't confident my body could hold up well. I knew that Saturn and Pluto were coming together in the sky right then, and I certainly seemed to be feeling it.

But over the next few days, I found myself increasingly mesmerized, even transformed, by the extraordinary richness of Chinese culture, with all its emotional depth and aesthetic subtleties. My bodily concerns faded in the face of all that. My first impression on arriving in Beijing involved the striking uniformity of all its citizens, since everyone was dressed in blue uniforms. There were virtually no cars, other than a few official vehicles, with the vast majority of citizens riding bikes.

The tipping point came for me during the performance of a Chinese ballet our group attended based on the famous Chinese tale "The Dream of the Red Room." I've never been particularly drawn toward dance as an art form, certainly not ballet, but this was dramatically different from anything I'd seen before. The entire production was stunningly arrayed, with colors and set designs that ignited my imagination. I sat there with tears running down my cheeks over what I was seeing and hearing, but when I turned to look at the other members of my tour, most were falling asleep in their seats. But then, they were likely dealing with a more dramatic form of jet lag than I was, since I'd been inching my way across the globe rather than all at once.

That became the start of a love affair I was to have with this country over those next few weeks. Every day it seemed as though I was confronted with some new site or performance that affected me in a deep way. China was a country of massive contradictions, I knew, but the fact of its problematic government in 1982 nearly seemed irrelevant in the face of that long cultural legacy. In fact, I even came to think that its relative isolation from much of the West over previous decades, due to its politics, was largely responsible for the country's retaining many of those older cultural forms that wouldn't have survived in a more progressive climate.

Like Ladakh, China had never really entered the modern world, and as I traveled through its cities I felt as though I could sense some of the powerful atmosphere that characterized it for thousands of years, and which would likely be soon lost with the advent of modernization. I referred earlier to something called the *spirit of place*, and it felt to me like that quality there extended back into the dimmest recesses of time. It was a sense of something ancient, a quality I glimpsed in equal measure while traveling through Egypt years later. In China, though, it struck me as having a certain *feminine* quality about it, which perhaps had something to do with the lush vegetation of its geography and the curved lines of its art and architecture.

A canal in Suzhou, China

To better taste the flavor of the country, I made an effort whenever possible to break away from the group and travel on my own to out-of-the-way locations, even if that just meant meandering down side streets and observing people going about their daily business. A few times, I went to movie theaters or musical performances where I could sit and watch shows shoulder-to-shoulder with the locals. It was strangely exhilarating to be the only Westerner in an audience composed solely of Chinese citizens. Though I never understood a word of what was being said up on the screen or stage, I enjoyed soaking up the regional ambience, since it was uniquely different from what I knew in America or Europe.

In the city of Xian, I sat with a group of students in the balcony of an old movie theater for a double-bill presentation, all of them dressed in their customary blue uniforms. The first movie was a thunderously dull state-sponsored documentary on food production, which no one in the audience paid the slightest attention to as they chattered amongst themselves. After the novelty of my presence wore off, the students resumed their animated conversations, frequently stopping to spit on the floor every minute or two. Spitting was very big in this country, that was obvious.

Suzhou, China

Then, with the start of the main movie feature, a romantic story set in Hong Kong, they all went silent and leaned forward in their seats *en masse*, eager to catch a glimpse of life in the modern world beyond their borders. At that moment I realized these people were starving for information about the outside world, and these Hong Kong films—however superficial in form—served as their umbilical cord to that universe, and to modern life itself. It helped me better understand that these people were not simply faceless cheerleaders for Mao but flesh-and-blood humans with many of the same core interests as everyone else on the planet.

Though I relished seeing the more traditional sights, I found some of the reminders from older China more unsettling. On one of my forays I saw an elderly woman struggling to make her way down the street, being helped by a younger woman. When I looked down, I saw that her tiny feet had once been tightly bound, as had been the custom in old China. It must have been a torturously painful procedure for women of that era, and some, like this woman, still contended with its sad legacy in her final years.

While we were there in Xian, our group paid a visit to the large hangar which houses the terra-cotta statues of soldiers from two thousand years earlier. It's a magnificent archeological site, yet on that day the real action seemed to be taking place just outside, since a Chinese film company was shooting a movie on the premises. They needed some tourists as extras to walk by the camera for one scene. A few of those in our group were asked to partake, to which we happily complied. As a result, somewhere in the vaults of a Chinese film studio lies the footage of my big screen debut.

In Guilin, we sailed downstream past the towering limestone formations that rise up out of the Earth along the river's banks, and which have featured prominently in Chinese drawings and paintings for thousands of years. I'd seen images of these formations years earlier, and dreamt of visiting this region—and now here I was, my wish having come true. That night I walked out by myself to a vantage point along the river to see the limestone formations looming up beneath the full moon.

Guilin, China

When we finally arrived in Hong Kong to close off our trip, it was like moving forward in time a good fifty years, because of that city's advanced technology and modern values. Yet even here, there were stark contrasts, and as I walked from our five-star hotel through some of Hong Kong's side streets, I was greeted by the sight of vendors hawking everything from snake meat to carved elephant ivories.

Japan

Upon arriving in Tokyo, I was startled by its neon wilderness and struggled to find my way around the sprawling maze of subway and elevated trains. To my surprise, I managed to find relatively inexpensive lodging from which I could launch my daily expeditions throughout the city.

Stimulated as I was by Tokyo, I found myself growing weary of its high-tech razzle-dazzle, which began to feel like Times

Square transplanted onto Japanese soil. I began craving more traditional sights and sounds, something more in line with the old Japan, and sought that out in more obscure venues. That led me to a beautiful Kabuki performance on the upper floors of an office building; various temple ceremonies, including a fire-walking ceremony at night; and an especially interesting display of traditional dances by performers from around the country in a Tokyo auditorium. I traveled by train for a day to the more traditional city of Kamakura, where I visited various temples in the rain and climbed inside the hollow giant metal statue of the Buddha housed there.

In Kamakura

That piqued my interest further, so at the end of that week I decided to travel to Kyoto, since I had been told that would come closer to showing me the old Japan. I took the bullet train to Kyoto, which had once been the capital of Japan, and submersed myself in that city for a week.

I wasn't prepared for the impact the city would have on me. Kyoto was entirely different from Tokyo, and I now felt I was getting a taste of the real Japan. Just one week earlier, I'd felt sure that no place could move me more than China had; yet here I was, even more awed than I had been there. It didn't seem accidental to me that I'd have some of the most powerful dreams of my life in Kyoto, featuring moments of hyperawareness along with symbolic depictions of the divine—things that normally never figure in my otherwise prosaic dreams.

I felt that much of the extraordinary energy I sensed there must be due to the sheer proliferation of gardens, temples, and shrines that blanket this city, and which collectively confer an aura of spirituality to its environs. I remember reading a story of how John Lennon once came here with wife Yoko and was reduced to tears on visiting some of the temples. That's what happened to me as well.

In my desire to soak up as much of this city as possible, I visited as many of those temples and gardens as I could fit into my schedule. Some of the credit for that local atmosphere should probably also go to the unique zoning laws here, which forbade any new buildings to be taller than the tallest temple. At the same time, I had the ominous feeling it was only a matter of time before progress caught up with this city and wiped clean that extraordinary vibration.

Here in Kyoto, I began to recognize subtle differences between the Japanese and Chinese personality, something I'd never given thought to before. Most Americans tend to see Orientals as being largely the same, but that's certainly not the case. In China, it wasn't unusual for me to see two people arguing on the street, even to the point of coming to blows. But in Japan, public displays of anger or emotion like that were nowhere to be found.

Kamakura, Japan

When I mentioned that to an American who had been living in Japan for several years, he offered an interesting analogy, saying that just as Britain is to America, so Japan is to China. Both Japan and Britain are island cultures, and thus more geographically contained. That sense of physical isolation may well have led both societies to be more restrained in their customs and manners simply for people to cope with one another. By contrast, the sprawling nature of the Chinese and American landscapes gave rise to characters that were more open and expressive. Interesting way to look at it, I thought.

Earlier in the year, my friend Bill Hunt in Illinois had told me of a temple in Kyoto called Myoshinji, which offered weekly Zen meditation sittings that were open to Westerners. As it turned out, their weekly meeting was scheduled the night I arrived in town, so after getting lost on the way there several times, I finally located the group in one of the structures on the temple grounds and nervously proceeded to take part in their meditation session. It was my first experience with Zen meditation, and though I found it difficult keeping my body still for the entire period, it triggered my interest in the methods of this system.

But the highlight of my stay in Kyoto proved to be of a very different sort, and was quite unexpected. Several days earlier, I'd learned of a state-sponsored program that arranged for tourists to visit the homes of local residents in order to experience the culture more directly and personally. I went to the government office in town and applied for this opportunity. When they contacted me the next day to tell me whom I'd be meeting, they said they were assigning me to the home of an elderly local artist, having based their decision on my background in art school. I was secretly a little disappointed, since I actually hoped to spend time with someone more directly involved with Buddhism, like a priest. But when I was told this artist was actually very famous in the country, I became more intrigued.

93-year old artist in front of a recent painting of his of Mt. Fuji

I made my way to the home of the artist, who was ninety-three years old and lived in a ranch-style home that seemed colossal by Japanese standards. He clearly wasn't poor or starving. Along with a young translator assigned to assist with our meeting, he greeted me at the door and began by showing me around his large home. The rooms were a model of tasteful simplicity, most of them with nothing on the walls or floors except plain mats, but the overall effect was deeply moving. He showed me his massive studio space, where I saw several huge canvases on display, including a sprawling painting of Mount Fuji done in a style reminiscent of Georgia O'Keefe. His work was beautiful, and the fact he did such work at his age was inspiring.

We eventually adjourned to a side room of his house, nestled amongst a grove of bamboo trees, where we spent the next few hours discussing art, spirituality, and global culture over tea. He was small in stature, with warm, sparkling eyes, and snow-white hair flowing down around his bald head, his body adorned with an elegant black robe. There was a certain wisdom in his comments that suggested a spiritual practice of some sort. He had traveled widely around the world, including Chicago, Alaska, and the Grand Canyon. He had seen many extraordinary things over the course of his life. But when I asked him what had been the most beautiful thing he'd ever seen, he replied, simply, "Every moment!"

His mind was sharp, his manner friendly. When I left his house, we warmly clasped hands, and I felt privileged at having met this remarkable soul. Sadly, I wrote down his name in a notebook I was traveling with, which I lost that following week. Since then, I've tried to track down his identity, but I've had no luck—though I hold out hope I may still come across that someday.

The next few days, I continued my explorations of Kyoto and its nearby environs, but the exhaustion of the trip, and my health problems, were taking their toll on me. At one point, I was walking through the grounds of an especially beautiful temple complex called Ryoanji, where I sat for a long time contemplating the rock garden on its grounds. It had a curiously hypnotic effect on me, and afterwards I proceeded to walk slowly around the temple grounds as the sun sank lower in the sky. It had been a beautiful autumn day, and as it grew dark, I noticed a young couple from the lodge where I was staying off in some nearby bushes kissing passionately. I'd noticed this woman that same morning before leaving for the day: she was a beautiful Argentinian who caught not only my eye but those of every other young man at the lodge, the straight ones anyway. Seeing the two of them embracing like that triggered a wave of loneliness that swept through me. I made my way back to the lodge and lay in bed that night simply longing to get home.

Rock Garden in Kyoto

Hawaii

After heading back on the bullet train, I caught a flight out of Tokyo back to the States the next morning. While planning out this trip several months earlier, I'd heard about a magnificent remote beach on the island of Kauai, accessible only through a narrow eleven-mile hiking trail. The scenery looked extraordinary, so I quickly added it to my itinerary. While planning out this entire trip, however, I hadn't banked on dealing with a lingering illness at this stage of the trip so I knew this could pose a real challenge for my body.

After puddle-jumping by small plane from the Big Island over to Kauai, I hitchhiked to the trailhead that leads to the beach and began my long trek along the Ne Pali coast with my backpack and rolled-up tent. The further I made it along the trail, the fewer people I saw. The rich colors of the Hawaiian landscape had an almost neon brilliance to them, from the luminous greens of the indigenous fauna to the rich blues of the sky. The trail weaved up and down along the coastline, and by late afternoon I was so tired I decided to pitch my tent and spend the night at the midway point to my destination.

The next morning I set out on the trail, and the lush green colors progressively gave way to a very different but equally beautiful landscape of red, brown, and green earth tones, punctuated by the sight of huge spires of volcanic rock jutting up to my left side. The cliffs alongside the trail to my right harbored drops of over a thousand feet to the ocean at points, but I was so exhausted that I didn't pay much attention, certainly not as much as I should have.

The hiking trail along the Ne Pali coast, Kauai

That inattentiveness was nearly my undoing when at one point I absentmindedly tripped on a rock and lunged forward towards the edge. I immediately reached for a large tuft of grass bordering the path, which just barely halted my rocksliding trajectory down to the ocean. I lay there, shocked, with one of my legs hanging

over the ledge. In the blink of an eye, it jolted me into full awareness, as I realized how just one brief second of mindlessness could
have ended my life.

I had plenty of time those next few hours to reflect what had
just happened. I initially found myself pondering what my parents would have felt upon hearing the news of my death that way.
(Would my body have even been found?) When you're young, and
foolish, you tend not to think of such things, of course. But I also
started reflecting on the fact I've spent most of my life living in
the future, that is, going somewhere rather than being anywhere.
Always looking ahead, rarely looking down. From that point on
during my hike, I watched every step of the trail with as much
mindfulness as I could muster, tired as I was, and frequently
thought back to that Japanese artist's line: "Every moment."

I finally arrived at the remote beach of my destination, set
against looming spires of green-laden rock arching up in the
background. I immediately recognized it from various movies
and TV shows I'd seen through the years. There were only a few
other hikers on the beach, and that night some of us built a camp-
fire on the sand while someone passed around a joint. I slept that
night under the stars, thinking that this was indeed some sort of
paradise.

I stayed there for two days and as I hiked back out, I passed
several people hiking in. As it turned out, a devastating hurricane
pounded that island the very next day, by which time I'd already
flown back to Honolulu. I couldn't help but wonder what happened to those individuals on the beach as that megastorm made
landfall. I still wonder about that.

Coming Home

After leaving Hawaii, I stopped off in Los Angeles for a few days
to visit my friend Paul Broucek, whose career was just starting to
take off, unlike my own. Besides Paul's wife, another old friend

from Oak Park, Demetrious "Mimi" Betinis, was staying at his house, so I was reuniting with him as well. As happy as I was to see both of them, I was even happier at the thought of heading back to Illinois and resting up after what had been a long year.

When I did finally arrive back home, it was initially disorienting. Everything in my immediate environment was exactly the same, yet looked strangely different, surely because the eyes seeing all of it now carried a very different set of memories and emotions behind them. Coming back from a long trip is, in some ways, a bit like coming down from a powerful psychedelic experience; after being confronted by constantly changing stimuli, adapting to a stable environment poses a challenge all its own. But it was a challenge I was only too happy to take on, after nearly sliding off a cliff one week earlier. I couldn't help but wonder how the effects of this trip would play out for me in the weeks and months ahead.

For now, though, I just needed to rest, so I crashed onto my bed and fell asleep, and dreamt that night of Ladakh and the sound of bells coming in from the fields.

CHAPTER 40

THE DIVINE ZODIAC ~ A WINDOW INTO GOD'S MIND, OR SIMPLY HUMANITY'S GREATEST WORK OF ART?

W hen I first became involved with astrology, a number of things intrigued or even startled me about this discipline. As I mentioned at the start of this book, one of those was the fact that it even was accurate at all and said things about me the astrologer couldn't possibly have known.

But over time, the one feature of astrology that came to fascinate me most of all, as much for aesthetic as for philosophical reasons, was the zodiac itself.

At first glance, it seemed like a simple enough system, at least if I went by what the newspapers said. It suggested that there were twelve basic personality types. Simple enough; nothing terribly mind-blowing about that.

But the more I learned about the zodiac over the ensuing decades, the more I came to see intricacies in this model that went far beyond any simple categorizing of personality types. Within that twelvefold pattern were overlapping layers of meaning and patterns of interrelationship that struck me as surprisingly complex. I've likened it in some ways to coming across one of those rare old watches that seems simple on its surface, but when you open it up, you discover a complex network of gears and springs that tells you not only the time of day, but lunar phases, Greenwich Mean Time, yearly calendars, and the positions of the planets (what the clockmaking trade calls the "planetarium function"). For me, looking into the zodiac felt much like that.

Image: Shutterstock

In fact, the complexity of the zodiac was such that I couldn't help but think that no human mind could have conceived it. It wasn't simply complex; it was transcendentally beautiful in its own way. If this were simply the result of random ideas and beliefs cobbled together over the centuries by random astrologers in different countries, it wouldn't have had that internal intricacy and perfection of interrelated parts, I felt. It all led me to ponder a question that I still think about:

Was the zodiac invented or discovered?

That is, was it simply a human concoction, like the English language or a Beethoven symphony, but with no *universal* validity? Or was it indeed a genuine archetypal pattern that humans simply *uncovered*, and which existed in some state or form before humans came along, therefore offering us a window onto something universal?

I'd like to suggest that we can think of the zodiac as a bit of both: a human construct, but one that incorporates something profoundly significant beyond any purely human level. Understanding it is a cosmic detective story, I came to believe, one that takes us even further into the hidden depths of consciousness.

Looking behind the Clockface

The twelvefold zodiac that we know today, with all of its associations and complexities, didn't appear fully formed all at once. Whatever the ultimate source or nature of the zodiac, humanity's *understanding* of it developed over centuries, even millennia. It's not my purpose here to chronicle that entire history, which rightly deserves a book in itself, so I'll say just a few words about it.

Some believe that the zodiac's roots extend back into the dimmest reaches of prehistory, based on scattered clues that have been uncovered over the last century. One of those involves indications that zodiacal signs like Taurus may well appear on the walls of prehistoric caves like those in Lascaux, France (dating back roughly 19,000 years); these show bull-type images positioned along with star patterns that resemble the Pleiades star cluster. So certain signs may have roots that go back many thousands of years earlier than generally believed.[1]

But our full-blown twelvefold zodiac seems to have arisen in Mesopotamia between roughly 3200 BCE and 500 BCE. Although there are many constellations scattered throughout the entire sky, with many myths assigned to virtually all of them, the early astronomers and astrologers of the Middle East began to focus attention on those constellations grouped along the ecliptic—the path through the sky traced by the Sun, Moon, and planets in their yearly movements.

Over time, that basic zodiac was modified by countries like Greece, Egypt, Persia, India, and finally Europe, having split along the way into two parallel zodiacs, one sidereal (star-based), the other more seasonal ("tropical"), while simultaneously acquiring the wide range of associations many assume have always been part and parcel of the zodiac.

Here I'd like to look at a few of those associations, consider how these fit together in our modern understanding of the zodiac, and from there see what this implies.

The Twelvefold Zodiac

Perhaps the most important fact about the zodiac is the one we most take for granted: its twelvefold nature. After all, why not divide the circle into eight sections? Or sixteen? Or twenty-four? As you'll see, this one fact underlies virtually all the subsequent layers of meanings we'll be looking at here and makes them possible in ways that other numerical divisions of the circle don't allow, at least not in the same way.[2]

What I find intriguing is how there seems to be an orderly sequence or narrative to this sequence, as if those twelve signs were telling a *story*, from simple to complex—a story that doesn't stand out quite as dramatically when approached from the reverse direction. In the next chapter we'll touch on Shelly Trimmer's belief that the zodiac expresses a mystical unfoldment of consciousness from the simple awareness of Aries all the way through to the complexities of Aquarius and Pisces. But I also remember when my first astrology teacher, Maureen Cleary, addressed this progression in her own decidedly psychological way, which I would paraphrase roughly like this:

Aries is like the birth of a child, a primal awakening of raw awareness, comparable to the first shoots of life emerging out of the ground during springtime. In Taurus, that awareness starts to grow and blossom further, with an expanding sense of the tangible world it sees around itself, along with a feeling of possessiveness about those things and people—a shift from "me!" to mine!" In Gemini, the earliest glimmers of mind and thinking start to appear, while in Cancer, the child is becoming increasingly aware of itself as part of a family and starts awakening emotionally. In

Leo, the soul is starting to discover its own creativity, as well as ego, but also begins to feel the first inklings of romantic love. In Virgo, the soul is becoming more discriminating about itself, its appearance, its choice of friends and associations, and possibly entering into the work or service phase of its life.

In Libra, it is now opening up to the possibility of committed partnerships and bonding with others. In Scorpio, that bonding and relationship instinct takes the critical step of physical intimacy and sexuality, while also becoming more aware of death, birth, and the transitory nature of things. With Sagittarius, the person begins to move beyond sexuality and personal desires into philosophizing and a broader expansion of horizons. In Capricorn, that perspective comes to include a sense of status in the world and a desire to forge a reputation and lasting achievements. In Aquarius, a far broader awareness of community beyond oneself enters in, and with it, the importance of contributing something of value to the world. Finally, in Pisces one's attention turns to ultimates, and the mysteries of spirituality and God.

The Elements

While there are twelve zodiacal signs, these boil down to four basic kinds, commonly referred to as the elements: Earth, Water, Fire, and Air.

Earth is practical and more oriented towards material and functional values; Water is more emotional and experiences life more through its feelings; Fire is about energy, assertiveness, courage, and primal self-awareness. Air is more involved with mind, mental experiencing, and social interactions.

There are three Fire signs, existing at 120-degree angles to one another: Aries, Leo, and Sagittarius. There are three Earth signs: Taurus, Virgo, and Capricorn; three Water signs: Cancer, Scorpio, and Pisces; and three Air signs: Gemini, Libra, and Aquarius.

These elements have varying types of relationships with each other. Signs of one element relate more harmoniously with certain other elements, while being more likely to clash with others. For instance, Earth signs get along well with other Earth signs, as well as Water signs, but experience more friction with Fire and Air signs. Air signs get along with other Air signs, as well as with Fire signs, but not so easily with Water and Earth signs.

The Modes

In contrast with the four elements, the three zodiacal modes of Cardinal, Fixed and Mutable relate to three *types of action,* and to how individuals of varying elements move into and through the world. Cardinal signs tend to initiate things: they're restless, they forge ahead into experience. Fixed signs are more likely to consolidate their status, and are more focused or even stubborn in temperament. Mutable signs are more flexible and adaptable and less focused than either fixed or cardinal signs.

When you couple these three modes with the four elements, you begin to glimpse much of what comprises the unique character of each sign. For example, when Earth is in its cardinal or initiating mode (Capricorn), it expresses itself as worldly ambition, planning in practical ways, and looking beyond the present. In its fixed mode (Taurus), Earth expresses itself more in terms of shoring up resources and maintaining security. In its mutable mode (Virgo), Earth expresses itself by adapting itself to situations and people, as well as to intelligently discriminating the various phenomena it perceives. In all three of those modes, it's the same element, but manifesting in uniquely different ways and with uniquely different aims.

The Polarity Principle

As we have already seen, each sign has its own unique identity, yet that identity is bound up with the sign directly opposite it.

An example I've used in previous books is that of the old comedy team of Laurel and Hardy. While Laurel had his own distinct personality, it can't really be seen as separate from that of his partner, and vice versa. There is an identity and a chemistry within that partnership that's distinctly different from what each of those figures represents solely on his own.

That holds true for each sign and its opposite as well. For example, Taurus is often related to the principle of personal wealth, while its opposite sign, Scorpio, is related to the principle of other people's wealth. Together, the two might be considered as dual expressions of the common principle of *resources,* as well as *security.*[3] Likewise, Gemini and Sagittarius are very different in many ways, yet together express the common principle of *communication,* and of *knowledge.* Although Leo and Aquarius harbor many distinct meanings of their own, both express the principles of *pleasure* and *creativity,* in the one case more personal, in the other, more collectively.

In short, there is a linkage of meaning between opposite signs that exists above and beyond any sign's role within the zodiac's twelvefold narrative or its relationship to other elements and modes. Some have even suggested we should think of the zodiac as actually being composed not of twelve signs but six, fanning out into dual expressions.

The Threefold Division of the Zodiac
Like a pie, the zodiac can be sliced up into three broad sections such that its first four signs—Aries, Taurus, Gemini, and Cancer—constitute the first third. Leo, Virgo, Libra, and Scorpio constitute the second third, while the last four signs—Sagittarius, Capricorn, Aquarius, and Pisces—represent the last third.

As I touched on in chapter 20, these three sections represent increasingly broad avenues of expression for each of the elements. Hence, while all the Air signs represent the faculty of mind, and mental forms of experience generally, Gemini is the most personal form, whereas Libra is more interpersonal, and Aquarius the most global and transpersonal of them all. In the same way, all of the four elements broaden out in their expression the further they move away from the earlier stages of the zodiac.

The Gender of the Signs
The ancient Pythagoreans believed that numbers possessed qualities of *gender*, that is, a positive or negative polarity. As such, the number 1 is masculine in nature, 2 is feminine, 3 is masculine, and so on into infinity.

By the same token, the signs of the zodiac can also be seen as possessing gender, with each possessing either masculine or feminine qualities. The alternating signs of Aries, Gemini, Leo, Libra, Sagittarius, and Aquarius are considered masculine or positive in nature; Taurus, Cancer, Virgo, Scorpio, Capricorn and Pisces are all feminine or negative. Of course, one shouldn't think of positive or negative here in terms of good or bad, but rather like the positive or negative poles of a magnet or battery. Masculine or positive signs are simply more extraverted and outwardly directed in nature, while feminine or negative signs are more inwardly focused.

The Human Body as a Zodiacal Map
Astrologers have long related the various signs of the zodiac to various parts of the body. Nor is this done in some haphazard way, so that Aries relates to one part of the body while Taurus relates to a completely unconnected part: there is a specific and regular order to how these all fit together, all the way from the head down to the feet.

The head relates to Aries; the throat to Taurus; the shoulders and arms to Gemini; the chest and breasts to Cancer; the heart and upper back to Leo; the stomach and abdomen to Virgo; the kidneys and lower back to Libra; the genitals and anus to Scorpio; the hips and thighs to Sagittarius; the knees to Capricorn, the ankles to Aquarius; and the feet to Pisces.

There is deep symbolism at work here. In their respective functions, all of those body parts embody the meanings of their corresponding signs to a remarkable degree, in a way that's clearly not arbitrary or random. In addition, how those body parts interrelate likewise says something about how the respective zodiacal energies interact. Just as the zodiac tells a certain story in its sequencing, the body tells what might be thought of as a biological story in its zodiacal symbolism. There is an exquisite holism in how these parts work together.

The Chakric Wheel

To my mind, perhaps the most striking layer of meaning contained within the zodiac—and one that's been a key feature of this book—is the uncanny way it relates to the esoteric model of the chakras. Indeed, the correlation is so precise that it's the one feature, more than any other, that led me to believe the zodiac is not simply a random product of the human imagination but instead expresses a set of eternal truths.

As we've seen, simply spin the zodiac around so that Leo and Cancer appear at the top, and line up the traditional planetary rulers along the middle of this wheel, and you find an astonishingly precise correspondence with what yogic mystics have described in connection with the chakras. Each chakra has its central, balanced expression, represented by the visible planets, as well as its masculine and feminine expressions off to the sides, these relating to the zodiacal signs. (More traditionally-minded astrologers will notice here the similarity of this arrangement to the *thema mundi*, considered to be a cosmic template of existence, the birth chart of the world itself.)

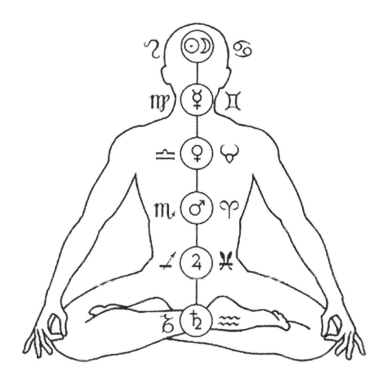

According to this cross-pollination of systems, we see that the zodiac represents a map of archetypal psychology, with the signs being associated with the various levels of consciousness along the spine. This correspondence further helps us to understand the notion of co-rulerships, and why certain traditional planets are linked to two different signs, rather than just one.

Whereas the Sun only rules Leo and the Moon only governs Cancer, Mercury traditionally rules both Gemini and Virgo; Venus rules both Taurus and Libra; Mars, both Aries and Scorpio; Jupiter, both Pisces and Sagittarius; and Saturn, both Capricorn and Aquarius.

Why should that be? The chakric model offers us a possible explanation, with the unique layout of its different centers.

Putting It All Together

These are just a few of the meaningful patterns associated with the zodiac, and there are still others, like decans, hemispheres, and lunar mansions. As I mentioned at the outset, all of these aspects of the zodiac overlap onto one another and create a multidimensional tapestry of meanings that interweave like systems of the human body—arteries, nerves, organs, the lymphatic network, the muscles, the skin—all working together organically to create a seamless whole.

In fact, so interrelated are these various layers and features that the meaning of any one sign is integrally tied into all these intermeshing layers and patterns. In other words, dig down deep enough into any one sign, and you automatically start tugging on all of these other threads. To illustrate that point, let's take one sign and examine it more closely—in this case, Aries.

- One of the most significant associations with Aries is specifically due to its position within the zodiac, as the perceived first of twelve signs; therefore this sign represents new beginnings and the early stages of all endeavors.
- Elementally, Aries is composed of Fire, which tells us a great deal about its fiery nature and its pioneering but famously hot-tempered tendencies.
- We also see some of its initiating nature in the fact that its mode is Cardinal, an orientation heavily focused upon doing, and on forging ahead into future undertakings.
- In terms of dividing up the entire zodiac into thirds, Aries represents the very first of the three fire signs, and therefore expresses the adventurous impulses of that element at their most personal and self-oriented.
- In terms of gender, Aries is an intrinsically masculine or extraverted sign; hence it is more focused on activity in the outer world than on the inner domain of feelings and reflectivity.

- Aries acquires some of its character through its position as a counterbalance to Libra at the other end of the zodiac. Whereas Libra is more passive and diplomatic, Aries is more assertive and decisive. When these two are viewed together, however, we realize that both signs relate to the broader principle of *relationship,* and the me/other dynamic in general. Aries represents the pure impulsive expression of self and Libra represents the mirror of "other" whereby self comes to know itself better—a point that isn't nearly as clear when examining Aries solely by itself.

- In terms of its symbolic position within the body, Aries relates to the head—the part of the body that governs the entire body via the brain. Thus this sign is the proverbial commander-in-chief, the four-star general of the zodiacal armed forces, as it were. This part of the body, and of the zodiac, is most identified with the "me!" part of the personality; if future scientists determined they could preserve only one part of your body, you would no doubt choose the head, because that's where the bulk of your awareness is focused. (Or would you say your feet, or your arms? Not very likely.) Likewise, Aries is the part of the zodiac that relates most to your basic identity, your conventional self and personality. Like the human head, it also holds the greatest concentration of awareness out of the entire twelvefold system.

- Aries relates to the third chakra, which has to do with basic drives, desire nature, and assertiveness. This chakric level concerns the emergence of the ego at its most primal and rudimentary; it's the awareness of "me" versus "the other." At its core, this chakra represents the warrior principle, with Aries representing the more masculine and extraverted side of that energy, in contrast with Scorpio (which, like Aries, is traditionally ruled by Mars), represents the more feminine, inwardly-focused side of that chakra.

In short, the meaning of Aries, like that of any sign, is really a combination of *all* these factors and layers. Take any one of those away, and you lose something of the sign's symbolic nuances.

Conclusion

As I hope has become apparent, there is an extraordinary design and elegance to how all these parts fit together. So was all of this invented, or was it discovered? To my mind, there are only so many ways to explain this multilayered construction.

One is to suggest that indeed the zodiac was consciously invented: it was all part of an intentional plan by a cabal of esoteric geniuses, working either independently or in collaboration, who rolled it out over many generations and across various cultural borders to its present stage.

Much more likely to my mind is the possibility that while the zodiac was created by human hands over time, its assorted ideas issued out of a divine intuition, a spiritual wisdom, in much the same way that our greatest myths—like the *Mahabharata*, the *Iliad*, and the *Odyssey*—arose from the minds of spiritual geniuses. I'm reminded here of Carl Jung's suggestion that astrology represents a repository of humanity's psychological knowledge projected onto the heavens, almost like a giant rorschach ink blot. But it's a rorschachian projection that taps into universal truths, drawing upon a body of divine wisdom that far transcends any one person or culture, much as the Biblical story of the garden transcends Jewish culture, or the *Iliad* and *Odyssey* transcend Greek culture. In turn, those truths may well tell us something important about consciousness itself, something we'll consider in the next chapter.

Furthermore, our understanding of the zodiac was shaped and verified over time *empirically*, by means of the efforts of astrologers testing these ideas out over centuries of time. After all, there have been countless conceptual tributaries feeding into this evolving body of astrological knowledge through the millennia.

Why did some of those ideas and techniques stick, while others fell by the wayside? The likely answer is that the ideas and associations that really worked were retained, while those that didn't were discarded. In the end, it's left us with a possible skeleton key into the mind of God.

But even if one doesn't accept that the zodiac holds some greater metaphysical importance, we're then entitled to pose another, very different question:

Could it be that the zodiac represents humanity's greatest work of art?

CHAPTER 41

ESOTERIC ASTROLOGY ~ A DISCOURSE BY SHELLY TRIMMER

*S*helly Trimmer was a teacher in the Kriya Yoga tradition. I studied with him from 1977 up to the time of his death in 1996, and whom I wrote about in **An Infinity of Gods**. Much of my own grasp of astrology, mysticism, and the occult came from my studies with him, as well as from his disciple in Chicago, Goswami Kriyananda.

It was well known among his students that Shelly had at some point dictated a tape recording expressing his thoughts and philosophy on the esoteric dimensions of astrology. What I heard about it through Kriyananda, who delivered a course on it that I attended, struck me as profound but also difficult to understand, at least initially. Several versions of the transcript of that recording were circulating, with slight variations amongst them, and since I was unable to verify which was the most faithful of those, I didn't include it in my book on Shelly.

Since that book's publication, however, I was able to get my hands on Shelly's original recording and have included my transcript of it here. I will present it just as I heard it on the recording, and I follow it with some explanatory notes of my own. The recording was old, and there were points where the sound quality was poor and difficult to understand. I've used square brackets, [ ], to indicate those parts where I was unsure of the words, and I've used round brackets, ( ), to insert words or terms of clarification which I thought would be useful to beginners.

Shelly Trimmer, circa mid-1960s (photo by Goswami Kriyananda)

I should first say a few words about esoteric astrology and what that really means. Over the years, I've come to realize that the term means different things to different astrologers, so I'll briefly explain some of those distinctions, which hopefully will help place Shelly's philosophy into a larger context.

In the broadest possible sense, esoteric astrology *refers to the notion that our conventional symbols of astrology—planets, signs, houses, aspects—conceal hidden levels of information and knowledge not readily perceptible to the casual eye, but which can be unlocked to the symbolically astute student. I'd suggest that this can be broken down to at least four different categories or approaches.*

1. For some, the term esoteric astrology *is essentially synonymous with karmic astrology—the study of how the horoscope reveals subtler clues to an individual's past lives. Over the decades I've encountered various systems which purport to do this, some of them focusing heavily on the Moon's nodes as indicators of past incarnations, others which look to the role of the twelfth house in the horoscope, while still others (as in the case of Goswami Kriyananda) involve a complex network of factors, such as noting the distance between the Sun and Moon, the gender of whatever sign the Moon is in, noting whether key aspects are approaching or closing, and many other symbolic clues.*

2. Yet another approach to esoteric astrology looks at how the horoscope represents a map of one's chakra system, the network of energetic centers along the spine of one's subtle body. I've touched on this concept throughout this book and dealt with it at greater length in some of my other works, but simply stated, its relation to astrology is this: the seven visible bodies of our solar system relate to the seven primary chakras, and the twelve signs of the zodiac correspond to various "compartments" associated with the masculine and feminine expressions of those chakras. Someone well versed in this system can study a horoscope and discern where the energies are focused within a person's chakric centers.

3. Mention esoteric astrology to most astrologers these days and it usually calls to mind the writings of former Theosophist Alice Bailey, who wrote a volume by that title. Hers was an extremely abstract system of ideas concerning the deeper "soul factors" which underlies astrology's principles, applied to either individuals or societies, and relies on a mystical philosophy concerning the field of space and time.

4. Finally, there is the form of esoteric astrology that Shelly Trimmer taught. It resembles Alice Bailey's work in some ways but is quite different in terms of specifics. Simply put, Shelly suggests that the essential principles of astrology symbolize the basic architecture of consciousness itself, or what he sometimes referred to as "the laws of self-conscious awareness." Of course, he's using the term "laws" here not in any legislative sense but much in the same way that we might talk about the laws of mathematics or the laws of geometry. In fact, his approach incorpo-rates a dimension of sacred geometry that suggests how different angles relate to different states of consciousness (an idea I touched upon in chap-ter 11 of The Waking Dream*). I should mention that his larger body of teachings on esoteric astrology also broached the zodiac/chakra corre-spondences mentioned above, but he alludes to these only peripherally in this particular discourse.*

Shelly's discourse is an admittedly difficult body of ideas to grasp on a single reading, especially for someone not already versed in astrology. Having read it now myself probably 100 times over the years, I've come to see it in a very different light now than early on. For those new to the subject, I'd suggest simply reading through it and letting the ideas plant their seeds in your subconscious, then coming back to it at a later time. For those who do take the time to delve into it more deeply, it can help shed light on the occult rationale behind some of the intricate patterns we discussed with the zodiac in the previous chapter.

Shelly was an extraordinary synthesizer, drawing on various tradi-tions to create a body of knowledge that was uniquely his own. Hopefully, my comments at the end will help you understand his ideas more clearly.
—R.G.

This is a discourse on basic astrology made as simple as pos-sible, even to the dangerous point of oversimplification.

What is astrology? Basically speaking, astrology is the lan-guage of the soul, an expression of the spirit, the law of Self. Each night, as you sleep, your dreams are composed of its language. It is You, and the basic laws of the You applied to this sector of time and space, on this planet Earth, in this solar system of soul, with this Sun.

To have a deeper understanding of the tenets of astrology, we should understand how the spirit formulated the soul into compartments, how the spirit hewed forth the laws of self-conscious awareness. For by understanding this, one can understand the maze of the Self and find his or her relationship to all that is, that was, and yet which shall be, and his or her position within this relationship. Did not the ancient sages speak and say "Know thyself"? Here is the basic key for the understanding of the You.

How shall we best start? Perhaps by understanding the law of meditation. Let us take a simple cube, a simple block of wood, and meditate upon it. The simple cube, the simple block of wood, becomes the object of meditation, and then there is you, who are doing the meditating; you are the meditator. Then there is the act of meditation. When these three become as one, then perfect meditation ensues. When we say "becomes as one," then the unity, the all, becomes the fourth factor.

Let us apply this now to the spiritual Self. There is you, the meditator, there is the object of meditation, which is the selfsame you as though you were the reflection of yourself; and there is the act of meditation, because you are meditating upon yourself; and there is the all of the meditation, which is the fourth factor.

Now when you are meditating upon yourself, you have four factors—two of which are the same—and arrange them in as many ways as possible, you will find that there are only twelve possible ways of arranging them. These become the twelve signs of the zodiac. And if we examine these variations of the spirit very carefully, we find that they arrange themselves into four groups, three in each group.

Each one of these twelve variations of self-conscious awareness is not just an abstract symbol; each is a symbol and a progressive stage in the basic awareness of the Self, following one another in the same way that the increase of unity produces the numerical sequence 2, 3, 4, 5, 6, etc.

These twelve variations of the basic You—the spiritual You—arrange themselves into a basic circle, sometimes symbolized on this Earth as a serpent feeding back upon itself, swallowing its tail, symbolizing the Self feeding back unto itself the eternal circle of its immortal existence.

Does not the Self meditating upon the Self become the Self all over again? By the very nature of its existence, the Self must eternally meditate upon itself. For if it ceased to do so, it would cease to be, and thus if it could happen unto one's spiritual being, it could happen unto all. And in the infinities of existence, if it could happen to one, it would already have happened unto all—and you would not now be here listening.

Since the Spirit is the basic You, the very kernel of your existence, let me explain concerning it a little deeper—the circle of spiritual awareness.

The spirit is the I AM AWARE THAT I AM THE SELF MEDITATING UPON THE SELF—this and nothing more. In this

Self-meditation, the observer becomes the observed, but the observed also becomes the observer. For which Self is truly the observer, and which Self is truly the observed? It is like saying that if the positive becomes negative, then the negative must become positive. For one thing alone and by itself has no existence, no meaning. And [happy?] wave or [happy?] cycle of spiritual awareness has taken place, and the observer which became the observed returns again to becoming the observer. And the observed, which became the observer, returns again unto being the observed, and a complete cycle has taken place. And so the beginning returns again unto the beginning.

And since the Self is the observer as well as the observed, the way of the Self moves about the circle in opposite directions. This action of the spirit, this Kriya of the spirit, produces the "Omic" sound, the Word.

Remember, the wave of Self moves in both directions at once, and the observed unit of Self becomes negatively existent in reference to the observer unit of Self. And if one unit of the Self is negatively existent, then it is equal to the observer times the act of observing. This is a basic expression of power—spiritual power in this case. Thus the spirit, by the very act of its nature, not only regenerates the existence of itself, but all the existences of which it is aware.

If we take these twelve basic variations of the Spirit and arrange them in a circle, and we observe in how many ways one may be related to the other, we will find that there are only seven possible relationships. The seven possible relationships are in this manner:

One state of spiritual variation may be related unto itself (conjunction).
The second unto the first two on either side of itself (semisexile).

The third unto the next two on either side of itself (sextile). The fourth unto the next two on either side of itself and the fifth unto the next two on either side of itself, and the sixth unto the next two on either side of itself (square, trine, and inconjunct, respectively).
This leaves one left, which is directly opposite from the beginning—the seventh relationship (opposition).

These are the seven possible aspecting relationships that exist like the diameter of a circle. The balancing mode of the spiritual arcs symbolize the seven chakras, the seven days of the week, and the idea which was written that the Great Spirit created all existence in seven days and on the seventh day the Great Spirit rested.
The seventh point is the point of equilibrium of balance. For here the two waves of the Self meet and each must be the reflection of the other, but must be balanced. And if we examine the seven possible aspects of relationship, we will find that five are dual and two are singular. These five are like the five elements of yoga—Earth, Water, Fire, Air, and Ether, or as some Moslems say, the plasma state of matter.
The two singles refer to the dual nature of the Self. They also refer to the seven planets of the ancients, five of which are dual, each one of the five ruling two signs, and the two singles each ruling one sign. And these seven possible aspects are a balancing diameter, holding in equilibrium the two arcs. One can see here that the circle of the Spirit is equal to twice the diameter and not the theoretical relationship of roughly 3.1416. . . times the diameter. Thus in the spirit, pi is equal to 2, while here on Earth, in this world of Assiah, pi is equal to roughly 3.1416 . . . This means that the Spirit is infinite in its power. It is also infinite in its reduction; it cannot be reduced to less. It is the unidimensional point of geometry through whose movement all dimensions are created. The

Spirit is composed of but four radions depicting the cross of the mystic and symbolizing again the four basic factors of its nature, which cannot be reduced to less.

To recapitulate, the spirit is composed of but four basic factors, two of which are the same which can formulate but twelve variations or phases of spiritual awareness. Any one of these phases or variations of spiritual Self-awareness may have but seven aspects. We are now ready to formulate (the) simple wave or simple cycle or simple circle of spiritual awareness.

The first movement of the Spirit is a simple act in the awareness of itself. Thus we have a beginning, the action of identity, the I AM, the identification of soul, the beginning of the soul. Thus is Aries associated with fire, fiery action, the commencement of new undertakings, the pioneering spirit, the identity of an existence or thing. The beginning, like the beginning of the zodiac, the beginning of the first house, the beginning of any new undertaking.

The second phase or variation of the spirit is the awareness of the soul, the awareness of the first act, fixed and sustained. A permanent record of the action of the spirit indelibly recorded in incomprehensible fabric of the spirit. Thus is Taurus associated with the ideas of fixed, endurable things, the memory track of the spirit. Hence spiritual wealth: the building block of existence.

The third stage of the spirit is oscillating. First it becomes aware of one and then another state of its existence. It oscillates or varies from one to the other. Thus is Gemini restless and changeable, like the air, and versatile in the area of communication.

We now come to the fourth phase of the spirit. There is a sensing of a difference between the soul and the spirit. The soul is reflective, responding to the slightest change of the spirit, feeling its every mode of expression. That the soul is the home of the spirit, because it's housing the expression of the spirit. Thus does Cancer makes sensitive, reflective, and domestic, like the negative polarity of the Self, which seeks to become the beholder.

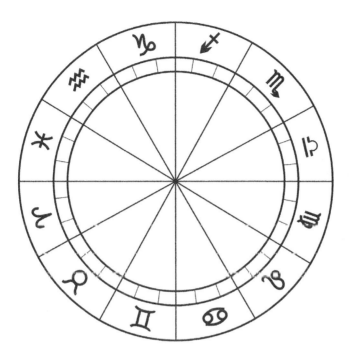

In the fifth phase, the spirit becomes aware of its nature due to the reflection of its acts in the soul. In that it is the generator of the soul, that the soul is the all-giving essence of itself; that it is a generating powerholder, amplifying all that it is aware of. Thus is Leo the sign of intense and noble love, and positive in its nature.

In the sixth phase, it measures and compares the nature of itself in the recorded acts of its soul. And the soul is quickened with living energy by the attention of the spirit. Thus does Virgo compare, measure, and analyze existence. And because of the quickening attention of the spirit does this phase, Virgo, become the mother of all living things. And because of the measurement of the soul and the spirit does the spirit know how it is adorned.

The seventh phase is a phase of the equilibrium and balance, for the positive and the negative wave of the Self meet here, and each is a reflection of the other. And though seemingly twain, each is the same self. Thus what happens unto one must happen unto the other. Here the observer becomes the observed, and the observed the observer. And the second half of the wave must return unto the beginning. Thus does the spirit weigh and balance the various phases of its nature; thus does Libra weigh and balance situations and thoughts and become uncertain in which way to act. Libra is introspective, for it speaks of balancing of Self; it is compromise and partnership, for it is a balancing and a meeting of the two waves.

The eighth phase is a phase of unitization. Because of the waves balancing and measuring, the spirit becomes aware that each phase is an exact unit, that it has a beginning and an end and the combining of more than one phase so that two or more may act as a single unit. Thus is Scorpio exacting and deals with ultimates—the beginning and end of things, the specializing of groups, the unifying principle.

We come now to Sagittarius, the ninth phase of the spirit. Here the spirit equates the nature of its existence and establishes the law or order of its spiritual dream. An awareness that one phase follows another phase in a natural sequence in the same manner that an increase of unity produces a mathematical series. Also the law governing groups, which act as a unit. Thus is Sagittarius a questing, a pursuing the meaning of nature and its existence and things. Thus it is sometimes referred to as the sign of the philosopher.

We now come to the tenth phase of existence—the phase of perspective. Here the spirit becomes aware of the importance of positioning in the order of things. Thus is Capricorn interested in its position and aware of the stabilizing influence of order, for it keeps all things in the correct perspective. For this reason, Capricorn is considered practical, for here is the facility of existence made manifest.

We now come to the eleventh phase of the spirit—that which is known as association. It associates each with each other and all with each other. This is the act of knowing, understanding, comprehending. Associating keeps all the parts together. For this reason is Aquarius is considered the brotherhood of man, the position of friends and acquaintances. Aquarius is a gathering together of information for all to partake.

We now come to the twelfth phase of the spirit. This is the phase of anticipation, because here the spirit knows that the other parts of its soul, the wave of Self returns unto the beginning. Thus does it anticipate that which is to be but is not yet so. Here is the order of existence projected into the unknown, into the abstract. Thus is Pisces the sign of believing, the nebulous, the unknown, the mystical, an awareness of that which is hidden or occult and not yet by normal means perceptible existence.

In the next phase (Aries), the beholder again beholds him or herself. And the cycle or wave is returned again to the beginning, and the beginning again commences. And one cycle is complete, and one cycle moves on to another cycle, ever increasing within itself like a spiral, and the spiral moves into infinity, ever compounding its basic nature into the maze of Self.

And as the spirit moves about in the awareness of the soul, it begins in the awareness of itself, and it becomes lost in the maze of things. And the spirit would forever be lost in the maze of the soul were it not for the eleventh and twelfth phase of its existence. For by associating and projecting one part with all the others in an abstract manner, it found its way, a path back unto itself. This is the Law of the Seven, for one part could be associated unto itself and unto the arcs on either side of itself, five of which are dual and unto the one which was opposite unto itself, the seventh part. This is like the diameter of a circle: the balancing path, the path back unto itself.

And the conjunction is like that of the Sun; and the 30 degrees on either side is like that of Mercury, and the 60 degrees on either side like that of Venus, and the 90 degrees on either side like

Mars, and the 120 degrees on either side like that unto Jupiter, and the 150 degrees on either side like unto Saturn, and the one single remaining, the opposition, like unto the Moon.[1] These are the seven aspects, and the aspects are after the nature of the planets. And these seven form themselves about the waves of the cycle of the spirit in an act of this manner:

In the fifth phase of the soul, the spirit—regardless of how dimly—is ever aware of itself. Thus is it in attunement with the spirit, a conjunction. And the fourth phase of Self is like a reflection of spirit which is most like that unto the Moon, reflective in its qualities. And if the Sun be considered positive, the Moon of necessity must be negative, and acting as a unit, as a head, if you will. On either side closest in the arc is Mercury, lying at the 30-degree mark. And even farther down on either side in the arc would be Venus, and further down on either side of the arc would be Mars, and still further down on either side of the arcs would be Jupiter, and still further down on either side in the arcs would be Saturn, which would occupy the last two. In this manner are the planets associated with the various phases of the soul, of the spirit.

These seven become seven states of awareness, balancing the maze so that the spirit might climb back unto itself. But each center must grow stronger than the maze to maintain its balance. This can only be accomplished through self-discipline. Neither by drugs or by magic may a being stand herein, save by the magic of self-discipline.

Saturn is the symbol farthest away in the arc from the spirit, the Sun. Saturn is the foundation, the first stepping-stone, the gross matter, the earth, the symbolic lead of the inert soul.

Next is Jupiter, order or law, like mathematics both abstract and practical. The first beginning of growth of the spirit in its upward climb, thus benevolent, bountiful, symbolizing water, and the metal tin, because it is more electropositive than the metal lead of Saturn.

Next in distance from the head is Mars, unitizing action, the symbol of fire. Here the spirit feels the first creative flames of freedom, which is symbolized by iron, which is still more electropositive than either tin or lead. If Mars becomes unbalanced, disruptive energies are the result.

Next we come to [the environment and love?] of Venus, the balanced memory of the soul. On one side lies the many splendored facets of the memories of spirit (Taurus) and on the other, the wavering balance of this and that (Libra), the associative uncertainties—the result of unbalanced selfishness or of balanced selfless love. Venus is symbol of air and the metal copper, which is still more electropositive than the three metals below it.

Next we come to the symbol of Mercury. It is closest to the spirit and communes with it the symbol of communication. On one side, it can fall away and oscillate first in one direction then in the other (Gemini). On the other side, it can fall away, criticize, measure and analyze the pros and cons of all things that exist within the maze of the soul (Virgo). In balance alone does it commune with the spirit. Mercury is like unto ether and the metal mercury, which is still more electropositive than the other metals below it.

We now come to the Moon, which is sensitizing and reflective. It is sensitive to and reflective of all things, and if the other five symbols below it are balanced, those dual symbols, then the Moon is reflective of the pure spirit alone. It is then the negative aspect of the Self and reflects the ultimate truth. It is silver in its nature, for silver is more electropositive than all the other metals below it.

Next is the radiant Sun—the amplifier of all that is below, if all else below it is balanced, and it beholds the reflection of itself and amplifies its own spiritual awareness. The spirit has now arrived at the pinnacle, the ultimate expression of itself. It may now move through the maze of Self, beholding its glories and wonders, never again becoming lost. For the spiritual awareness of Self is ever greater than the awareness of the things in the maze.

And the All of Itself is held in the equilibrium of balance, and that is the concealed mystery of Self, that is the equilibrium of Self. And the King of things is dead and its crown is found no more. And the spirit may behold the All of Itself in balanced equilibrium, and the golden wave of Self-creating eternal bliss. The Sun is symbolized by the metal gold, which is more electropositive than all the other six symbolic metals below it. This is what the alchemists meant by transmuting base lead into spiritual gold.

What then about the other three planets in the solar system of soul—Uranus, Neptune and Pluto, which lie beyond the orbit of Saturn? how do we account for them?

Uranus occupies the same symbolic position that Saturn does. Neptune occupies the same symbolic position that Jupiter does. And Pluto occupies the same symbolic position that Mars does. They symbolize a more awakened state of the positions, not only for the individual but for the masses who are aware of them. In this world of Assiah, in this position of time and space, Uranus leans more unto the sign Aquarius than unto the sign Capricorn. Thus it is like a new foundation, revolutionary in its action. And Neptune leans more in the direction of Pisces than that of Sagittarius. And Pluto—there's still a controversy as to which direction Pluto leans, and so unto the various schools of thought which differ, I leave them to decide which direction Pluto leans mostly. But know you that the true position is [the same as?] Mars.

From all which I have said here in the foregoing, you can see that whatever you have been aware of, whatever you are aware of, or whatever you shall be aware of, as its position and aspects within the nature of the soul and the spirit, that whatsoever you do unto others, you cannot help but do unto yourself. For this is the law of the Self. And this be true in either thought or deed. And though you may hide in different shells, in different places, in different times, you can never escape from the face of You. And the seeds you have sewn, you must sometime balance or reap back unto yourself. All states of awareness are placed within the twelve compartments of the soul, and these twelve basic states of spiritual awareness are called houses, and their movable states are called signs.

(End of transcript)

Closing Comments by Ray Grasse

Having studied Shelly's teachings extensively over the years, it's clear to me what Shelly says in this discussion is the tip of a much larger body of thought not only about astrology but consciousness and the cosmos at large. (For further discussion of these, I recommend reading An Infinity of Gods, *as well as chapters 10 and 11 of* The Waking Dream.) *Shelly sometimes said that mathematics and geometry represented the purest language we can use to transmit universal truths over time, and we glimpse some of that perspective in this text. Having said that, I'd like to point out a few things that may bring some clarity to this material. For those who feel like Shelly's words themselves are clear enough on their own, none of the following is really necessary, but for those who feel the need for some more explanation, perhaps these comments will help.*

At its most fundamental, Shelly suggests that the planets and zodiacal signs symbolically express the basic architecture of consciousness. It boils down to the four essential parts of self-conscious awareness:

1. **The viewer:** *the observing consciousness you experience as yourself right now while reading this.*
2. **The viewed:** *the world you perceive before and around you at this moment, and which you believe to be separate from you, although in fact these are two aspects of the same thing.*
3. **The act of viewing:** *the state of consciousness with which you see your world is something distinct unto itself and is constantly changing.*
4. **The "all of the parts":** *also sometimes described as being the "memory track" of all the changes experienced by consciousness.*

One way I've found it helpful for explaining this fourfold concept is with a simple mathematical equation, say, three-fourths, or 3/4. There is the numerator, 3, which for the sake of discussion can be equated with the viewer. There is also the denominator, 4, which can be equated with the viewed. Then you have the relationship between *those two, which is the specific function indicated by the line separating the two, which can be equated with the act of viewing. Finally, you have the overall equation itself, the proportion we call "three-quarters," which represents something above and beyond any of those individual parts. In other words, you can talk about the number 3 by itself; you can talk about the number 4 by itself; you can talk about the principle of the fraction which relates those two numbers; and finally there is the "all of the parts," which is the meaning of the proportion implied by the overall equation and isn't limited to any one of its parts.*

Shelly associates these four parts with the Tetragrammaton, the four-lettered name of God, or IHVH, as described in the Jewish mystical tradition of the Kabbalah. Two letters, the two H's are exactly the same, which relates to the fact that the viewer and the viewed are one and the same.

These four parts can be rearranged in twelve different ways, representing the "twelve variations or phases of spiritual awareness," and they comprise the basic vocabulary of existence. They can also be seen as representing a natural progression of consciousness from its simple stages (starting with Aries) all the way through to its most complex (Aquarius and Pisces). At this point, the cycle starts over again and repeats itself. He says:

In the next phase (Aries), the beholder again beholds him or herself. And the cycle or wave is returned again to the beginning and the beginning again commences. And one cycle is complete, and one cycle moves on to another cycle, ever increasing within itself like a spiral, and the spiral moves into infinity, ever compounding its basic nature into the maze of Self.

Shelly relates this overall process to the ancient symbol of the ouroboros, the snake eating its own tail. For Shelly, this symbol expresses the mystery of self-consciousness as a process of eternal self-regeneration. Here Shelly makes the following profound (but mysterious) statement:

These twelve variations of the basic You—the spiritual You—arrange themselves into a basic circle, sometimes symbolized on this Earth as a serpent feeding back upon itself, as a serpent swallowing its tail, symbolizing the Self feeding back unto itself—the eternal circle of its immortal existence. Does not the Self meditating upon the Self become the Self all over again? By the very nature of its existence, the Self must eternally meditate upon itself. For if it ceased to do so, it would cease to be. And thus it could happen unto one's spiritual being, it could happen unto all. And in the infinities of existence, if it could happen to one, it would already have happened unto all—and you would not now be here listening.

Shelly also introduces an idea that is central to his philosophy, when he speaks of the "maze of the soul," or "the maze of Self." He says:

And as the spirit moves about in the awareness of the soul, it begins in the awareness of itself, and it becomes lost in the maze of things. And the spirit would forever be lost in the maze of the soul were it not for the eleventh and twelfth phase of its existence. For by associating and projecting one part with all the others in an abstract manner, it found its way, a path back unto itself.

The "maze of Self" concerns the universe of one's nature as represented by the twelve signs and houses of one's horoscope. Right now, you perceive reality as a complex ocean of inner and outer impressions, ranging from your wealth and siblings to your friendships, fears, desires, family, spiritual values, and so on. All this is constructed out of those four basic" building blocks" of Self we described earlier, in varying combinations.

Within that arena of diverse phenomena, your basic personality represents but one part—symbolically, one twelfth of your universe, represented by Aries. This might be thought of as the simple I AM principle, versus the more developed I AM AWARE THAT I AM principle of awakened consciousness. The other eleven houses relate to all the other aspects and phenomena of your existence.

It is all too easy to become lost in this maze, in which we lose a clear sense of our own nature and instead become engrossed in the world of "things," whether they be inward or external.

But Shelly says there is a way out of this maze, whereby one can return back to the awareness of one's true nature. That way involves putting all the parts of the maze in order, which happens by balancing the various states of awareness, and using that to then climb our way back to our true Self.

It's here he begins a discussion of sacred geometry, and the range of angular relationships within a circle and their various meanings, of which there are five dual and two single. Rather than delve into that material here, which would have most readers' eyes glaze over in short order, I'll jump ahead to what I think is the underlying message—namely, the law of the Twelve versus the law of the Seven.

The Law of the Twelve has to do with the peripheral states of consciousness associated with the chakric compartments along the right and left sides of the spine, which are the twin channels of **pingala** *and* ida, *the domains of waking and sleeping consciousness. It's here where most* *of us live, in terms of acting out the energies in those peripheral chan-nels and being constantly swayed by the impulses of the horoscope, of the maze. But it's on the wheel that we are "crucified," Shelly sometimes explained.*

By contrast, the Law of the Seven concerns the balanced states of consciousness within the center of the spine (which Shelly relates to the diameter of a circle in sacred geometry). It's the shorter and more direct path to self-realization. Using self-discipline to resist the lures of phenom-ena within ida and pingala, one can eventually return to a true aware-ness of the Self. Here he says:

These seven become seven states of awareness, balanc-ing the maze so that the spirit might climb back unto itself. But each center must grow stronger than the maze to main-tain its balance. This only can be accomplished through self-discipline. Neither by drugs or by magic may a being stand herein, save by the magic of self-discipline.

Shelly is referring to the mystic process of balancing and lifting one's consciousness through the various chakric level until one finally reaches the pinnacle of Self-awareness within the third eye, or ajna chakra, sym-bolized by the element of gold. He says:

Next is the radiant Sun—the amplifier of all that is below if all else below it is balanced, and it beholds the reflection of itself and amplifies its own spiritual awareness. The spirit has now arrived at the pinnacle, the ultimate expression of itself. It may now move through the maze of Self, beholding its glories and wonders, never again becoming lost. For the spiritual awareness of Self is ever greater than the aware-ness of the things in the maze.

And the All of Itself is held in the equilibrium of balance, and that is the concealed mystery of Self, is the equilibrium of Self. And the King of things is dead and its crown are found no more. And the spirit may behold the All of Itself in balanced equilibrium, and the golden wave of Self-creating eternal bliss. The Sun is symbolized by the metal gold, which is more electropositive than all the other six symbolic metals below it. This is what the alchemist meant by transmuting base lead into spiritual gold.

Shelly thus views the essential principles of astrology as providing us with not only a symbolic diagram of our essential nature, but at the same time gives us a road map of how we can return to our essential nature. At which point the "stars align" and harmony is restored to the kingdom of one's being.

CHAPTER 42

THE UNIVERSE IS AWARE OF YOU

A few years back I read about a popular quantum physicist out of the University of Toronto by the name of Deep Prasad, who related an experience he had one morning that sounds for all the world like an encounter with alien intelligences.[1] In a lengthy Twitter thread, he wrote:

> Near the beginning of this year (February 1), I had the most absurd, world-changing experience of my life. It happened in broad daylight at 9:40 in the morning in my home. More specific details will be for another time when I have a better safety net and can expand more. But to put it simply: I was paralyzed against my will, could not move, and saw 3 entities that had no-chill.* Could I be crazy? Sure. Do I think I am? Obviously not. Could this have been a hallucination? I can't prove it wasn't or I wouldn't be so worried about sharing this.[2]

Coming from this fellow, known more for his brilliance with scientific facts and theories than anything alien-related, it made for an especially intriguing account. He went on to give more details of what he experienced (along with drawings), but in elaborating on that encounter he shared this follow-up comment:

> I felt this weird light hitting the top of my head. And suddenly I got hit with the most blissful, euphoric feeling I

---

* The online Urban Dictionary defines "no-chill" as "Acting without regard to how others feel or see you."

have ever felt. I will try my best to describe it: *It felt like the Universe was sentient and aware of my existence.* (emphasis mine)

It's easy to gloss over that last sentence, but we shouldn't. Whatever the objective reality of his anomalous experience, it succinctly expresses an important mystical truth that's been expressed by mystics and saints throughout the ages:

The universe is sentient, and is aware of your existence.

We tend to think of ourselves as somehow separate from the universe. As D.H. Lawrence said, "We have lost the cosmos." Not only is the universe dead, but it's somehow completely indifferent to our existence. However, mystics have long suggested something different. The world is not only alive but embodies a vast intelligence—and we are directly connected to that intelligence. We are one with the cosmos, the cosmos responds to us, and it is *aware* of us, because in a sense it *is* us.

Shelly Trimmer expressed a similar idea when he said that when one attains "God consciousness"—that is, a fully awakened realization of one's true nature—an almost complete inversion takes place, whereupon the universe is now *looking in at you, rather than you looking out at the universe.* Goswami Kriyananda put it a little differently but made the same essential point: "Realize that everything you see is part of you. You are not apart from life, but a *part of* life."

I've only had tiny glimpses of that awareness myself, but those were just enough to convince me of the truth of what these teachers have said. The implications are vast and multileveled, and one of them is this:

You are never really alone.

APPENDIX I

FOUR APPROACHES TOWARD UNDERSTANDING THE GREAT AGES

Over the course of my studies into the Great Ages, I've noticed that researchers on this topic tend to fall into one of four categories. I'd like to summarize those basic approaches and their relative value in the simplest possible terms. While there is often considerable overlap between these in real-life situations, their focus is distinct to speak about their unique aims. They are as follows:

The Astronomical Approach

This approach focuses on the bare-bones science of how the Great Ages happen in terms of calculating and explaining the movement of the vernal point and the precession of the equinoxes, the influence of the Earth's wobble on precession, determining the boundaries of the constellations, exploring extraneous influences on precession (such as exploring whether our Sun is part of a binary star system, as proposed by Walter Cruttenden), and so on. Of all the different approaches, this one is the most purely scientific, looking chiefly at the hard astronomical facts behind the Great Ages doctrine.

The "Timing" Approach

This focuses predominantly on determining when the various Great Ages start or end, how long they last, what secondary and tertiary triggers factor may be involved, and similar questions. This might involve calculating when the vernal point crosses over key stars in the constellations along the ecliptic, establishing the varying sizes of those constellations, the role played by planetary cycles as triggers, the role (and duration) of sub-cycles within each Great Age cycle, and so on.

Whereas the astronomical approach is more focused on questions of *how,* this approach is focuses more on questions of *when.* Essays or sometimes even entire books have been devoted solely to this one concern, such as establishing a particular year or even date for the start of the next Great Age, or determining significant dates within that transition.

The Historiographic Approach
What is the cultural legacy of the beliefs and myths surrounding the Great Ages, and the Aquarian Age specifically? This approach takes a more scholarly stance toward determining such things as the first recorded instance of beliefs about the Great Ages, or how our modern conceptions about these epochs fit into the larger body of Great Year teachings through history from around the world, as in ancient Greece or India. Likewise, at what point did theories about precession merge with those about the Great Ages, since these weren't always synonymous in people's minds like they are now? This approach explores the mythologies and folklores from different cultures concerning the various constellations and the role these played in the influence of our understanding of precession over time. A prime example of that is the controversial work *Hamlet's Mill,* by Giorgio de Santillana and Hertha von Dechend, which suggested possible correlations between mythological traditions through history and the astrological ages. While that work touches on factors of both astronomy and timing, the authors primarily focused on those traditions and beliefs and less upon the symbolic implications of the ages themselves—such as we'll see in our next, and final, approach.

The Symbolism or "Meaning" Approach
It's one thing to talk about the Great Ages in terms of when they start or end, or the astrophysics involved in their dynamics, or

the historical record of what people believed and theorized about them through the centuries; it's quite another to focus on what any Great Age *means*, symbolically, and how it's actually manifesting in the world.

For instance, when the Age of Aquarius fully sets in, how will its influence actually appear throughout society and culture? This is not simply a matter of examining peoples' beliefs or theories about the Great Ages, but it's rather about looking at the deeper implications and actual manifestations of these epochs on the world. For example, what key themes will be weaving their way through movies, literature, politics, and religion in the coming decades or centuries? What is the deeper archetypal significance of those themes, and of Aquarius itself as a zodiacal principle? What are the highest and lowest potentials of the Aquarian mythos? Can these in turn be related to other doctrines, such as we've seen with the chakras? What are the dynamics of the transition from one Great Age to another? Questions like these are problems of symbolism and meaning. They require a more interpretive or hermeneutic mindset than those involved with our previous three approaches, which instead tend to be more scholarly or quantitative in nature.

My own interest has always leaned towards this last approach—understanding the Great Ages in terms of their symbolism and the symbolic phenomena which manifest during them. Taking that approach, it seems obvious to me from developments like space travel, the Internet, and the rise of modern democracy that the Age of Aquarius has to some extent already begun, even if its full unfoldment may still be several centuries away.

Nonetheless, all four of these approaches have something important to offer and should to be taken into account in any fuller investigation into the Aquarian Age. Whatever your preferred method, I'd keep a close eye on these next two thousand years if I were you; it could get very interesting!

APPENDIX II

THE GREAT AGES AND THE ASCENDING/ DESCENDING ARCS

As we've been seeing, one way to understand the complex developments of history is through the astrological doctrine of the Great Ages. This suggests that roughly every 2100 years, the global zeitgeist shifts into a new zodiacal epoch, based on the backward movement of the vernal equinox into a different constellation. Accordingly, we are now at the end of the Piscean Age and moving progressively into the Aquarian Age. Viewed together, twelve of these Ages comprise a roughly 26,000-year period, sometimes known as the "Great Year."

In an even broader way, though, it's possible to divvy up the entire 26,000-year Great Year into *halves*: into two distinctly different arcs lasting roughly 13,000 years each. A close analogy would be how an ordinary year can be divided into two halves, one waxing, the other waning. During six months of the year, extending from the first day of winter on December 21 to the first day of summer on June 21, we see a gradual expansion of light in the world (in the northern hemisphere, that is, since the seasons are reversed in the southern hemisphere). During the other six months of the year, from the first day of summer to the first day of winter, we see a progressive diminishing of light.

Applying this approach to the larger Great Year, we can likewise divvy up the roughly 26,000 cycle into two 13,000-year-long halves: one "ascending," the other "descending." This suggests that the ascending arc (spanning just six of the entire twelve Great Ages), would involve an expanding awareness of *spiritual* light, whereas in the descending arc (spanning the remaining six Great Ages) there would be a lessening of that light and a growing focus on material or conventional interests.

The question then becomes: where do we establish the starting and ending points for those ascending or descending arcs within this 26,000-year era?

During a regular twelve-month year, it's easy enough to declare that the ascending arc of increasing light begins with the winter solstice, and that the descending arc begins as daylight starts diminishing with the summer solstice. But it becomes more complicated when we turn our attention to the Great Ages, since there doesn't seem to be any convenient starting or ending points for those waxing or waning phases, as you have with an ordinary year.

Reevaluating Sri Yukteswar's Legacy

Here we might turn our attention to the Kriya Yoga teacher Sri Yukteswar, who had his own thoughts on the matter. Unlike most Western astrologers, he framed his discussion of the Great Year in terms of the Indic concept of the *yugas*.

This ancient Hindu and yogic model views history as unfolding in certain long "chapters," in way vaguely similar to the Western model of the Great Ages. But *unlike* the Western model, which is based on the astronomical phenomenon of "precession," the yuga system is based less on actual astronomy than pure numerology: *the ratio of 4:3:2:1*. And instead of the twelve ages we normally think of, there are just four yugas of varying length: *Satya* (the Golden Age), *Treta* (Silver Age), *Dvapara* (Bronze Age), and *Kali* (Iron Age). Traditionally, these yugas have generally been seen as lasting for monumental periods of time, together adding up to create a longer yugic "Great Year" (or *chatur yuga*) lasting a whopping 4,320,000 years.

Sri Yukteswar had his own novel take on the yugas. It's beyond the scope of this piece to explain all of its details, except to say that he regarded the yugas as lasting for much shorter time frames than most Indic traditionalists do, leading to an overall Great Year that's closer in length to that of the Western model: 24,000 years in total duration (versus the roughly 26,000-year Great Year described in the Western zodiacal system).

This raises a question many have struggled with: how does the yuga system correspond to the Western zodiacal model, if it does at all?

For instance, which yuga corresponds to the zodiacal Age of Pisces? Or that of Aquarius? Because of the wildly uneven lengths of the yugas, the two systems have posed huge challenges for anyone trying to integrate them, since they clearly don't match up in any precise way.

Yukteswar's revised length for the entire yugic Great Year made this task slightly easier because of the closer correspondence between the overall duration of both the Eastern and Western models. But the individual zodiacal ages and yugas still don't really match up. That led to a dual model that looks something like what you see in this illustration below: Aries and Pisces correspond to the very top of the yugic wheel, roughly coinciding with the Golden Satya (also called Krita) Age. Virgo and Libra line up at the very bottom, roughly corresponding to the Kali Yuga.

We are here
(according to Sri Yukteswar's formulation)

Using this model, Sri Yukteswar proposed an ascending arc starting with the latter portion of the Kali Yuga and progressing all the way up to the Satya Yuga. The descending arc would start at the tail end of the Satya Yuga and drop progressively down to the Kali Yuga. By his calculations, we are moving away from Kali Yuga, not entering into it.

In terms of their equivalents within the Western zodiacal system, Yukteswar's ascending arc would run roughly from the Age of Virgo up through the Age of Aries, while the descending arc would run from the Age of Pisces down to through that of Libra.

I have a couple of serious problems with the yuga model, and with Yukteswar's formulation in particular (which is slightly awkward for me, since I've had a longstanding connection to his particular lineage through my teachers Shelly Trimmer and Goswami Kriyananda).

First, as I mentioned in my book *StarGates*, the yugic model doesn't have as much of a foundation in hard astronomy as the Western model of the Great Ages, which is connected to the movement of the vernal point through the constellations. As I mentioned at the outset, the yuga model is based on a mathematical ratio, such that the Satya, Treta, Dwapara, and Kali Yugas are of decreasing lengths based on the 4:3:2:1 proportion. That doesn't necessarily negate its validity, since there are quite a few techniques and concepts in astrology that have no basis in "hard" astronomy but rely on pure symbolism or numerology (for example, you can't go outside and actually show me someone's eleventh house cusp; nor can you demonstrate any scientific or astronomical basis for secondary progressions). But it certainly puts the yuga system on a very different footing than that of the Great Ages model.

Another difficulty lies in the fact that there isn't a strong consensus of opinion amongst Vedic astrologers about the actual lengths of the various yugas, or of the entire yugic Great Year in general. While Western astrologers may disagree as to precisely where the Piscean Age may have begun, they are at least in broad agreement in suggesting it was around the beginning of the Christian era. But the differences of opinion amongst Vedic astrologers as to where any given yuga starts (or how long it lasts) can vary by as much as tens of thousands of years!

I have yet another concern with Yukteswar's model, which I didn't mention in *StarGates,* and it's a particularly critical one. When calculating where humanity is presently situated within the yugic cycle, Yukteswar consistently used the *autumnal equinox* as his marker rather than the *spring equinox*, as most Westerners do, without ever fully explaining his rationale for doing so. This obviously makes an enormous difference in how we approach this subject. Because the autumnal equinox lies at the exact opposite end of the zodiac from the spring equinox, using the former as one's reference point completely changes where we see ourselves within the larger scheme of things, not only in terms of which yuga we're in, but which zodiacal Great Age we're moving through.

For example, using the autumnal equinox as our starting point, as Yukteswar does, we'd naturally conclude that we've been slowly moving away from the Kali Yuga over recent centuries and ascending towards Dvapara Yuga and then Treta Yuga, and finally up into the Golden Age of Satya (or Krita), which is still many thousands of years down the road. But if instead we use the *spring equinox* as our reference point, we'd conclude that we're actually *still within* the Golden Age of Satya—for thousands of years more, in fact—and heading eventually downward towards Treta, Dvapara, and finally Kali, which is far off in our future.

For those of us working with the Western model of the Great Ages, using the autumnal equinox as our reference point, rather than the spring equinox, would suggest that we're not entering the Age of Aquarius at all, but moving into the Age of Leo instead!

Which of the equinoxes we choose to use as our markers makes a massive difference in terms of where we currently see ourselves in any "ascending" or "descending" arc model. Using the autumnal equinox, we would conclude that we are currently moving upwards in an ascending arc; but if we use the spring equinox as our reference point, as I believe is more appropriate, we'd conclude that we're actually starting downwards within the descending arc.

To be clear, I'm not arguing that one of these approaches is correct and the other wrong so much as trying to clarify a problem that's been largely ignored in discussions of Yukteswar's work. I personally believe that *all four* seasonal points—the two solstices and two equinoxes—have their own importance as markers in the unfoldment of the Great Ages. Nonetheless, I strongly believe the spring equinox does hold special importance as a key marker for our collective consciousness, analogous to the role played by the Ascendant in the personal horoscope—a role distinctly different from that played by the autumnal equinox, or for that matter the Descendant in the personal horoscope. To simply ignore the difference between these markers doesn't strike me as a rigorous way to approach any serious evaluation of Yukteswar's contribution.

Reevaluating the Arcs in Light of the Chakric Model

In light of these distinctions, I'd like to propose a different way of framing the ascending/descending arc problem than what Yukteswar proposed. To my mind, that can be done by placing it within the context of the zodiac/chakric model we've been considering throughout this book.

Seen through this lens, the shifting of the Great Ages corresponds to the coursing of collective awareness through those
different chakric levels, and in turn gives us a better sense of
where we are now as a society. As we saw earlier, Aquarius occupies a point on the lowest rung of the chakric ladder, along with
Capricorn, whereas Leo and Cancer occupy the spiritual "penthouse" at the very top.

With this vertical system as our reference point, I'd suggest
that we view the ascending arc as extending from the Age of
Capricorn below all the way up through the Age of Leo above (in
other words, starting roughly 2,000 years from now and running
all the way through to 14,000 years from now), and the *descending
arc* as extending from the Age of Cancer down through to the Age
of Aquarius (which would have started roughly 10,000 years ago
and in turn will run up through the next 2,000 years).

Because the vernal point is starting to enter into the constellation of Aquarius, we would conclude that we're currently moving down into the "basement" of the chakric system, and that
the great turnaround which inaugurates the ascending arc won't
really start for another 2,000 years.

Beyond Good or Evil
But as I have suggested, it would be simplistic to regard the higher
or lower levels of the chakra system as being either "good" or
bad." While the ascending arc may involve a growing awareness
of spiritual energies and expanding light, and the descending arc
may involve a diminishing of spiritual light, each of these plays
an important role in humanity's evolutionary drama.

Calling the lower chakric ages "bad" and the higher ones
"good" is akin to calling winter bad and summer good, or like
labeling midnight bad and noontime good. Rather, all the seasons and daytimes have their own unique qualities, lessons, and
virtues to offer. That undoubtedly holds true for the Great Ages

as well. The fact that we're moving into the proverbial basement of the chakra system may indeed pose certain existential challenges, but *every* age and chakric level poses certain existential challenges of its own, just as the scorching heat of summer poses different challenges than the frigid cold of winter.

On the other hand, every age and chakric level holds its own *creative potentials* as well. Precisely because Aquarius *is* a root chakra sign, it may simply mean we are entering into a more secular era, one not as thoroughly dominated by religious institutions or dogma as before. As noted in an earlier chapter, this shift could be concerned with bringing spiritual values and principles down into materiality and ordinary life, and applying them in everyday, practical ways. This could become a time when we're learning to see the Divine in more here-and-now terms rather than being relegated to some distant heaven far removed from us. The coming era will definitely be a more technological and scientific one, and at its best, that could possibly indicate the emergence of a more spiritualized science which aims to understand the world in terms of occult principles and sacred geometry. I'd like to believe it could also mean that astrology will experience a pronounced surge of interest and intense study, like astronomy has experienced, though whether it will ever be embraced by the scientific mainstream as fully as astronomy is much less certain, due to the fact it requires a symbolic perspective above and beyond what astronomy demands.

All in all, the fact that we're moving into those Great Ages associated with the bottom of the chakra system could signify that we're coming to know the Divine in a way quite different from anything experienced before. Perhaps it will be a time when we learn to find the Divine presence out on Main Street as much if not more than in all our churches, mosques, or synagogues.

APPENDIX III

THE DRAMA OF AMERICA AND RUSSIA ~
AN ARCHETYPAL PERSPECTIVE

The following mini-essay was originally penned as a submission to the now-defunct Whole Earth Review *back in 1987, where it was eventually published as a letter-to-the-editor. I wrote it during a point of high tensions between the U.S. and Russia, not long before the fall of the Soviet Union. As things eased up on that front, I put it aside and essentially forgot about it until things began heating up again between these two nations recently. The present book had been fully typeset and ready for publishing when I remembered that early piece and pulled it out of my files to include it here as an appendix, feeling it might have something useful to add to the discussion. I've cleaned it up a bit and added a few more thoughts at the end, to flesh things out slightly.—RG*

When one looks at the volatile relationship between the United States and Russia, it's hard not to wonder whether there isn't something deeper at work taking place in that geopolitical dynamic. Is it possible that within the historic dance between these two superpowers a more archetypal drama is being played out?

With that in mind, I'd like to suggest that within the relationship of the U.S. and Russia we're witnessing the two key descendants of the ancient Roman Empire having survived into modern times. For while the institutions of the Empire have long since disappeared, the spirit of Rome lives on in these two superpowers, each with its own imperialistic ambitions and cultural forms.

Consider the fact that in the year 293 A.D, the Roman Empire began dividing into two parts: one centered in the east, Byzantium, the other centered in the west, Rome. In its architecture (e.g., the

Kremlin) and alphabet (Cyrillic), the modern Russian nation is the chief inheritor of the Eastern Roman Empire. (Remember, too, the word "Czar" stems from the word "Caesar.) On the other hand, the United States, via England, has its roots in the Western Roman Empire, something visible not just in its architecture (the Capitol building in D.C. having been inspired by the Roman Pantheon), or its alphabet (Roman/Latin), but in its political vocabulary ("Senate," "Republican," and so on).

Seen in this way, the tensions between these two superpowers reflect the working out of a schism that actually extends back two millennia.

But what, really, is "Rome"?

If we take a hint from depth psychologists like James Hillman, Carl Jung, and Sigmund Freud, the Roman Empire wasn't simply a political entity but also a *particular state of consciousness*. In the symbolism of its monumental architecture and imperial policies, Rome reflected a new sense of identity and ego-awareness taking shape in the world; for just as any empire strives to assimilate and dominate the regions of its environment, so the ego strives to assimilate and dominate the outlying regions of the psyche itself.

That rudimentary sense of self-awareness represented an important stage in the evolution of consciousness, and with it came an extraordinary range of new possibilities—but also a new range of problems. That's because inherent in that ego-awakening was a profound sense of *duality*, a heightened sense of the self/other dynamic that naturally inclines toward "war," towards defensiveness and expansionism. There is a battle inherent within the dynamics of the ego, in other words, which compels it to defend its own boundaries while broaching those of others. The rise of empires around the world, like those of Rome, China and Egypt, were but the tangible expression of that primal ego-awakening, writ large.

Not surprisingly, all of this reached its climax during the Age of Aries, which lasted roughly from 2100 BCE to 1 AD—the zodiacal era associated with humanity's ego-awakening. But while the Arian Age may itself be long gone, we're still contending with its mixed legacy and that internal sense of the self/other conflict.

In a sense, you could say that in the nuclear dance between the United States and Russia, we're witnessing the myth of the "warring brothers" who originally seeded the Roman Empire—Romulus and Remus—now being played out on the global stage. Our relationship as rival nations is thus a deeper and more fraternal one than we've suspected. Sharing in the psychic bloodlines from both parents, we're like split-off portions of an original whole, who faintly sense in each other the missing half of our own nature.

As it so happens, the current stage in that ongoing drama of the ego's evolution is now transposed onto the current Great Age mutation taking place, as we grapple with the seismic shift from Pisces to Aquarius. As a result, one of these two superpowers (Russia) is noticeably more attuned to the mythos of the fading Piscean Age, not only with its collectivist sensibility and identification with suffering but its deeply religious roots; whereas the other superpower (United States) is more attuned to the Aquarian mythos and its more individualistic, capitalistic, and secular values. The resistance of Russia to the United States is, more broadly, a resistance to the modernized West and all that represents, while the antipathy of the U.S. to Russia issues out of a resistance to the archetypal values of the fading Piscean Age.

Seen in this perspective, the tension between these two powers on the world stage may well represent the birth pangs of a new ego-identity struggling to be born, one that's poised between those two extremes of the collective and the individual, between belief and empirical rationality, between religion and science. What form that new mode of being will take, and whether it will ultimately prove a more constructive or destructive force in the world, remains to be seen.

Postscript: In 2019, I wrote an extended article for the Mountain Astrologer magazine on the possible effects of the United States' "Pluto return," which I mentioned would be firing for the first time in late February of 2022. (I eventually included that essay as a chapter in my book StarGates.) Among the seven predictions I made for that transit was this one: "As I pointed out, during its last Pluto return England was embroiled in a number of military conflicts in various parts of the world, and it's possible America could likewise find itself embroiled in one or more conflicts, too, whether that involve Iran, Korea, Venezuela, or another country. But considering the more covert, even under-handed side of Pluto, this could just as easily manifest through acts of sabotage, terrorism, or cyber-terrorism directed at the U.S. rather than conventional battlefield conflicts." As it turned out, virtually to the day the Pluto return first became exact, the United States found itself essentially on a war footing with Russia—which initially appeared "cold" but with the potential for becoming a "hot" war. (I was naïve not to include Russia on that list of possible opponents, but things seemed to be on a relatively even keel with them in 2019. Live and learn.) As of this writing, March of 2022, it's difficult to say how the Ukrainian situation will play out, but as far as the U.S. is concerned I'd pay particular attention to the next few triggers of the Pluto return later this year, which are as follows: 1) late April into very early May, when Pluto stations and changes direction; 2) the second week of July, when the Pluto return fires exactly again; 3) the second week of October, when Pluto goes stationary again; 4) finally, the period around New Years of 2022, when the Pluto return technically fires for the last time. (Though that will be the last of the exact triggers, the effects of the Pluto return will undoubtedly extend long into the future, for better and/or worse.)

ENDNOTES

(All URLs accessed in early 2022)

Chapter 4: The Beatles - Harbingers of the Aquarian Age?

1. See chapter 3 of my book *Signs of the Times: Unlocking the Symbolic Language of World Events* (Hampton Roads, Virginia, 2002).

2. See chapters 2 and 8 of *Signs of the Times.* In fact, Aquarius represents the *dynamic between* the group and the individual, rather than just one side or the other. With that in mind, I'd suggest that whereas the Beatles represented the more group-oriented side of that emerging Aquarian paradigm, Bob Dylan, on the American side of the Atlantic, represented its more individualistic side. There was even a curious mirror-like symmetry between their careers and joint evolutions as performers. For example, precisely as the four Beatles started becoming more individualized during the mid-1960s, Dylan started moving away from solo performances to working more with groups. Likewise, exactly as the Beatles began working more acoustically on records like "Yesterday" and albums like "Rubber Soul," Dylan was shifting from recording acoustically to a more electrified approach (epitomized in his controversial performance at the Newport Folk Festival in 1965).

3. https://www.theguardian.com/music/2013/apr/20/beatles-soviet-union-first-rip-iron-curtain

Chapter 5: Brain Koan

1. From *An Infinity of Gods,* chapter 32.

Chapter 7: Classroom Earth

1. As I've noted in earlier books, the "Goswami Kriyananda" I refer to throughout this work isn't to be confused with *Swami*

Kriyananda, also a teacher in the Kriya Lineage, and founder of Ananda Village in northern California.

Chapter 11: A Few Questions (and Possible Answers) about Reincarnation and the Afterlife

1. In the years before his death, movie critic Roger Ebert had a web page in which he generously interacted with readers on assorted matters—not just film-related, but anything at all. He was staunchly anti-metaphysical, and even claimed to be an atheist, and I got into heated debates with him over the validity of NDEs (near death experiences), among other things. He invariably shot those accounts down as unreliable. But in an interview with Esquire Magazine after Roger's death, his wife Chaz said this about his final days and moments: "The one thing people might be surprised about Roger is that he didn't know if he could believe in God. He had his doubts. But toward the end, something really interesting happened. That week before Roger passed away, I would see him and he would talk about having visited this other place. I thought he was hallucinating. I thought they were giving him too much medication. But the day before he passed away, he wrote me a note: 'This is all an elaborate hoax.' I asked him, 'What's a hoax?' And he was talking about this world, this place. He said it was all an illusion. I thought he was just confused. But he was not confused. He wasn't visiting heaven, not the way we think of heaven. He described it as a vastness that you can't even imagine. It was a place where the past, present, and future were happening all at once." (https://www.esquire.com/entertainment/tv/news/a26606/roger-ebert-final-moments/)
2. *The Divine Romance*, by Paramahansa Yogananda, Self-Realization Fellowship, 1986, p. 55.
3. Paramahansa Yogananda, *Ibid*, p. 287.

4. Regarding the question of what happens to one's pets and the afterlife, another anecdote which comes to mind here involved a young woman I knew whose father was a distinguished professor and mother a respected journalist. Like her parents, she was extremely intelligent herself, but notably skeptical about anything paranormal or metaphysical. When I tried discussing phenomena like ESP, ghosts, or life-after-death with her, she invariably took a more nuts-and-bolts approach, saying there was no hard evidence to back up such ideas. I lost touch with her for several years, but when we eventually got back in touch she told about something strange she had seen which she was unable to explain. There was a man in the condominium complex where she lived who took his dog out for a walk around the central lake every day, and she'd often look out the kitchen window and see the two of them enjoying their walk together. Eventually the dog died, and the man continued his daily walk around the park, without the dog. But one day she happened to be looking out the window when she saw the man on his walk— and next to him this time was the phantom image of his recently deceased dog, prancing around the man's feet like he always did before, with the man seemingly being unaware of the ghostly canine. This continued for a number of seconds until both the man and phantom dog disappeared from view. My Norwegian friend was clearly shocked by this event, since she wasn't at all predisposed to believe in this sort of thing. Needless to say, that made her story all the more compelling to me.

Chapter 13: On the Mysteries of Soul

1. We sometimes use the term "old soul" to describe a man or woman of great depth, or who we might even suspect has experienced many past lives. But notice that we never use the term "old spirit" to describe such individuals! Esoterically speaking, that makes good sense, because while some individuals

may indeed have a far greater backlog of past-life experiences and soul-memories packed under their karmic belt, the spirit is itself, by contrast, timeless and eternal. As a result, terms like "young" or "old" have no meaning when describing it.

2. For more on this, see chapter two of my book *An Infinity of Gods*.

3. For more on this distinction between humans as *children of God* versus as *brother or/sisters of God*, again, see *An Infinity of Gods*, particularly Appendix I.

Chapter 15: The Meeting of Jupiter and Neptune in Pisces

1. My thanks to Richard Smoley here for calling my attention to Eliphas Levi's book.

Chapter 17: When Someone's Saturn is on Your Sun

1. The astrologically savvy reader may notice a recurring theme with some of the "disappointments" I've described in this book. That includes my let-down with *Apocalypse Now*, the processing mishap with my own experimental film at the Chicago film lab one year earlier, and these near-misses with the rock musicians mentioned in this chapter. What links these (and still others not mentioned)? They all involve *Neptune* symbols—the planet governing both films and music. As it so happens, my birth chart shows a strong Saturn/Neptune/Moon connection, a pattern which can show disillusionments or setbacks in Neptunian areas, particularly.

Chapter 18: The Astrology of Hollywood's "Golden Year"—1939

1. The correlation between America's Neptune return and the "Golden Year" of 1939 holds true whether we employ the tropical, non-precession corrected degree of Neptune or its more sidereal, precession-corrected position. It's beyond the scope

of this article to explain the finer details of that rarefied debate here, but a decent starting point for those wanting to learn more would be the following link: http://skyscript.co.uk/forums/viewtopic.php?t=6044. As I pointed out, the first U.S. Neptune return, calculated tropically, took plae on Oct. 28 of 1938, and it fired again on August 29, 1939. But according to sidereal, *precession-corrected* standards, the Neptune return first took place first on Nov. 3, 1939, then again on February 23, 1940, then one last time on Sept. 3, 1940. As a result, one could really attribute the cinematic explosion of 1939 to the influence of *either* the tropical or sidereal positions of Neptune during that return, since their impact was so broad as to essentially overlap on one another. But it seems clear to me the astonishing synchronicity of Welles' radio broadcast and the premiere of *The Wizard of Oz* occurring so close to those two *tropically-*determined dates certainly underscores the value of the non-precession-corrected approach. I'll have to leave it for others to search out equally impressive examples to support to the sidereal, precession-corrected dates; I've yet been unable to find any myself, but perhaps others will have more luck.

2. It's worth mentioning that film director Francis Ford Coppola was born during one of the key trigger points for the United States' Neptune return: at his birth on April 7, 1939, Neptune was stationing at 21 Virgo, one degree away from the U.S. Neptune, and turned direct five days later on April 12.

3. My thanks to Richard Smoley for pointing out the timing of the WWII connection.

4. I'll add one more synchronicity to the mix. My late friend, Lynne Wachowski, mother to Lana and Lily Wachowski, directors of the *The Matrix*, was born on Oct. 29, 1938—roughly 24 hours after that first exact U.S. Neptune return (and one day before Welles' infamous radio broadcast). Considering that timing, I find it fascinating she'd later give birth to children

who would eventually become famous for a film series based on the idea that the world around us is really an illusion.

Chapter 20: Twenty-One Things Worth Knowing About the Aquarian Age

1. Though I personally learned about the chakra/zodiac model from teachers in the Kriya Yoga tradition, there are numerous writers from outside that tradition who have written about it as well, such as David Frawley, Marc Edmund Jones, Jeffrey Wolf Green, and Rico Baker.

2. When discussing America's role in the coming Great Age with students or even colleagues, I've sometimes heard it said, "But the U.S. is a Cancer nation, not an Aquarian one, since it was born on the 4th of July!" My response is that the importance of the U.S. in world affairs—or that of any nation—is more than just a simple matter of Sun signs. (That's true when it comes to personal horoscopes as well—i.e., not every writer is a Gemini or Virgo, nor every prizefighter is an Aries, nor every banker is a Taurus. Sun signs are just one facet of someone's personality, albeit an important one.) However, there usually *are* indications of a nation's attunement to incoming Aquarian trends in its horoscope, such as a prominent Uranus or an emphasis on Aquarius—both of which are the case with the July 4 horoscope for the U.S.

3. See Carl Jung's *Answer to Job*, para 758. During the early 1980s, I wrote a letter to the Jungian psychologist and author, Marie-Louise von Franz, asking for her general thoughts on Carl Jung's views about the impending Aquarian Age. Though she was elderly at the time, she was kind enough to write me this short but enigmatic reply: "Dear Mr. Grasse, The processes underlying history in the collective unconscious, at least for the Western civilization, have been worked out by Jung in his book *Aion* in that strange self-renewing process of the Self.

Astrologically, we are moving from Pisces to Aquarius and in the process moving from Christ to the Lapis. That's all I can shortly tell you. All my best wishes for your work. Sincerely, Marie-Louise von Franz." The "lapis" is a term familiar to students of alchemy, but since that's a field I've never been particularly well-versed in, I decided to ask the opinion of Dr. Aaron Cheak, a respected authority on the subject, who provided this insightful comment: "The lapis is the philosopher's stone (*lapis philosophorum*), the agent of transmutation which restores our primordial, immortal wholeness through the unification of opposites. It is the consummation of the great work (alchemy) and of individuation (analytic psychology). For Jung, Christ and Lapis were both expressions and images of this wholeness, which he called the Self, and both involved an alchemical marriage of opposites. I would say that the precessional shift from Christ to Lapis (or Pisces to Aquarius) indicates a shift away from the collective emphasis on Christ as god image (and on external salvation through adherence to religious dogma), and towards the realisation of the god image within through the dynamics of psychological alchemy. This is in accordance with Jung's suggestion that the Self may in fact be a more primary reality than Christ (i.e., Christ is simply an image of the Self, not the other way around). Either way, the shift to an emphasis on the Lapis is a shift not only to a new god image, but to a more explicitly internal path of alchemical realisation."

4. Joseph Campbell, *The Masks of God, Vol. 4: Creative Mythology.* New York, Viking, 1977, p. 36.

5. I've come to regard the rise of modern psychology as representing a blending of influences from *both* the Piscean and Aquarian Ages. To a great extent, modern psychology truly began with an investigation of the "unconscious"—that mysterious ground of being which underlies our conscious emotions

and motivations. But in previous centuries, that dimension of being was largely understood in terms of that mysterious thing called "soul," and it was invariably perceived in strictly religious or supernatural contexts. From out of that previously religious framework emerged the completely secular notion of a personal "unconscious," which shared some similarities with the older notion of "soul" but now with nothing intrinsically spiritual or theological about it. Later on, psychologists like Carl Jung and Roberto Assagioli amended this by introducing more spiritual and archetypal elements into the picture, but the "unconscious" was still largely viewed through a rational, analytical lens. At such, I regard modern psychology as a hybrid: on the one hand, reflecting the legacy of the Piscean Age with its more inwardly-focused concerns, and on the other hand expressing the more rational and scientific orientation of the emerging Aquarian Age.

6. For a more in-depth discussion of how Jean Gebser's theory relates to the emerging Aquarian mythos, see my book *Signs of the Times*, chapter 15.

7. It's worth noting that the Piscean Age, like the Age of Aries, also introduced a certain level of individualism into our collective experience, as a result of Christianity's notion of a personal relationship with God—a God who numbers all the hairs on your head, in fact. But this, too, was a highly *qualified* type of individualism, since it still required the mediating influence of an external savior or church authority, without which one's individual essence was essentially valueless.

Chapter 27: Walt Disney's "Sorcerer's Apprentice ~ A Cautionary Tale for Our Times

1. Not surprisingly, Walt Disney's *Fantasia* was released at the tail end of America's first Neptune return (as discussed in chapter 18), but it also reflected the pivotal Uranus-trine-Neptune in effect from the late 1930s through the early 1940s.

Chapter 29: Some Passing Thoughts on Sacred Architecture

1. I discussed these and other ideas in more detail in a lecture delivered at the Theosophical Society in 2016, titled "The Spirit of Place," viewable here: https://www.youtube.com/watch?v=4Wys5c1jrnE

Chapter 30: The Genius of Citizen Kane, Part I

1. *Bilge Ebiri, The Once and Future Kane," The Criterion Collection, Nov. 21, 2021:* www.criterion.com/current/posts/7613-citizen-kane-the-once-and-future-kane
2. *Boehnel, William (May 2, 1941). "Citizen Kane", New York World-Telegram.*
3. In recent years it's become increasingly common to hear comments along the lines of, "I don't see what's so special about *Citizen Kane*. I've watched it and it just doesn't do much for me." To some extent, that's understandable, since we all have different tastes. But I also don't think it accidental that fewer and fewer people are seeing *Kane*—or *any* of the older films, for that matter—in theatrical settings, instead viewing them primarily on small-screens, whether on TV sets or smart phones. A film like *Citizen Kane* is one of those that really should be seen in a larger setting to appreciate its impact. I've likened it to the difference between hearing Beethoven's Ninth Symphony in a concert hall versus hearing it on a smart phone. Having watched Welles' film both on TV and in theaters many times myself, I know full well the difference, and encourage anyone who has the opportunity to see it in a larger setting to do so.

Chapter 34: A Two-Tiered Approach to History ~ Mundane Astrology and the Great Ages

1. For more on this subject, see my book *Signs of the Times: Unlocking the Symbolic Language of World Events* (Hampton Roads, 2002), particularly chapter 2.

2. The written transcript of Armstrong's complete talk can be found here: https://www.hq.nasa.gov/alsj/a11/A11CongressJOD.html

Chapter 35: "Midnight Mass," the TV Series
1. Rosie Knight, "Midnight Mass's Final Line is Full of Hope" (series review), https://nerdist.com/article/midnight-mass-last-line-full-of-hope/

Chapter 37: Is Astrology Really Nothing More than Divination?
1. Geoffrey Cornelius, *The Moment of Astrology: Origins in Divination*. The Wessex Astrologer, 2003 (Revised edition), p. 305.
2. https://www.youtube.com/watch?v=C6k7xa1NrCc
3. Richard Tarnas, *Cosmos and Psyche: Intimations of a New World View*. Viking Books, 2006, p. 409.
4. In both *The Waking Dream* (chapter 4) and *Under a Sacred Sky* (chapters 1 and 16), I myself argued that astrology was indeed a form of "divination," but more in the sense that it involved a symbolic reading of the universe and its phenomenon, and less so in the strongly participatory or "daemonic" sense implied by Cornelius. While that daemonic side is certainly involved in many instances (especially with horary astrology, which calculates a horoscope for the time a question is presented to the astrologer), it isn't the sole or overriding factor. For that reason, I suggested the usefulness of positing a *spectrum* of divinatory processes ranging from "low-information/high-subjectivity" systems like crystal ball gazing and tea leaf reading, where one has little outside data to work from, to comparatively "high-information/low-subjectivity" methods like astrology, where one has an enormous amount of objective data to draw from. In his book, Cornelius seems to suggest that astrology is basically a "low-information/high-subjectivity" system, whereas I would

suggest that astrology is a comparatively "high-information/low-subjectivity" discipline.

Chapter 40: The Divine Zodiac

1. The fact that the names and forms associated with the different signs may have emerged at certain times in history doesn't necessarily mean those underlying principles aren't themselves timeless, eternal archetypes. To use an analogy, Albert Einstein came up with his ground-breaking Theory of Relativity early in the 20th Century but the underlying principle he was codifying obviously existed in nature before he came along and gave it a name. Likewise, even if we accept that the first known depiction of Taurus may have taken the form of bison images in the 19,000-year-old caves of France, that doesn't mean the *archetype* of Taurus itself didn't exist before then.

   Another example: John Anthony West suggested that the Great Sphinx of Egypt may well have dated back to the Age of Leo, or possibly even the previous age of Leo. But one might ask whether the symbol of "Leo" even known or formulated that far back in history. What if that constellation was only christened as "Leo" by the Mesopotamians thousands of years later? Perhaps it doesn't matter, because if indeed the zodiacal principles we're now familiar with are eternal in nature, the "Age of Leo" existed whether or not it was fully and consciously labeled as such by the astrologers long after the Sphinx was created.

   Along similar lines, it appears that some signs have changed their forms or names over time, as in the case of Aries, which was originally known to the Babylonians as the "Hired Man" and later replaced by the Greeks with the symbol of a Ram. Likewise with Libra, which in its earliest stages was viewed as an extension of the constellation Scorpio and given its present symbol of "the scales" by the Romans. Does that by itself negate the eternality and timelessness of these zodiacal principles? Not at all. We can interpret this as either reflecting humanity's gradually-evolving understanding of the true meaning of these constellations, or perhaps as suggesting there is a deeper link between the meanings of those earlier and later forms than meets the casual eye.

2. Do the meanings of the twelve signs correspond with the meanings of the twelve houses of the horoscope? Since the revival of Hellenistic astrology in the 1990s, some traditionally-minded astrologers have argued that the meanings of the houses (or "places") historically arose in such a dramatically different fashion from those of the zodiacal signs that the two should *not* be seen as interchangeable or even similar in their meanings. For example, whereas most modern astrologers believe the 10ᵗʰ house has a resonance with both Capricorn and Saturn (in what some refer to as the "alphabet" system of correspondences between planets, signs, and houses), some traditionalists believe that these principles are in fact very different, if not diametrically opposed. For instance, whereas the 10ᵗʰ house is a place in the horoscope classically associated with honor, fame, and good reputation, Saturn is traditionally associated more with dishonor and scandal.

I respectfully disagree with the logic of that critique, because while it may have its roots in certain traditional theories and systems, I don't believe it's been borne out by the trial-and-error, empirical experiences of astrologers over time. Staying just with that one example, take some time yourself to watch how Capricorn and Saturn manifest in people's horoscopes and you'll quickly see that they're deeply ambitious energies, often seeking fame and reputation, in a way that's *entirely* resonant with 10ᵗʰ house symbolism. The fact that there are often problems in those very areas (as far as potential falls from grace or a loss of "honor") doesn't negate that correspondence, but simply reflects the problematic and double-edged nature of both Saturn and Capricorn in *whatever* areas they touch.

In the end, it all comes down for me to whether one believes the 12-fold model of astrology is a true archetypal pattern or not; because if it is, then it's natural to assume the meanings of the 12 houses would closely reflect those of the 12 signs. But if one believes that the meanings assigned to the houses and signs arose in some comparatively random way, then I can see why some would think there's little connection between these symbols. Needless to say, that isn't my view.

3. My thanks here to Dave Gunning for his feedback on this passage.

Chapter 41: Esoteric Astrology

1. On several occasions over the years I've heard other astrologers suggest a relationship between the different angles (or aspects) and the various planets, in a way quite similar to what Shelly suggested here, though generally with a difference. Whereas Shelly associated Saturn with the inconjunct and the Moon with the opposition, the other astrologers I've come across equated Saturn with the *opposition*. On its surface, that's understandable, since it is the furthest point away from the Sun on the wheel. However, Shelly's logic on this point was subtle, since he regarded the opposition as not really being "on the wheel" but as part of that axis *beyond* phenomenal reality. By contrast, the inconjunct, or 150° angle, is actually the furthest point away from the Sun or 0° *on the wheel* (i.e., phenomenal reality)—hence it would be better associated with Saturn, the symbol of material reality.

Ray Grasse

Chapter 42: The Universe is Aware of You

1. This interview by George Knapp gives a good overview of Deep Prasad's experience (in three installments): https://www.krqe.com/home/alien-presence-came-knocking-when-scientist-deep-prasad-least-expected-it/

2. Quoted from Prasad's original Twitter account, where he explains his experience in a lengthy multi-part thread: https://twitter.com/Deepneuron/status/1200280316306321408

ABOUT THE AUTHOR

Ray Grasse is a writer, photographer, and astrologer living in the American Midwest. He is author of several books including *Under a Sacred Sky, An Infinity of Gods, StarGates, Urban Mystic,* and *Signs of the Times,* and contributor to numerous anthologies. His first book, *The Waking Dream,* was called "a masterpiece" by Colin Wilson. He worked on the editorial staffs of Quest Books and The Quest Magazine for 10 years, and has been associate editor of The Mountain Astrologer magazine for over 20 years. He received a degree in filmmaking from the Art Institute of Chicago under Stan Brakhage, and studied under teachers in both the Kriya Yoga and Zen traditions. His websites are www.raygrasse.com and www.raygrassephotography.com.

Made in the USA
Monee, IL
01 May 2022

95703609R00223